PRAISE FOR *Get Into Any College*

"*Get Into Any College* delivers invaluable information ranging from the elimination of admission myths to successfully tapping into scholarship funds. From start to finish, the Tanabes provide informative step-by-step information combined with their experiences at Harvard."

—*Leonard Banks, The Journal Press*

"What's even better than all the top-notch tips is that the book is written in a cool, conversational way and even offers anecdotal bits in their *Stories From Real Life* section."

—*College Bound Magazine*

"When you consider the costs of a four year college or university education nowadays, think about forking out $16.95 for this little gem written and produced by two who know."

—*Don Denevi, Palo Alto Daily News*

"The chapters on essay writing with examples are excellent for students who never know how to begin. Examples of essays, both strong and weak, go a long way to help students who are stuck."

—*Lynda McGee, College Counselor, Downtown Magnets High School*

"The first college admissions strategy book that actually shows you how to get into college. *Get Into Any College* features the strategies and stories of real students who have been accepted to the country's top colleges. . . . The book is filled with student-tested strategies to help applicants write better essays that stand out from the pile, promote themselves during college interviews, ace the SAT and ACT and find free cash for college."

—*Pam Costa, Santa Clara Vision*

"The Tanabes literally wrote the book on the topic, having authored the award-winning book, *Get Into Any College*."

—*Bull & Bear Financial Report*

"The Reading List: Offers advice on writing a good entrance essay, taking exams and applying for scholarships and other information on the college experience—start to finish."

—*Town & Country Magazine*

"Applying for college can be a drag for high school seniors who don't always know exactly what admissions officers are looking for. Now there is a book that can help."

—*The Daily News*

GET INTO ANY
COLLEGE

TWELFTH EDITION

- Step-by-step instructions on how to get into and pay for any college

- Learn from the true-life successes and failures of real students

- Successful admissions essay examples, application forms and interview questions

- Comprehensive—The only resource you will need to get into the college of your dreams

GEN and KELLY TANABE

Harvard graduates and authors of
Accepted! 50 Successful College Admission Essays
and *The Ultimate Guide to America's Best Colleges*

Get Into Any College: The Insider's Guide to Getting into a Top College

By Gen and Kelly Tanabe

Published by SuperCollege, LLC (www.supercollege.com)
2713 Newlands Avenue
Belmont, CA 94002
650-618-2221

ISBN 978-1-61760-160-6

Manufactured in the United States of America

10 9 8 7 6 5 4 3 2 1

Library of Congress Cataloging-in-Publication Data

Names: Tanabe, Gen S., author. | Tanabe, Kelly Y., author.
Title: Get into any college : the insider's guide to getting into a top
    college / Gen and Kelly Tanabe.
Description: Twelfth edition. | Belmont, CA : SuperCollege, LLC, [2020] |
    Includes index. | Summary: "A resource for high school students and
    parents on how to apply to selective colleges. Covers strategies on
    college selection, college applications, essays, interviews,
    standardized tests and scholarships and financial aid. Outlines what
    selective colleges look for in applicants. Includes more than 20 essay
    examples"-- Provided by publisher.
Identifiers: LCCN 2019058520 | ISBN 9781617601606 (paperback)
Subjects: LCSH: College choice--United States. | Universities and
    colleges--United States--Admission. | Universities and colleges--United
    States--Entrance requirements.
Classification: LCC LB2351.1 .T36 2020 | DDC 378.1/61--dc23
LC record available at https://lccn.loc.gov/2019058520

TO OUR FAMILIES.

TO HARVARD.

To the many students and friends who shared their college admissions experiences, secrets, successes and failures.

Also, to all those who will soon embark upon one of the most exciting journeys of their lives—college.

CONTENTS

Rewrite and Edit Again, with Help from Editors • Step 5: Polish Your Essay • The Essay-Writing Absolute Don'ts • Totally Dumb Topics to Avoid • Specific Tips for Specific Questions • Next Up: The Magic of Recycling and Examples of the Good, Bad and Ugly . . . Essays that Is

CHAPTER 6: RECYCLE YOUR ESSAYS WHEN APPLYING

Presto-Chango! Turn One Essay Into Two • The Common Application: The Easiest Way to Recycle • How to Answer Any Question With Only One Essay • Recycling in Action: A Case Study • How to Shorten a Long Essay • How to Build a Longer Essay • A Final Warning About Recycling

The College Essay in the Real World • Magnum Opuses: Essays that Opened College Doors • Seven Disastrous Essays That Spelled Rejection • A Final Note on the Essays That Bombed • Do You Have a Good Essay?

The Interview Nightmare • Secrets of the Interview • Make the Most of Your Sweaty Palms • Interviewers Are Real People Too • Don't Just Talk About You • Creative Digressions and Connecting: How to Become Bosom Buddies With Your Interviewers • Listen, Too • Your Interview Homework • Cheat Sheet of the Most Commonly Asked Questions • The "No-No" Topics • Know the World Around You • Is Religion a Taboo Topic? • No Snoozing Allowed • The Mock Interview • Leave the Halter Top and Short Shorts Behind • A Safety Pin, Aspirin and Other Emergency Supplies • Show Time! Psyche Yourself Up for the Real Thing • Why Blowing It Is Not Blowing It

CHAPTER 9: CRITICAL FINAL STEPS BEFORE

You Are Done! (Well Almost...) • Do a Once, Twice and Thrice Over • The Big Send-Off • Thank All of Your Helpers

How to Survive the SAT and ACT • Myth #1: Standardized tests make or break your chances. • Myth #2: You have to score in the top 90 percent to get into a selective college. • Myth #3: There is nothing you can do to prepare for the tests. • The Ingredients of the Alphabet Soup of Tests • The SAT • The PSAT • The SAT Subject Tests • The ACT • Duel of the Three-Letter Acronyms: The SAT vs. ACT • Advanced Placement Tests (APs) • International Baccalaureate Program • TOEFL • How to Increase Your Scores • How to Master English and Reading Tests • Number Hunching and Crunching: How to Be a Math Whiz • The Day Before the Big Event • Test

SPECIAL FEATURES

Stories from Real Life

These short stories about the successes and failures of real students are both entertaining and enlightening. They reveal how the college admissions and financial aid process really works!

Special Highlights

CHAPTER 1

WHAT SELECTIVE COLLEGES REALLY WANT FROM APPLICANTS

Getting Into Your Dream School

If you ever visit Harvard, you will find nestled among the red brick buildings in the heart of Harvard Yard a statue of John Harvard. Like a miniature Lincoln memorial, old John is seated in a chair upon a pedestal, dressed in the latest 18th-century fashion and clutching a large encyclopedic book. John has greeted millions of students and visitors alike and has the reputation of being America's third most photographed statue. (He has also had the dubious honor of being painted blue by those rascal Yalies during the Harvard-Yale football game.) There are three things about this distinguished statue, however, that are commonly referred to as the "three lies" of John Harvard. They are as follows:

#1   The date inscribed for Harvard's founding is incorrect.

#2   The statue is not of Mr. Harvard but of a better looking stand-in.

#3   Harvard University was not founded by John Harvard—although he did donate a lot of money.

Along with these "three lies" we would like to add a fourth:

#4   You have to be a superstar to get into Harvard.

The truth about colleges (even those in the elite Ivy League) is that many high school students who apply have the brains to succeed academically. However, within this large group of qualified students, only those few who can convey their abilities, talents and personalities in the short space of the college application will have a chance of getting accepted. The five percent of applicants who got into Harvard last year, for example, were not the only ones capable of doing Harvard-quality work. In reality, this five percent— whether accidentally or intentionally—were best able to market themselves through their applications, and this convinced the admissions officers that they deserved to be admitted.

Whether you are applying to a school that accepts five percent or 60 percent of its applicants, you need to know how to write an application that not only maximizes your strengths (while minimizing your weaknesses) but also ensures that you stand out from among the masses—and that's what this book will show you how to do! So, if you have decent grades, don't bomb the SAT or ACT, are a reasonably hard worker and (most important) are willing to challenge yourself academically, then you have what it takes to get into a great school.

At this point you might be asking yourself, "Is writing a compelling college application something that can be learned?" The answer: "Absolutely!" And we, who have done so, will teach you how.

If you've read other books on college admission, you may have encountered the traditional "top-down approach" which is filled with useless lectures by supposed "experts," many of whose firsthand experiences are decades old. This book is built on the actual tips, strategies and secrets discovered by today's students who have gotten into top private and state universities. Through their experiences and techniques, you will learn how to create that winning application that gets you into your top college choice.

So let this book be your guide through the college admissions process. We will show you what works and (almost as important) what doesn't. By the time you finish you will have produced the best possible college application, and with a little luck, (you always need luck in this game!) you will receive in the spring that beautiful thick envelope with an acceptance letter from the school of your dreams.

How this Book Is Superior to All Others:
A Shameless (But True) Testimonial

We know you have many choices when it comes to buying a book on college admissions. If you are standing in the bookstore reading this, we hope the following short paragraphs will highlight what makes this book better than all of the others you see on the shelf. If you have already bought this book, then you may skip this section, or read it if you want to see just how smart a purchase you've made!

A down-to-earth radically different approach from any other guide. Unlike other books written by so-called "experts," this book was written by those who have actually done it. With the help of hundreds of students from both elite private and highly selective public colleges, we share with you the secrets of how to get accepted. All of the strategies and tips in this book have been proven successful by students like you. Plus, we're not shy about revealing mistakes that can turn an otherwise strong application into a guaranteed rejection.

Absolutely essential examples, samples and illustrations. Any how-to book worth the paper it is printed on should provide many examples so that you can see how the tips and strategies are actually used. Not only have we included examples from actual applications, but we have even added 25 real admission essays and an entire completed application.

No useless fluff or padding. This guide gives you all the right information— comprehensively and concisely. You will learn the essential strategies on how to get into college. We know no high school student has the time (or desire) to read a book that doesn't get to the point.

Stories from real life: The successes and failures of actual students. There is no better way to understand the sometimes mysterious process of college admissions than through the experiences of those who have already done it. Learn from the grand successes and grave mistakes of actual students through their uncensored and honest confessions. Each short story not only reveals how the admissions process really works but is also quite entertaining. (We promise at least a few laughs—not an inconsequential point considering the work ahead of you!)

Easy (and dare we say) fun book to read. You may think college admissions is the diametric opposite of the word "fun," but if you're going to spend your valuable time reading this book, the least we can do is make it entertaining. That's why throughout each chapter you'll find many personal stories and anecdotes that, aside from teaching you more about college admissions, are also pretty funny.

A Sneak Preview to What's Inside

Now that we have shamelessly praised our book, let's take a quick look at what's inside. In general, each chapter gives step-by-step, easy-to-follow instructions on how to complete a particular section of the application. Along with essential Do's and Don'ts you will also learn about common pitfalls—many of which were painfully discovered by the students you'll meet inside.

Being the perceptive authors that we are, we have designed the chapters to be read in sequence or independently, depending on your personal needs. So, feel free to skip to the chapters that deal with areas in which you think you need the most help.

Chapter 1: What Selective Colleges Really Want from Applicants. What you are reading right now.

Chapter 2: How to Pick the Perfect College for You. The two most common questions we're asked are these: "Where should I apply?" and "Will I get in?" Our strategy will help you make these critical decisions and ensure that you maximize your chances for admission into the best college possible while leaving nothing to chance.

Chapter 3: Create a Compelling Admissions Application. Here we will take you on a guided tour of the blanks, spaces and boxes of the application form and show you how to fill it out correctly. There are many Do's and Don'ts for the application form and by learning what information to list and what to withhold, you can create an application that will stand out from the pile of other applications. Plus, we'll share the truth about applying early and whether or not it gives you an advantage.

Chapter 4: How to Guarantee Excellent Evaluations. There is plenty that you can do (none of it unethical, of course) to ensure that your teachers write glowing evaluations. This chapter answers the two most important questions: "Who are the best people to ask for evaluations?" and "How can you be sure that they will write unique and positive reviews?"

Chapter 5: How to Write an Irresistible Essay. How can you possibly write about the past 17-odd years of your life in fewer words than are on the back of a cereal box? We'll show you how in this essay-writing workshop. Here you will master the secrets to writing a compelling personal essay that will have admissions officers begging for more. The essay is one of the most important parts of the application, and if you only have time to read one chapter, this should be it.

Chapter 6: Recycle Your Essays When Applying to Many Colleges. This chapter will save you weeks if not months of time. Recycling is the all important—some would claim even magical—technique that allows you to use only a few quality essays for all college applications. Following the simple editing strategies in this chapter, you can apply to as many schools as you want using only a handful of original essays.

Chapter 7: Example Essays: The Good, Bad and Ugly. This chapter contains—you guessed it—the example essays. Included are 15 essays that worked as well as 7 that didn't. A short commentary follows each essay written from the perspective of an admissions officer. You can use the good essays as models to compare to your own. The bad ones, of course, show you how *not* to write an essay.

Chapter 8: The Secrets to Crushing the Interview. Are you worried about going one on one with an admissions officer or alumnus? Well, don't be. After reading this chapter, you will understand why you don't have to stress over interviews. You will also get a sneak peek at the kinds of questions your interviewers will ask, learn how to present yourself as the intelligent and motivated applicant that you are and find the solution to the all important issue of what to wear.

Chapter 9: Critical Final Steps before Submitting the Application. Whew! You have worked hard and now have a set of outstanding applications. But before you submit the applications to the colleges, there are some important things you need to double check. Here you will find a check-off list of everything you need to remember as well as what to do if (oh, my goodness) you miss the deadline!

Chapter 10: How to Ace the SAT and ACT. Standardized tests are dreaded parts of college admissions. Here we discuss how important these tests *really* are and give you hints on how to increase your scores. This chapter has everything you ever wanted to know about the SAT, ACT, SAT Subject Test, PSAT, TOEFL, AP and IB exams.

Chapter 11: How to Win Free Cash for College. If you thought getting in was difficult, consider for a moment how you (and your parents) are going to foot the bill. Fortunately, there is more money out there to help you pay for school than you may think—$241.3 billion to be exact. Financing your education can come not only through college and government funding and outside scholarships, but also by negotiating in the right way with the university to increase its share of the cost. This chapter is devoted entirely to the many ways to finance your education—a topic particularly popular among parents.

Chapter 12: Admissions for Special Groups. In this chapter, we cover the special considerations for athlete, transfer, international and home- schooled students and students with special needs.

Chapter 13: Get Started Before Your Senior Year: What Freshmen, Sophomores and Juniors Need to Know. With the growing competition to get into college, it is very important to get a head start. To help, we have designed this chapter especially for you on how to plan your remaining years in high school to maximize your chances of being admitted into a good college. Included are keys to picking challenging classes, getting your teachers to love you and choosing how and to what degree to get involved with extracurricular activities and sports.

Chapter 14: Prepare Your Child for College: What Every Parent Needs to Know. Many parents want to help their child get into college but don't necessarily know what to do (besides pulling out the checkbook). In fact, some forms of parental involvement can be detrimental to getting a child admitted. If you are a parent, then you will find this chapter (along with the rest of the book) especially enlightening. You will learn everything you need to know about helping junior or juniorette get into the right school as well as how to pay for this education without having to take out a second mortgage.

Chapter 15: Decide Which College to Enter. Here we skip ahead to when you hear from all of the colleges. We give you some advice on how to decide which offer to accept as well as how to deal with (the words every student dreads), the *wait list.*

What Colleges Consider in Deciding Whom to Admit

It may seem obvious what criteria colleges consider when they're weighing admissions decisions. Naturally, all of the pieces you submit or participate in are judged: transcript, application form, essay, recommendation letters/evaluations and interviews.

But college admissions is like an onion; there are many layers. Once the first layer is peeled away, there are more beneath it. This means that colleges don't just consider your grades but they measure other factors as well such as your class rank, school report and the difficulty of the courses you've taken. It's important to understand not only what factors the colleges consider but how they consider them and in what context.

Academics

Grades. Of course grades are a given since they are one indication (many admissions officers say the strongest indication) of how prepared you are for college courses. However, grades are not measured in a vacuum. The admissions officers want to know the difficulty level of the courses you've taken, how you've excelled in comparison to the other students at your school and how your school's courses and grading system stack up against other schools.

Class rank. Fewer schools are ranking students than in the past because of the competition it creates. Schools with high academic performers feel that their students are disadvantaged because students who are in the middle of the class

WHAT COLLEGES CONSIDER IN DECIDING WHOM TO ADMIT

Academics
Grades
Class rank
Difficulty of courses
SAT, ACT scores
SAT Subject Test scores
AP and IB test scores
School report

Student Life
Extracurricular activities
Talents
Awards
Public service
Work experience
Athletics, especially if you are
    being recruited

Personal Characteristics Demonstrated By
Essay
Interview
Recommendation letters/evalua-
    tions

Other Factors
Under-represented racial or ethnic
    background
Geographic background
Socio-economic background
Legacy
Demonstrated interest
Challenges

rankings at their school might have been at the top of the class rankings at less rigorous institutions. Because of these discrepancies, colleges might use the ranking information to see how you've excelled in comparison to other students at your school rather than to parallel performances of students from several schools. Students from high schools that don't provide class rank may be assessed by colleges through the use of other measures such as test scores and the school report.

Difficulty of courses. More important than the actual grades you receive are the classes you take to receive those grades. Admissions officers want to see you challenge yourself in classes and that you take advantage of the advanced classes your school offers. It's better to receive a mixed GPA and have a challenging course load than a higher GPA with an easy course load. Most high schools will reflect the difficulty level of the classes that you take with a weighted GPA that gives more strength to AP, IB and honors classes.

SAT, ACT scores. Admissions officers know that high schools have different methods of grading and that an A at one high school is not the same as an A at another high school. College entrance exam scores allow the colleges to have a standardized way of measuring students' academic preparedness across different high schools.

SAT Subject Test scores. Similarly, SAT Subject Test scores provide a standardized way for colleges to look at students' academic performance. These scores, however, may help determine your fit for a specific major since they are subject specific.

AP and IB test scores. Not all colleges require that AP and IB test scores be submitted, but those that do use the scores as another standardized way to measure students' performance. In addition, they indicate how well a high school prepares students in a specific subject area.

School report. High schools provide this report to the colleges to detail their grading system, courses offered and student body composition. The school report may outline the average number of AP, IB or honors courses that students take and a breakdown of GPAs for your class. Colleges use this information to get an idea of how competitive your school is, how you've taken advantage of its offerings and how you may compare to other students. This is especially helpful if your school doesn't provide class rankings.

Student Life

Extracurricular activities. Colleges want to know what you do both inside and outside the classroom. As you'll see in Chapter 3, they don't want to see the quantity of activities that you participated in but rather the quality. Leadership, making a special contribution to an activity or receiving an honor or award for an activity will help you stand out.

Talents. Colleges want their students to have diverse special talents including visual and performing arts, math and sciences, writing and more. Whether in the application form or in the essays, you'll want to highlight special talents you have or areas in which you may excel.

Awards. Awards help the colleges put into perspective how you have distinguished yourself in a given field or surpassed the competition in an activity. While it's fine to write in the application that you play the piano, it's more impressive to detail the awards that you've won for the application of this talent. This shows the college the degree of your talent or achievement, as well as your dedication to perfecting your skill.

Public service. Admissions officers like to know that you are involved in the community. They'd rather see that you have made a meaningful contribution in your volunteer work, either through a tangible result or by the number of hours you've committed, rather than reading that you have volunteered one or two times. In other words, leading a group of students to serve meals every week at a homeless shelter will set you apart far more than doing it by yourself once or twice. Some students feel compelled to volunteer to impress the colleges even when they don't have a desire to do so. We recommend that if you don't want to volunteer, you don't. It's better to do what you enjoy because that's where you'll excel.

Work experience. Work experience exhibits responsibility, your ability to work with others, leadership if you supervise others and any skills you may have learned on the job. Admissions officers like to see that students hold jobs, whether during the school year or summer, and take into account the time expended. They realize that if you hold a job, especially during the school year, you don't have as much time for other extracurricular activities.

Athletics. Participating in athletics demonstrates mental and physical commitment and your ability to work as part of a team. If you are in a position to be recruited by a college, this can play a strong role in your admission, depending on the role of athletics at the school. Even if you will not play intercollegiate athletics, having participated in high school can make you stand out.

Personal Characteristics

Essay. Chapters 5 to 7 cover the essay in great detail, but we'd like to note that the essay is an opportunity for you to share something about yourself beyond the numbers, scores and one-sentence descriptions in the application form. This can be a pivotal piece of your application. It can push your application from borderline consideration to acceptance.

Interview. You will learn much more about the interview in Chapter 8. It's important to remember that the interview is another opportunity to relate your strengths in a personal way. If you have the chance to do an interview either on campus or with a local alum, you should do so. Also, if the interview is optional or recommended, consider it to be a requirement if you're able to meet with someone locally.

Recommendation letters/evaluations. The evaluations are designed to provide others' assessments of your strengths and weaknesses. Your teachers and counselor will write about your academic and extracurricular achievements and about your leadership and character. They may be asked to compare your standing with those of other students they've taught. It's important that these key people know who you are and what you've accomplished. Chapter 4 covers the evaluations thoroughly, and there's a worksheet in the appendices to give your counselors and teachers helpful information for writing these.

Other Factors

Underrepresented racial or ethnic background. Colleges want to create diverse environments and may give weight to your application if you are from an underrepresented group. These groups are usually African Americans, Latinos and Native Americans. Asian Americans may or may not be considered as underrepresented, depending on a school's criteria.

Geographic background. Again to create a diverse environment, admissions officers may select students who are from geographic areas that are not as well represented. The geographic backgrounds that are underrepresented will vary by college. For example, a New England college may not have a large pool of students from the West Coast, whereas a Midwestern college may seek more students from the South. The most selective public colleges usually don't follow this pattern however and instead promote standards in which out-of-state students must be more competitive than in-state students.

Socio-economic background. Colleges want to give opportunities to students from a range of socio-economic backgrounds. It is important that you include this information.

Legacy. Many colleges take legacy into account when considering applications. "Legacy" means that you are the son or daughter of an alumnus. At Ivy League colleges, up to 35 percent of freshmen are legacies. According to a recent article in *CNBC*, children of alumni are admitted to Harvard at five times the rate of non-legacies. While this may seem unfair, especially to students who are not legacies, colleges do this with the bottom line in mind. They know that parents whose students are not accepted to their alma mater will not be as generous with their donations. Plus, the colleges say that children of alumni tend to be more qualified overall because of their parents' focus on education and socio-economic standing. What does this mean for you? While you can't change the colleges that your parents attended, you can consider whether you'd like to apply to their alma maters.

Development. Along the lines of legacies, colleges also take into account development, or how likely your family is to make donations to the college. The colleges say that this is a factor for an extremely small number of students. In most cases, this doesn't come into play unless there is the potential for donations that are seven figures or larger.

Demonstrated interest. Some colleges keep track of how much interest you show in their colleges. This is known as "demonstrated interest." Their notes on an individual student may include items like attending information sessions, calling to ask questions, visiting the college and other contact that you make with the college. Demonstrated interest may help your chances of being admitted because colleges want students who are the most likely to accept their offer of admission. There are more details about demonstrated interest in Chapter 3.

How Colleges Make Their Decisions: Behind the Closed Doors of the Admissions Office

When you think of the admissions officers making their decisions, you may envision a group of white haired, bespectacled old men dressed in tweed and bow ties. The men heatedly discuss each applicant, vote and then throw applications into piles for acceptance or denial. This may have been closer to reality several decades ago, but it is far from the truth today. In fact, admissions officers are a diverse group designed to reflect the varied student body, and the admissions process is not as simple as a quick read of the application and a toss into a designated stack.

Who Are the Admissions Officers?

If you were telling a joke to a friend, a teacher or your grandparent, the content of the joke would probably differ based on who you were telling it to. It's always a good idea to know your audience, and college applications are no exception. Many students wonder who their audience will be for applications, who will be reading their heartfelt essays and what personal opinions the admissions officers will hold.

Admissions officers come from a variety of backgrounds. They are an ethnically and geographically diverse group with both genders represented. However, there are some traits that tend to be common among this group. In general, admissions officers probably skew younger than you might expect. So you can pretty much eliminate that image you have of the group of old men dressed in tweed and bow ties. Some have worked in higher education, some plan lifelong careers in admissions and many are recent graduates of the college who are not as likely to make working in admissions a lifelong career. Occasionally a faculty member is asked for assistance, especially when an applicant has a specialized talent such as in the arts or sciences. A faculty member may have a better understanding of the student's specialized talent.

Why You Need Face Time with the Admissions Officers

The title of "admissions officer" is a misnomer. They do far more than the name suggests. Admissions officers not only decide who's accepted but also do outreach for the college to garner more applicants. They spend much of the fall months visiting high schools, meeting students and parents and giving informational sessions. It's not unusual for them to give three to five talks a day about their college at different schools and community centers.

What does this mean for you? First, it is an opportunity to get some valuable face time and make an impression on the admissions officer. There have been countless times when just a handful of students show up for a talk, even for some very selective colleges. If your school has a visit from a college you're interested in, you should definitely make the effort to attend the session. Stay after to chat with the admissions officer. Explain a little bit about your background and why you can see yourself as a fit at the college. Ask thoughtful questions, and ask if you can email the admissions officer with any follow-up questions. Admissions officers make notes about their visits, and if you make an impression and eventually apply to the college, the note that he or she makes can make a difference.

There's a second reason it should matter to you that admissions officers do school visits. This is the time for the admissions officer to learn more about your school and glean information that is not as easily conveyed in a high school report. Your counselor can explain just how difficult the grading system is, that Ms. So-and-so's class is particularly difficult or that many students hold part-time jobs and don't have as much time to participate in activities.

What Happens Behind the Closed Doors of the Admissions Office?

Just like the admissions officers themselves probably don't reflect the image you previously held of them, the actual admissions process probably doesn't either. While there can be heated discussions at times, more decisions are made via written notes. And while you may spend weeks, even months, perfecting your application, a decision can be made in less than a half hour. To take the mystery out of the process, here's what happens behind the closed doors:

Your file is created. Every applicant has a file. Every piece that is submitted for your application is date stamped. The file will include the application form that you submit as well as your high school report and transcript, evaluations and interview reports that others submit. As you can imagine, there is a mountain of files from the thousands of applicants.

All the numerical data is collected. Once your file is ready, the numerical information such as grades, test scores and classes is collected. This makes it easier and more uniform for the admissions officers to review.

Your application is read. It's typical for each application to be evaluated by two or three different readers. The readers write notes on the application parts that are not data entered such as essays, evaluations and interview. The first readers are usually assigned from your geographic region since they know the area best. They often can add insight about specific high schools since they may have visited them. Even if they don't have personal insight to add about your specific school, they will review the high school report to better interpret how you rate against your immediate peers. This is especially helpful for high schools that don't rank students. The reader summarizes your evaluations, interview and special achievements and gives a recommendation whether to accept, waitlist or deny you. The second reader also interprets your data but spends less time because the first has already written a summary of your non-numerical information. Second readers also write notes summarizing plus and minuses and give a recommendation for acceptance or denial.

You are rated. During this process, students are rated. The rating system may vary, but here's an example:

HARVARD'S ADMISSIONS RATING SYSTEM

Academics

1. Genuine scholar, Summa potential. Top grades and scores near 800
2. Excellent grades and scores in the low- to mid-700s
3. Solid grades and scores in the mid-600s to low-700s
4. Average grades and scores in the low-600s.
5. Marginal ability

Extracurricular/Athletic

1. Top leader with accomplishments on the state, national or international level
2. Major contributor
3. Active with minor offices
4. Some participation
5. Little interest
6. Unable to participate because of work or injury (This is not counted against the applicant.)

Personal Qualities

1. Rare interview
2. Outstanding interview
3. Average interview
4. Somewhat neutral or slightly negative interview
5. Poor interview

HARVARD'S ADMISSIONS RATING SYSTEM (CONTINUED)

Overall

1. Superior for admission
2. Clear admit
3. Reasonably strong applicant
4. Capable applicant
5. Not recommended

Other colleges have different rating systems, and some set a bar above the norm that all students with a high enough rating are usually admitted.

Some decisions are made. At some colleges, decisions may be made without the applicant ever going to committee. Decisions may be made based on the two or three readers alone or the readers' recommendations with one of the director's approval. Some students are so outstanding, or on the other hand so under-qualified, that the decisions are made solely by the readings, and the students are never discussed in committee. After these decisions are made, the number of acceptances is added up and the rest of the applications go to committee.

Your application may go to committee. Going to "committee" means that instead of being evaluated by two or three individuals separately, an application is discussed by a group of people. The committee may be the whole admissions staff and may even include faculty members. More often the committee is a smaller group such as a handful of admissions officers. At some colleges, all applications go to committee, but more often only the applications that are not clear acceptances or denials go to committee. Taking into account how many spots have already been filled, the committee is usually given direction of approximately how many students should be admitted.

The Admissions Gamble and the Role of Luck

In all of our experience helping students get into college, one very clear fact about college admissions has become apparent: There are no guarantees. Many well-qualified and deserving applicants are denied. The exact criteria that admissions committees employ on the individual level are just too diverse to predict. And there is clearly an element of luck and circumstance that can help or hurt a student's chances. This can be viewed both positively and negatively. On the one hand, just because you didn't get a perfect SAT score doesn't mean you won't get into your first-choice school. On the other hand—even if you are well qualified and you do everything right—for reasons beyond your control, you can still be denied:

We can not guarantee in any way admittance into any school. No one can make such a guarantee. If you meet someone who does, don't walk but run in the opposite direction. What we do promise, however, it that the information in this book will help you craft the best possible application, which is essential to maximizing your odds of getting accepted.

Who We Are and How We Will Help

You may be wondering who we are and what special credentials we have to write a book about college admissions. Well, since you've twisted our arms–ouch!–we suppose we will have to do a little bragging—which, by the way, is an important "art" you will have to learn to write a successful application.

Between the two of us, we were accepted by all of the Ivy League schools plus Stanford, Berkeley, Duke, Rice, Pomona and a host of other prestigious state and private institutions. We were also a part of a minority of students who were not rejected by any college or university. Having won dozens of merit-based scholarships worth over $100,000, we left Harvard debt-free and our parents guilt-free. Both of us graduated Magna Cum Laude. Since graduating we have dedicated ourselves to helping students learn from our experiences. We have authored 14 books on college planning and have traveled across the country to give more than 800 free workshops at high schools and bookstores on being accepted and then paying for college.

We should also mention that this book draws on the collective experiences of students too numerous to name individually but who generously shared their time, shamelessly contributed their personal stories (both good and bad) and allowed us to print their application essays. Without the gracious cooperation of these students, this book would not have been possible.

Enough about us. Let's take the first steps toward getting you into your top choice college!

STORY FROM REAL LIFE
YOU CAN BE NORMAL AND STILL GET INTO HARVARD

You don't have to be an academic superstar to get into a great school. But you do have present your strengths to the college and give them a reason to let you in. —Gen and Kelly

I am living proof you don't have to be a superstar to get into Harvard. Although I went to a competitive high school, I was far from being an outstanding student. Unlike my friends who had perfect 4.0s, my report card was littered with "A's" and "B's." I got average SAT scores. They weren't terrible, but they weren't great either. I have to admit that when I filled out my college applications even I was shocked at how "average" I was on paper.

My only chance I felt was to work really hard on the essay and get good teacher evaluations. I don't know what my teachers wrote, but it must not have been that bad. I was the kind of student who always tried hard. I also spent a lot of time on my essay and must have written and rewritten it a dozen or more times. But still nobody imagined that I would get into Harvard.

In April even I was stunned when I opened the acceptance letter. Soon after I arrived at Harvard my roommates and I had a late night discussion about how we got in. We began to compare SATs, grades and anything else to see why we were chosen. When I told them what I had gotten, they couldn't help but tease, "How in the world did you get in?"

It was obvious that it was not my grades, scores or even activities that got me in. I think I owe it mostly to my essay and evaluations. I hope all of you who are thinking about applying to competitive schools will not be discouraged just because others have better grades, higher scores or are more active in clubs or sports. As I found out, it's not a prerequisite for you to be school president, valedictorian and football team captain all at the same time to get into Harvard.

Harvard does take normal people too. At first I was embarrassed by my low scores and grades. But now I freely admit my "averageness." And Harvard must know a little something about success since I have consistently gotten better grades than my roommates who, based on their high school records, are far more outstanding than I am.

—Eugene, who is at Harvard and is still normal

STEPS TO SUCCESS

YOUR ADMISSIONS TIMELINE

9TH GRADE

Fall Semester

❑ Explore various extracurricular activities to find what you enjoy.

❑ Challenge yourself academically by taking difficult courses.

Spring Semester

❑ Plan the next three years of your academics by identifying which AP, IB or Honors courses you want to take. Know what prerequisites you'll need, if any.

❑ Meet your counselor to discuss your goals and ask what resources your school has to prepare for college.

❑ Take the PSAT 8/9 if offered at your school to help get familiar with the PSAT test.

Summer Vacation

❑ Find a summer job, do volunteer work or attend a summer program.

❑ Instead of TV, try reading for pleasure to build your vocabulary.

10TH GRADE

September–November

❑ Take challenging courses including AP, IB or Honors classes. Keep up your grades—aim for "A's."

❑ Start narrowing down your activities. Begin to dedicate yourself to a few extracurricular activities, and work toward leadership positions. If you haven't found activities that you are passionate about, think about starting a club or special project. Don't forget to look outside of school at community activities.

❑ Compete in matches, contests and competitions to rack up awards.

❑ Inquire about taking the PreACT at your school to prepare for the ACT test or the PSAT/NMSQT to get practice for taking the exam in the eleventh grade.

December–February

❑ Start attending college fairs, browsing college guidebooks, attending visits by college reps and checking out college websites.

❑ Meet with your counselor to discuss colleges that may be a good fit and ask what you should be doing to prepare.

March–May

❑ Inquire about taking the PSAT 10 at your school. It will help you get familiar with the PSAT/NMSQT, which you will take in the eleventh grade.

❑ Take the AP tests in May in subjects that you have completed.

❑ If you feel prepared enough, take SAT Subject exams (usually in May or June) for courses that you have completed.

Summer Vacation

❑ Find a summer job, do volunteer work or attend a summer program.

❑ If you go on a family vacation, visit colleges in the area.

❑ Study for the PSAT/NMSQT that you must take next year.

❑ Read books for pleasure (and vocabulary building).

STEPS TO SUCCESS

YOUR ADMISSIONS TIMELINE

11TH GRADE

September–November

☐ Take the PSAT/NMSQT in the fall to practice for the SAT and to be eligible for National Merit Scholarship awards.

☐ Continue to take challenging AP, IB or Honors courses.

☐ Take the SAT, especially if you are applying for Early Admission or Early Decision.

☐ Discuss with your parents how you will finance your education. Learn about federal financial aid, and ask your counselor about local scholarships. Visit www.supercollege.com to search for scholarships that fit your background.

☐ Get to know your favorite teachers well. Start thinking about whom you might ask to write evaluations.

☐ Focus on becoming a leader in a few extracurricular activities—run for an office, lead a team or start your own club, business or service project.

☐ Get a copy of some college applications to preview.

☐ Continue to compete in matches, contests and competitions.

☐ If you think you will play Division I athletics in college, register at the NCAA Eligibility Center at www.eligibilitycenter.org.

☐ Get a preview of how much financial aid you'll be likely to receive by completing the FAFSA4caster at https://fafsa.ed.gov/FAFSA/app/f4cForm.

☐ Attend college fairs and college representative visits to your school and visit colleges. Ask questions!

December–February

☐ Continue to research colleges.

☐ Register and prepare for the SAT or ACT and SAT Subject exams. Think about taking review classes or set up your own preparation schedule.

March–May

☐ Take the SAT (usually in March, May or June) or the ACT (usually in April or June).

☐ Take AP exams in May and the SAT Subject exams in May or June.

☐ Visit your counselor to discuss your preliminary plans for applying to college and sources of financial aid.

☐ Write to your U.S. Senator or Representative if you would like to attend a U.S. military academy or participate in an ROTC program.

Summer

☐ Find a summer job, do volunteer work or attend a summer program.

☐ Plan family vacations so that you can also visit some of the colleges where you might want to apply for admission.

☐ Get applications from colleges by writing letters, requesting them online or downloading them from the colleges' websites.

☐ Register for the SAT or ACT and SAT Subject tests. Set up a study schedule or take a test preparation class.

☐ Read books for pleasure (and vocabulary building).

STEPS TO SUCCESS

YOUR ADMISSIONS TIMELINE

12TH GRADE

September–November

- ❑ Continue to take challenging courses and keep up your grades. Be careful of the "senior slump."
- ❑ Decide which schools you will apply to and list the deadlines.
- ❑ Take the SAT (usually in October or November) or the ACT (usually in September or October).
- ❑ Take the SAT Subject exams in October, November or December.
- ❑ If you are applying for early admission, finish taking the required standardized tests. The November tests are typically the last that you can take to be eligible.
- ❑ Submit Early Action or Early Decision applications. Deadlines are typically around November 1, but check to confirm the cut-off dates.
- ❑ Ask teachers and counselors to complete your Evaluation Forms and School Report. Approach them early, and make clear the deadlines for each school.
- ❑ Request transcripts and test scores be sent to the colleges.
- ❑ Brainstorm and write your essays, and enlist editors to help you perfect them. (Start this as early as possible!)
- ❑ Arrange college interviews and practice for them.
- ❑ Attend college fairs and college representative visits to your school and visit colleges. Ask questions!

December–February

- ❑ Send off your applications—Deadlines are typically in January, but check with each school.
- ❑ Complete the necessary financial aid forms, including the FAFSA and CSS/PROFILE. Both are typically due in February to be eligible for financial aid from the college.
- ❑ Continue to apply for scholarships. Don't forget to check with your counselor, civic groups, local businesses and your parents' employers.
- ❑ Ask your counselor to complete any necessary Mid-Year School Reports. They are typically due in February.

March–May

- ❑ You are done (almost)! Now it's time to wait it out. You will typically receive notification letters at the end of March. (Remember, good news usually—but not always—comes in thick envelopes.)
- ❑ If you are placed on the wait list, write a letter reiterating your interest in being admitted.
- ❑ Decision time: With help from your parents, teachers and counselor decide where you'd like to spend the next four years. Consider the financial aid offers and contact the schools if you have additional extenuating financial circumstances.
- ❑ Take part in "pre-frosh" events and visitations. Notify the schools of your decision and send in your deposit to your new college.
- ❑ If you haven't already, send thank-you letters to all of your helpers, and inform them of where you have decided to attend college.

Summer

❏ Enjoy your summer of freedom. Congratulations and good luck as you
embark on four of the most exciting
years of your life!

IN THIS CHAPTER

● The "right" number of schools to apply to

● Hedging your bets: How to spread your choices intelligently

● Essential questions to ask about each college

● Making sure the college "fits" you

● The truth about early action and early decision

● The pitfalls of rankings

CHAPTER 2

HOW TO PICK THE PERFECT COLLEGE FOR YOU

Your First Challenge: Deciding Where to Apply

We've heard almost every reason imaginable for why a student would pick a college. For example, we know one student who decided to apply to a college because during the campus tour he noticed that there was a Krispy Kreme donut shop right in the center of campus. We even know of another student who wanted to get so far away from home that she took out a compass and a map and drew a 400 mile circle around her house. She vowed never to apply to a college within that circle. Depending on your personal priorities, these may or may not be good reasons to pick a college. But since we all have our own personal preferences, it's important to remember that the same factors that make one school a student's dream college may make it a nightmare choice for you.

In this chapter we will not be so presumptuous as to assume we know what is important to you. What we will do, however, is present the factors that we feel you should consider when deciding where to apply to college.

But only you can say if the availability of hot donuts, for example, is reason enough to keep a school on your list.

Besides worrying about where to apply, many students also stress over how many schools they should apply to. While there is the occasional student who applies to more than 20 schools—we know of one student who applied to 37—we feel that this is definitely overkill. Most students should apply to between eight and twelve schools. This is a reasonable number, especially considering the fact that each school charges between about $35 and $90 just for the privilege of applying. Plus, by "recycling" your essays (more on this in Chapter 6) or using the Common Application, applying to this number of schools should be fairly easy.

The Neapolitan Ice Cream Approach to Picking the "Right" Colleges

Imagine that colleges are Neapolitan ice cream. (Just bear with us a moment and the value of seeing colleges as that tri-flavor ice cream will become clear.) For our families, the strawberry ice cream was always the least desirable and the last flavor to be eaten, the vanilla was likable and delicious, but

---

COLLEGES AS NEAPOLITAN ICE CREAM

Strawberry: These are schools to which you are almost sure that you will be accepted, where you know that your grade point average is well above the median and that have less strenuous requirements for admission. Strawberry schools are sometimes known as "safety schools."

Vanilla: These are the schools that you are pretty sure you will be accepted to and that you would like, but perhaps not love, to attend. They are the schools that fulfill most of your preferences.

Chocolate: These are your top-choice schools for which you would give up all your earthly possessions to attend. Most likely these are the schools to which it is the most difficult to gain admission. Even if you think that you don't have a chance, apply anyway. The admissions officers might find you to be more remarkable than you believe you are. (Some of the most extraordinary students are also the most modest.)

Most students pick a few colleges as their strawberry flavor. The majority of schools are usually of the vanilla variety. Depending on how competitive they believe their applications are, students may have a few or many chocolate schools. Regardless of how your list turns out, just make sure that you have schools of each flavor and that they are schools that generally meet your preferences. By doing this, you set your sights high while ensuring that you have a school where you will be happy to attend in the fall.

the chocolate was the flavor that everyone fought over. While your order of preference may be different, the analogy of Neapolitan ice cream applies to colleges, which can also be divided into three categories of desirability.

The strawberry schools are your least desirable schools but also the ones that you are sure you can get into. The schools that you wouldn't mind attending, but that may also be a little more selective, are the vanilla schools. Your top choice schools, those that may also be the most difficult to get into, are your chocolate flavor schools. Regardless of how you divide your college preferences, we recommend that you have two to three of each flavor.

The Neapolitan Ice Cream Approach ensures that you definitely have a place to go to college; yet you don't have to sell yourself short by not trying for your top choice schools.

Which School Has the Best Parties and Other Important Questions You Need to Ask

One student we met used the *U.S. News & World Report* annual college rankings as her only criteria for applying to college. She was accepted by three of the five colleges to which she applied. Only one problem: She realized later that she didn't want to move to the East Coast, where the schools were located! She discovered too late that although you can choose schools by reputation, it is better to have concrete reasons for applying.

How can you find out if a college (given all of the intangibles) will make your college years rewarding academically, socially and culturally? Here are some sources of information:

- **College brochures.** One of the first places to look for more information about a college is in those beautiful full-color brochures that the colleges may mail or that you can download. These brochures are filled with lots of useful information, but remember, they are biased and will tout only the positive aspects of the school. Always view the college's brochure with a healthy dose of caution.

- **College directories.** There are both books and websites that offer profiles of colleges. Often you can find information about the student population, activities, majors offered, costs and financial aid, as well as some useful statistics—such as how many freshmen are admitted each year. The best directories go beyond the numbers and statistics to give students' feedback, narrative descriptions and in-depth profiles of the colleges. Our book *The Ultimate Guide to America's Best Colleges* has detailed profiles of more than 300 colleges.

- **College fairs.** Don't just settle for pictures and printed words. Go to college fairs and speak with the college representatives. For a schedule of national fairs, contact the National Association for College

Admission Counseling (www.nacacnet.org). When you go, don't be shy about asking the representative all of your questions about the college—that's why they are there. Rather than trying to meet with every college, focus on a handful with which to spend quality time. Ask for the representatives' business cards, and follow up with email reiterating your interest and sharing more information about yourself.

- **Campus visits.** The single best way to learn about colleges is to visit, but don't just settle for the official tour. Take time to do your own investigation by walking the campus, sitting in on a class, eating in the cafeteria and talking with some students who are not tour guides. If you can, arrange ahead of time to meet with an admissions officer and contact the department of your major. The best time to visit is when school is in session. It's hard to get a feel for a college when it's empty! Also, if you don't have the budget to travel to all of the schools or the more distant ones, visit those closest to you—even if you aren't interested in applying. The more campuses you visit, including those that are not on your list, the better idea you'll have for what you really want in your dream college.

- **College rep visits.** When college reps visit your high school, attend the meetings. It's worth giving up your lunch time for an opportunity to get more in-depth information about the college and to form a more personal connection with the reps. Be sure to ask questions, and speak with the reps afterward. Again, ask for business cards, and follow up. The relationships that you build with the reps will help with demonstrated interest, which is described in Chapter 3.

- **College students.** Speak to recent graduates of your high school and ask them what they think of their school. If the school is close to you, visit the campus, take a tour and ask to be put in touch with a current student to be able to ask questions. If you call the office of admissions they might be able to put you in touch with a "student ambassador" who is a current student and can answer your questions by phone or email.

- **Counselors and teachers.** There's help close to home too. Your teachers and school counselors have helped thousands of students get into college and can share what they've learned over the years. If you haven't already, make an appointment to meet with your counselor.

- **Websites.** Visit colleges' websites to learn about their admissions and financial aid policies, academic offerings, student life and campus surroundings. To get a preview of student life, take a look at the websites of their campus newspaper, student organizations and even the individual homepages of students. These student sections are where you'll find the true portrait of the college beyond the marketing hype.

While perusing information about the schools, keep the following questions in mind:

What Are Your Academic Goals?

- *Do you want to be trained for a specific line of work or do you want a more general liberal arts education?* A pre-professional education prepares you for a specific job and includes areas such as engineering and pre-med. Some schools like MIT have very strong programs for those interested in the sciences but might not be right for someone interested in literature. A liberal arts education, on the other hand, aims to equip you with general knowledge and reasoning skills suitable for many jobs.

- *What might you major in?* Most universities are stronger in some areas and weaker in others. While it may be too early for you to know whether you want to major in English or history, check out how strong the programs and professors are in the various fields you are considering. Investigate the courses offered and required, how many students are majoring in your area of interest, the professors' areas of research, whether you need to apply to enter the major and whether a thesis is required. In addition to speaking with a professor or administrator in the department, ask to speak with a student currently in the major.

- *How many years does it take to graduate?* Most schools graduate their students in four years, but some majors may take longer. For the same major, different schools have different requirements for the number and difficulty level of courses. Laboratory work, research, senior theses, tutorials or seminars may be requirements for your field. All of this can affect how long it takes to finish.

- *Do you prefer a small college or large university setting?* Most students find smaller classes that allow more active participation to be more rewarding than large, impersonal lectures. But larger institutions also have advantages, such as more resources and often (but not always) more famous faculty.

- *What do you plan to do with your degree after graduating?* Whether you want to go directly to graduate school or work for a non-profit organization after graduation affects what you look for in a college.

STORY FROM REAL LIFE
WHY I WISH I HAD CHOSEN BETTER

The glossy brochures and flashy websites from colleges never tell the entire story. Gather as much information as possible from other sources and you won't be surprised when you arrive on campus. —Gen and Kelly

When I was a senior in high school I had no idea where I wanted to go to college. I remembered someone saying good things about "California College." (This is a fictitious name since I do not want to offend this very real school.)

One day I received an information packet from California College. Inside was a beautiful full-color brochure that unfolded into this gorgeous picture of the school. There were dozens of testimonials praising the small student-to-teacher ratio and wonderful extracurricular activities. After reading all these good things, I just had to apply.

When I received my acceptance letters, I only had to look at the happy students in the California College brochure to make up my mind. I wanted to be one of those smiling students. On August 25 my parents and I flew into the Los Angeles airport. We rented a car and headed off to my new home for the next four years.

Following the instructions that the college sent, we drove for hours, switching from freeways to state highways then to city streets and finally turning onto what looked like a country road. As we got farther away from civilization I grew more uneasy. When we finally reached the school it was so far from any town—much less a city—that I wondered how it could have looked so urban in the picture. I took out the brochure. Sure enough there were the three modern looking buildings as pictured, but what the brochure didn't show was that these were the *only* buildings on campus. Everything else looked like residential homes or forest reserve. There was so much nature and the campus was so quiet. I suppose that if I had been raised in an isolated hamlet in the Sierra Nevada mountains I might have found this place reminiscent of home. But being from a rather large Southern city I had wanted to go somewhere a little more cosmopolitan.

Ultimately, I went crazy and decided to transfer. This time I made sure that I visited the campuses before I made a decision. It cost me my first two years of happiness, but I had learned my lesson.

—Aaron, who is now a happy urban student at UCLA

Investigate what recent students have done post-graduation, and learn about what those who work in your future career studied in college.

Do You Want to Attend Party Central?

- *Do you want to have three Greek letters emblazoned on your chest everywhere you go? Does the school have a Greek system?* Some students are inclined to joining a fraternity or sorority, while others feel that their existence on campus is overbearing for those who choose not to go Greek.

- *Does the school offer extracurricular activities that you would enjoy?* If you join the Hasty Pudding Club at Harvard, you'll have the chance to cross-dress and sing on stage at its famous annual performance. It's important that your future college offers activities you'd enjoy.

What Type of Digs Do You Want?

- *Do most students live on campus or commute?* Whether students spend most of their lives on campus or off makes a big difference in the social atmosphere of the college.

- *Can you live with strangers?* Can you bathe near strangers? If you lived in the dorm, would you have roommates? How modern or ancient are the dorms? Does each room have its own bathroom or do you use a shared facility? These are questions you'd want to explore.

What Kind of Campus Environment Do You Want?

- *What size student body fits you?* Some students like the intimate feeling of a small school where they know the names of all of their classmates, while others prefer the diversity of a large student body.

- *Is the campus in the inner city, countryside or somewhere in between?* Is it a college town where the college is the social center of the city? Is it in the middle of nowhere, where you have to drive 40 miles just to see a movie? If locality matters to you, then you'll want answers to these questions.

- *What is the weather like?* If you've never endured a minus-20 degree winter or a 90 percent humidity summer, you might want to think twice about how the weather will affect your life (e.g., being able to sunbathe between classes vs. literally not seeing the sun for months at a time).

- *How far is the college from home?* Do you want to remain geographically close to your family and friends or do you want to venture into the world of collegedom solo? What are the chances of your parents dropping in for a surprise visit? Is this a good thing? (It can be if they are willing to do your laundry!)

- *Is the school known for attracting students of a particular political view?* Most schools have a surprisingly even balance of conservative and liberal students. However a few have a noticeable imbalance. While you should keep this in mind, don't let it be an overriding factor since you will always find others who share (and oppose) your views.

You will not be able to find answers to all of these questions, but asking them should help you narrow down your list of prospective colleges. Also, some of these questions may not be important to you and recognizing that is also helpful when picking colleges.

Your goal when choosing colleges is to find schools that offer what is important to you. The only way to do this is to first ask yourself questions like those posed above and then do some detective work to find schools that match your needs. Refer to Appendix B for a College Search Worksheet that will help you summarize your research on the colleges.

Applying Early . . . or Should I Sign My Life Away?

Okay, so you won't really sign your life away, but you may have to commit to attending the college if you are accepted. These early bird specials in college admissions allow you to apply—as you may have guessed—earlier. Typically this means you must turn in your completed application and finish all of your testing by November, and you will receive notification in December or January that you have been accepted.

There are three forms of applying early. With all three you apply early and receive a decision early.

- **Early Action:** You are not bound to attend the college.

- **Restrictive Early Action:** While you are not bound to attend the college, you are often not allowed to apply to another college Early Action or Early Decision. When you are restricted from applying to another college early, this is known as "Single Choice Early Action."

- **Early Decision:** You are bound to attend the college.

The advantages of applying for Early Action or Early Decision are: 1) You demonstrate to the college that it is your top choice; 2) You will find out sooner if you are accepted and thus may not have to apply elsewhere and most importantly, 3) Many colleges have higher acceptance rates for Early Action

EARLY ACTION AND EARLY DECISION FAQS

How should you decide whether or not to apply early?

Have you really done your homework on the college? In other words, have you visited or at least spoken with a college representative, alum or current student? Have you done the same for other colleges too for comparison?

What are your reasons for applying to the college early? Apply early because you truly want to attend the college, not because you think that this is the best strategic move that you can make.

Are your grades and test scores at their peak? If not, it may be better to allow yourself to take another round of standardized tests.

How does applying early affect your financial aid package?

One of the biggest disadvantages of Early Decision is that you won't receive other financial aid packages for comparison. However, if you find that the financial aid package is not enough, contact the financial aid office. Explain why the package is not enough, and be ready to back up your case with numbers. If in the end the financial aid office is not able to meet your family's need, you can get out of your commitment to attend the college.

Will applying early really give you an edge?

The answer is both yes and no. Yes, statistically colleges typically accept a higher percentage of students early than they do during the regular decision time. A study of early admissions found that applying early was the equivalent of scoring 100 points higher on the SAT. However, at the same time, the caliber of students applying early can also be higher, making the competition tough. We recommend that you don't apply early solely as an admissions strategy but that you do so because the college is truly your first choice.

or Decision applicants than regular admissions applicants. Keep in mind, however, that the applicant pool for Early Action or Decision is usually of a higher caliber.

The disadvantages are that: 1) For Early Decision, you are committed to attending that school if you are accepted and must withdraw your applications to all other schools. (For Early Action, you don't have to make this commitment); and 2) You will not be able to compare financial aid packages since you have to make your decision early. If you apply during the regular action cycle, you can compare financial aid packages which may differ significantly and therefore influence your final decision in selecting which college to attend.

We suggest that you use these early bird specials, especially the binding Early Decision, only if you are sure that the school is your first choice, you definitely want to go there and you are not concerned greatly about financial aid. Otherwise, stick with the regular admissions schedule.

The Dreaded Deferment

One possible outcome of applying early is neither acceptance nor rejection. It is a deferment. Being deferred means that your application was not strong enough to be an "instant accept" but was still competitive enough that the college will re-evaluate it during the regular admissions cycle. It is impossible to say how many "deferred" applicants ultimately get accepted. If you are deferred, there are three things you should do:

Start applying to other colleges. Don't count on the deferment turning into an acceptance. While it is possible, you need to protect yourself from having no other choices by applying to other schools.

Send an email to the admissions office to let them know you are still interested. At the same time, provide them with an update on any new accomplishments since you submitted your application. Some students take deferment personally and lose interest in the school. By sending an email reiterating your desire to attend, you reassure the admissions officers that you are not one of these students. Also, since your application was not strong enough during the early round, it can only help if you add a few more achievements. Even if your update is reporting good grades during the semester, it's important to let the admissions officers know this.

Ask your counselor to contact the school on your behalf. The admissions officer may give an indication of what your weakness is. If the admissions officer mentions that your SAT scores are below the median, you know it's time to start preparing and take the exam again.

Don't Worry About Money (Yet)

Until now, we have not discussed perhaps the biggest factor in determining where you will go to college—money. Yes, it is true that college costs a bundle, with private colleges being especially guilty of exorbitant prices. It is not uncommon for parents to take out a second mortgage on their homes or for students to have loans for years after they graduate. And unfortunately, costs are only rising.

However, at this point, do not let costs dictate your goals. Even if money is tight, don't make it your primary concern just yet. (If you have trouble paying for the application fee, ask your counselor about a fee waiver.) The reason that money should not be an issue now is that while tuition is expensive there is also a ton of financial aid available. Just last year over $241.3 billion in financial aid was given to students to help them pay for college. The real question is not how much a college costs, but how much you'll have to pay out of pocket after taking into account scholarships and financial aid.

Once you get accepted, you can work with the college to put together a financial aid package that will make the school affordable. This is why you need to wait until you are accepted by the college and they determine what kind of financial aid package they can offer before making cost a limiting factor. Be sure to check out Chapter 11, *How to Win Free Cash for College*, to see what kind of support is available and how you can maximize your aid package.

Your college education is one of the most important investments in your future and you need to know all of the information before making the right decision.

THE PITFALLS OF RANKINGS

It is true that rankings can be helpful. They offer a quick snapshot of useful information such as costs, enrollment, acceptance rates and academic ratings. In this sense, they can provide a starting point for your college search. However, we strongly recommend that you don't use the rankings as your only source when selecting colleges. Here are some key factors that the rankings may miss:

Specific academic department. Rankings of this kind may provide an overall academic rating of the college or even the ranking of a specific graduate department at a university, but many departments are left out. Additionally, the undergraduate experience is not well covered. If you know what you'd like to major in, it's better to select a college based on your specific academic department rather than the college's overall academic ranking.

Specific professors. Similarly, rankings do not portray teaching styles of specific professors at a college or explain how they interact with their students. There may be professors who are conducting research or who teach a series of courses that completely match your interests, yet you would never know from the ranking information that is published. You may crave having professors who know all their students by first name, invite students over for dinner or involve undergraduate students in research. These are examples of characteristics that aren't captured by rankings.

Student life and activities. Naturally college is about more than what you learn in the classroom. There is no better way to determine whether a college's student life and activities are a match for you than to visit the college or speak with students about its offerings.

THE PITFALLS OF RANKINGS (CONTINUED)

Internship opportunities. The rankings may take into account the overall availability of internships, but they don't factor in the specific internship a prospective student might like to hold. Whether at a magazine publication in New York City or at the Smithsonian in Washington, D.C., these are opportunities that you might like to know about.

Location. You may feel it is important to know whether the temperatures are sub-zero for months at a time or whether the college is in a vibrant metropolis or laid-back suburban city. Even if everything else were equal, location could play a large role in your college experience, yet this is another factor that the rankings don't cover.

Your out-of-pocket costs. While the rankings do provide general statistics such as the average amount of financial aid given, they aren't able to supply the actual out-of-pocket costs for you or your individual family. There are online calculators to help you predict this, but they aren't as specific as the financial aid package that you'll receive from the college. From this, you'll be able to determine how much your family will need to pay, which is far more important than the average amount of aid outlined in the ratings that is given to thousands of students.

While it can be helpful to use rankings as one tool in selecting colleges, remember that there are so many aspects that the rankings just can't cover. The best approach is to make your own rankings based on your individual preferences such as those for academics, career path, student life, location and cost. You know yourself better than any researcher at a news magazine ever will!

IN THIS CHAPTER

● Discovering the secrets of creating a killer application

● How to beef up and prioritize your accomplishments

● The "correct" way to brag

● When to leave something blank

● An example application that worked

● How to show demonstrated interest

CHAPTER 3

CREATE A COMPELLING ADMISSION APPLICATION

How to Write a Killer Application

We confess. The actual application form is hardly sexy. It lacks the challenge of the essay, the stress of the interview and the personal touch of the teacher evaluations. We won't deny that it is a monotonous chore with an annoying number of questions, blanks, lines and boxes.

It is precisely for this reason that many students make careless mistakes and do not carefully consider how to strategically present their information. These deficiencies, while they may seem small, are often magnified in the eyes of the admissions officers and can take the edge off an otherwise perfect application.

The application form is your personal stats sheet, much like those of professional athletes. Instead of the number of rebounds or yards per run, your stats include test scores, years of participation in extracurricular activities, number of awards won and, of course, grades. The admissions officers use your application as both a summary of your achievements and a way to quickly compare you to all the other applicants. From your application they will learn about your education, test scores, extracurricular activities, volunteer work, honors, employment and family background. That's a lot of important information, so you better not rush when filling out this very critical form.

The goal of this chapter is to show you how a little planning can not only save you time, but ensure that your application stands out from the masses. (To get a sense of the word "masses," try imagining the 135,000 applications that a school like UCLA gets each and every year!)

We begin with how to request or download college applications. Then we'll look at format, style and strategy. At the end of this chapter, you'll find an example of a completed form of a successful applicant. Be prepared to limber up those typing fingers.

Get Your Very Own Applications

Your first step is to get a copy of the application. Typically, you complete an online form to register on the college's website. Some colleges allow you to download applications from their websites to print out and complete while almost all allow you to fill out and submit the applications online. If you choose to complete your applications online, be sure to read the section with our tips and strategies for these virtual applications.

Save Time With the Common Application or Coalition Application

If you were to apply to nine colleges, this would normally mean completing nine separate applications. The Common Application and the Coalition Application can cut the number of applications you need to complete and save you time. More than 900 colleges have agreed to accept the Common Application, and more than 150 colleges accept the Coalition Application. For these schools, you only need to complete the application once and then submit the same application electronically via the Internet.

You may complete the Common Application on the website of the National Association of Secondary School Principals (NASSP), which administers the Common Application, at www.commonapp.org. The website also offers materials in Spanish and a virtual counselor with questions and answers about college planning and financial aid.

The Coalition Application is available at www.coalitionforcollegeaccess. org. Starting in ninth grade, you may use the website to start entering personal and school-related achievements. The Coalition Application also offers an online "Locker" to hold papers, videos and images and a "Collaboration Space" for getting feedback from teachers, counselors or parents.

For both applications, remember that some colleges have supplemental forms that you will also need to include with either your Common Application or Coalition Application.

Get Ready to Be a Neat Freak—Even if You're Not

If you aren't a neat freak, try to pretend that you are. Otherwise you'll end up with a (virtual or literal) mountain of papers and brochures liable to take on a life of their own. Here are a few quick and easy things you can do to keep yourself organized and efficient. First, get a binder or folder to house all the forms and brochures or create a folder on your computer. Then create an Excel or spreadsheet file with the following:

- List all of the colleges you are applying to and their deadlines. Note which colleges require their own applications, the Common Application or Coalition Application or the Common Application or Coalition Application and supplemental materials. If you are undecided if you will apply early, include both the early and regular deadlines. Pay attention to priority deadlines for financial aid or scholarships.

- Note if the school has a rolling admissions policy. Schools with rolling admissions policies admit and deny students as they receive their applications. When their class is full, they stop admitting. Thus, if the school employs rolling admissions, get your application in well before the deadline. You don't want to miss out because you procrastinated.

- For each college, list all of the materials required. Don't forget to include the actual application form, fee, transcript, financial aid form, evaluations, school reports, mid-year school reports and standardized test score reports. This will ensure that you don't omit any materials, which could delay the processing of your application.

Your Online Personality

While your friends may enjoy looking at photos of the last party you attended or your proclivity for documenting outrageous stunts, admissions officers will not. Take a look at your online presence—blogs, Facebook, Twitter and the other sites du jour—and remove any questionable content. At the very least only allow your closest friends to have access. In a recent survey, 35 percent of admissions officers said that they viewed applicants' social media accounts. It's better to be safe. While you're at it, sign up for an email account with a professional name. Hotchick18 or URanIDiOT14 isn't something you want the admissions officer typing in when composing an email to you.

Beef up Your Extracurricular and Academic Life

The most important parts of the application form are the areas that make you shine. You can probably guess which parts these are: your extracurricular activities, jobs and honors and awards (which we will discuss later). These are the sections that can really set you apart from other applicants. Anyone can take an English honors class, but not anyone can start an adult literacy program or become the manager at Wayne's Weenie World.

Since you don't have space to list everything that you have ever done on the application, you need to first decide which activities you want to highlight. Begin by making a list of all your extracurricular activities, summer activities and jobs. List everything big and small. Significant and insignificant. Don't forget that extracurricular activities include experiences like teaching all those hyper kids at Sunday School, whacking the ball around on the Ping-Pong team, playing the triangle in band, leading a sit-in against animal fur or volunteering as a candy striper at the hospital.

For every activity, job and sport, try to list as much of the following as possible:

- Name of the organization, program or business.

- Dates you participated or worked.

- Number of hours per week you spent on the activity or job.

- Leadership positions you held and your responsibilities.

- Major accomplishments you made while in the organization.

● Special projects that you initiated or oversaw. These could be either long-term or one-time projects.

Although you are far from senility, you will still find that it is surprising what other people remember that you have overlooked. Be sure to show your list to your parents, teachers, siblings, friends and advisors. Ask them to help you add anything that you may have forgotten.

Prioritize Your Activities

Now that you have a list, it's time to select which activities and jobs you are going to highlight and in what order. You probably will not have enough space to list everything, and even if you do, you should only present those activities in which you made a contribution. Don't give the impression that you did a little of everything. Rather, emphasize the depth of your participation in a few activities.

Rank the activities in the order of importance based on those in which you were a leader or had responsibility. Even if you were not an officer in the club, if you took charge of a special event or project, note that on your list. After these items come activities where you dedicated a lot of time and made a contribution. Next, note which activities are academic in nature as well as display volunteer service.

Keep in mind the dates of your participation. If possible, include activities that span all four years so that you present a consistent pattern of participation.

Depending on how much space you have, add some diversity. If your top five activities are all related to your passion for calculus, add your membership in the cross country team (even if you are a terrible runner) to show that you are interested in more than quadratic equations.

Here's an example of an application form in which you are given only a small amount of space:

PLEASE LIST YOUR EXTRACURRICULAR AND VOLUNTEER ACTIVITIES

Student Council President (12th); Class President (9th); NHS secretary (12th); Big Brothers Volunteer (9th-present); Key Club Volunteer Tutor (10th); Tennis Team (9th-11th); and Charity Tennis Tournament Organizer (9th).

Here's an example of a more generous application that gives you more room to explain:

PLEASE LIST YOUR EXTRACURRICULAR AND VOLUNTEER ACTIVITIES

President, Student Council—chairs monthly meetings, serves on district council, initiates and organizes Toys for Tots donation drive, founded student concerns program, oversaw implementation of revised student constitution. (12th grade).

Secretary, National Honor Society—publishes monthly minutes, serves on fund-raising committee, established and maintains website, chairs new members selection committee. (12th grade).

Volunteer, Big Brothers & Sisters—meets twice each week to tutor little brother at Oaks Elementary School; teaches basic math, reading and composition. (9th-present).

Varsity Tennis Team—top-ranked singles player; placed 2nd in district in 10th grade and 4th in state in 11th grade. Organized school's first "Charity Tennis Tournament." (9th-present).

Leadership is Always Better Than Membership

We mentioned that activities in which you displayed leadership should be ranked high on your list. To see why, put yourself in the shoes of an admissions officer. Imagine that you are looking at your 551st and 552nd application of the day. Whew, time to call it a day! But, before you go home, you need to make a decision about these last two. Here are some things that each mentioned in their list of activities:

Applicant A

1) Reporter for school newspaper

2) Speech team member

3) Young Voter Club Member

Applicant B

1) Editor-in-chief of school newspaper

2) Organizer of city-wide speech contest for 1,000 children

3) Director of Young Voter Registration for Democrat Club

Whom would you admit? Given other factors are equal, Applicant B! The activities in which you have leadership roles or responsibilities are the most memorable. Applicant B demonstrates her leadership and dedication through her accomplishments while Applicant A only catalogs his participation.

Keep in mind that leadership does not mean you had to be an elected leader. If you organized a fundraiser on behalf of your soccer team, helped to direct a play for church or decided to print t-shirts for the cheerleading squad, these are all examples of leadership. We've seen some amazing applications that display a ton of leadership by students who have never been an elected "anything" in their lives!

When describing your activities, don't be afraid to brag a little about what you have contributed. Admissions officers like to see students who are initiators both inside and outside of the classroom.

Tastefully Bragging about Your Honors and Awards

Do you remember how your mother would react when your Aunt April started bragging about how precious your two highly competitive cousins were and how they were being showered with praise from their teachers? If your mother was like ours, she would probably have started firing back her own barrage, cataloging every award you had won since the 3rd grade in alphabetical order: Aardvark Lover of the Year, Boy Scouts of America Volunteer Award, Certificate of Merit for the Science Fair . . .

When it comes to writing about your honors and awards in your applications, you need to borrow a little from the persona of your proud mother. Don't be afraid to brag about your accomplishments as if you are proving

HOW TO RANK YOUR ACTIVITIES AND JOBS

To prioritize which activities should come first on your application form, use the following criteria to rank their significance: (Given in order of importance)

#1 Activities, organizations, projects or businesses that you initiated or founded. These should always be listed first.

#2 Activities in which you were the leader—president, secretary or captain—or jobs in which you oversaw others. Even if the form does not provide a space, note your responsibilities (e.g., Smithtown Public Library—Children's Reading Program Coordinator).

#3 Activities or jobs in which you made a special contribution (don't forget to note that contribution in a few words) or sports in which you have excelled.

#4 Activities of academic importance (e.g., National Honor Society Member) and public service.

#5 Other non-academic activities or sports in which you did not make special contributions or particularly excel.

#6 Everything else.

that you are indisputably better than your cousins (which you already know is true).

Just as when listing activities, there are guidelines for determining which awards and honors to list first. Start with awards that carry the most weight, such as national or state recognition. After that, list awards that very few students get or that are highly prized in your school or community. Academic awards of any kind should be high on your list followed by awards for leadership, community service, club activities and athletics.

When listing any award, highlight its significance by stating how many received the award each year or for each region. Descriptions such as, "one awarded each year," or "one award per district" emphasize the importance of the honor. It's impressive if you won an award for your commitment to community service, but it's even more impressive if you note that only one student from each school receives such recognition.

Be sure to add explanations for those awards with titles that are not immediately recognizable. For example, "Stallion Award Recipient" could be an award for academic achievement, community service or excellence in horse breeding. Make sure the purpose of the award is clear.

Here's an example of a well ordered, yet concise summary of an applicant's honors and awards:

ACADEMIC HONORS
Briefly describe any scholastic distinctions or honors you have won since the 9th grade:

1st Place Oratory: State Speech Tournament (12th); Outstanding Junior: 1 awarded/year (11th); 2nd Place Research: Science Fair (11th); 1st Place Creative Writing Contest: 2 per grade (11th); Principal's List (9th-present); Certificate: French Class (10th).

When to Leave It Blank

Application forms are not like art: White space is not aesthetically pleasing. If you do not have enough activities to fill all the spaces, then try adding more description to those that you are listing. This way you not only expand on those activities that are impressive but you also minimize the white space. It is perfectly valid to substitute quality for quantity.

Don't be afraid to reach back into the past and list a few things you did during your freshman year. Sharing that you were a member of the Square Dancing Squad adds an interesting and unique personal touch—especially if you went on to become a 250-pound nose guard for the football team.

One warning: If you really have no other significant contributions to list, resist the temptation to fill your form with meaningless information. It is better to leave a few blanks than to write about how you donated a can of tuna to the holiday food drive. Descriptions of activities that lack significance will only reveal your desperation to fill up the space and will make the admissions officer question your ability to gauge importance.

More often you will find that you don't have enough space on the application form to include everything. You may have to make some difficult choices and not include some important activities. But before resorting to axing some good activities, try to creatively shorten your longer sentences.

Nip and Tuck in All the Right Places

The limited space on the application form will force you to rely on your most creative skills of manipulation. Most students find that the spaces on the application forms are hardly wide enough for a single sentence let alone a complete description of their activities from the past four years. The key is to be clear, yet concise, by nipping and tucking wherever possible. For example, you should not write:

> As vice president of the National Honor Society, I helped to start and run a canned food drive to benefit a local charity dedicated to helping senior citizens.

Instead write:

> National Honor Society (VP). Organized charity food drive.

This second sentence is concise, to the point and much stronger than the first example.

If the application form provides only a small box into which you must list your activities, list the important ones first, include your leadership positions in parentheses, and separate the activities with semicolons. For example:

> Smith High Recycling Coalition (Founder); NHS (Pres.); Student Council (VP); Math Club (Meet Organizer); BSA (Eagle Scout).

You can abbreviate activities that are nationally recognized or well known among educators. There are some schools brimming with generosity that allow you to use extra sheets. Take advantage of the gift of space, but remember that economy of words is important. Admissions officers don't have the time to read excessive explanations.

Leave No Question Unanswered

Check and double-check to make sure that you have filled in every blank and checked every box. In the spaces that are not applicable to you, type a dash so that you know that you have not left the space blank by mistake. If your form is incomplete, it could be returned to you and will certainly reflect poorly on your attention to detail.

Zap! Tips for Applying Online

In the pre-Internet days, applying to college meant lugging out the typewriter and investing in a couple gallons of correction fluid. Now, students can apply to colleges online. Instead of typing the answers on an actual form, you fill out online forms via the Internet. Usually, you are able to save what you've written and use the same information to apply to multiple schools.

Here are some tips to help you avoid some common mistakes:

Preview the application. Before you start completing the application, take a peek at it so you know what questions are asked and what information you'll need to provide. Don't just jump right into filling out the application sections without knowing what the entire form looks like.

Prepare your answers in advance. Because you know what the questions are, you can compose and organize the information in advance. Spend time on the answers. Just because you can apply instantly with the click of a button doesn't mean that you should craft your answers as speedily.

Gather the information and materials you need. It helps to have all of the information and materials you'll need at your fingertips. For example, for the Common Application, you will need a copy of your high school transcript, a list of your extracurricular activities, test scores and test dates and parent or legal guardian information such as educational background, occupation, etc.

Compose your essay in a word processing program first, then upload it. Don't try to write your essay at the time that you are submitting your application. You'll learn more about essay strategies in Chapters 5 through 7.

Be careful about typos or mistakes. It's easy to make careless mistakes when you submit your applications online. Take time to review your work.

Don't neglect the editing process. It's tempting to hit the submit button to send the application on its way as soon as you finish. However, you need to have someone look at it first. Print out a copy and read it yourself and get someone else to read it too. You'll catch many more errors (and believe us, there will be many) in your application if you and your editor can review a hard copy as opposed to just viewing it on the screen.

Keep a hard copy or an electronic copy of your application. You can refer to it when applying to other colleges and to scholarships.

Read the instructions for any information you need to submit offline. You may be able to submit your application electronically. Still, you may need to send additional information like letters of recommendation or transcripts by regular mail. Follow the directions carefully.

Finally ... Don't Forget to Sign

One last thing before you put the application aside: Do not forget to autograph it in all the right places—whether electronically or with ink. There are probably several forms that require your signature, and without it your application will *not* be processed.

An Example Application That Worked

This chapter could not be complete without an example of an actual application. Please note that names and identifying information have been changed. Also, this is just one example of a good application. It is meant to be an illustration of the strategies described in this chapter. Please remember that unless you are this applicant's identical twin sister, your application will be different.

Also, due to the size differences between the application and this book, we re-formatted and edited the form to fit.

STUDENT INFORMATION

Full legal name: Katherine Peters
Prefer to be called: Kate
Are you applying as a: X freshman or ❏ transfer student
Address: 1248 Center Drive, Hometown, CA 94022
Telephone number: (650) 555-1212
Email address: kate@supercollege.com
Social Security number: 123-45-6789
Date of birth: 10-06-96
Place of birth: New York   State: NY   Country: U.S.
Citizenship: U.S.
If you are not a U.S. citizen and live in the U.S., how long have you lived in the country? N/A
Are you a permanent resident of the U.S.? N/A
If you are not a permanent resident, have you applied for permanent resident status? N/A
If you are not a permanent resident, what is your visa type? If you will need a student visa, check F-1. N/A
❏ F-1 ❏ H-4 ❏ J-1 ❏ A-2 ❏ Other:
Visa expiration date: N/A
How many years have you been in the U.S.? N/A
Are you a U.S. veteran or a dependent of a U.S. veteran? No.
Have you been ❏ convicted of a felony ❏ dismissed for disciplinary reasons

Area(s) of academic major: English   or undecided ❑
Possible career plans: Journalism   or undecided ❑
Will you apply for financial aid? X Yes   ❑ No

OPTIONAL INFORMATION

First language, if not English: N/A
Language spoken at home: English
Please identify your ethnic group:
X White, non-Hispanic   ❑ Black, non-Hispanic
❑ Hispanic/Latino   ❑ Asian or Pacific Islander
❑ American Indian/Native Alaskan ❑ Not listed here
Gender X Female   ❑ Male

FAMILY INFORMATION

State of legal residence of your parents, spouse, or legal guardian: California
Since: 09/84
Parents' gross annual income: $110,000
Student gross annual income: $2,000 (Summer wages)
Family size: 5
Mother's full name: Karen Peters
Occupation: Accountant
Name of business: Hometown Accounting
College: U.C. Santa Barbara
Degree: B.A.   Year: 1998
Professional or graduate school: U.C. Berkeley
Degree: M.A.   Year: 2000
Father's full name: Aaron Peters
Occupation: Engineer
Name of business: Ace Technologies
College: U.C. Irvine
Degree: B.A.   Year: 1997
Professional or graduate school: U.C. Berkeley
Degree: Ph.D.   Year: 2003
Parents are X married   ❑ separated   ❑ divorced

EDUCATION

Secondary school : Smith High School   public X private   ❑ parochial ❑
Date of entry: 09/2017
Address: 1234 Main Street, Hometown, CA 94022
CEEB/ACT code: 12345
Date of expected graduation: 06/2021
Overall GPA for all courses completed/attempted to date: 3.8
College counselor: George Lee
Counselor's phone: (650) 555-1234
Counselor's fax: (650) 555-1235
Other secondary schools, including summer schools and programs:
Name of school: DeSoto Academy
Location: Somewhere, CA

Dates attended: Summer 2019, Summer 2020
Colleges at which you have taken courses for credit:
Name of college: N/A
Location: N/A
Degree candidate? N/A
Dates attended: N/A
If, following high school graduation, you were not enrolled in a college or university for one or more terms during any academic year, use the space below to list the dates and briefly describe your activities during the period(s) you were not attending college: N/A

TRANSFER STUDENT INFORMATION

Please list all post-secondary institutions you will have attended prior to enrollment.
Name:
Location:
Dates attended: Total credits: GPA: CEEB code:
N/A
Type of school where you are currently enrolled or were last enrolled:
❑ Community/two-year college   ❑ Four-year college/university
Indicate the total number of credits you expect to earn from all colleges before enrolling.

TEST INFORMATION

ADVANCED PLACEMENT EXAMINATIONS

AP Exam name: English	Date taken: 5/2020	Score: 5
AP Exam name: Chemistry	Date taken: 5/2019	Score: 4
AP Exam name: U.S. History	Date taken: 5/2020	Score: 4
AP Exam name: Spanish	Date taken: 5/2020	Score: 5
AP Exam name: Euro. Hist.	Date taken: 5/2019	Score: 3

INTERNATIONAL BACCALAUREATE (IB) EXAMS

IB Exam name:	Date taken:	Score:
IB Exam name:	Date taken:	Score:
IB Exam name:	Date taken:	Score:
IB Exam name:	Date taken:	Score:
IB Exam name:	Date taken:	Score:

ACT

Date taken/to be taken:
English score: Math score: Reading score:
Science score: Composite score:

Date taken/to be taken:
English score: Math score: Reading score:
Science score: Composite score:

SAT

Date taken/to be taken: 3/20
Reading score: 700   Math score: 770   Writing score: 720
Date taken:
Reading score: Math score: Writing score:

SAT SUBJECT TESTS

Date: 6/2020   Subject: Math Level 1   Score: 750
Date: 6/2020   Subject: Spanish   Score: 720
Date: 6/2020   Subject: U.S. History   Score: 680
Date: Subject: Score:

TEST OF ENGLISH AS A SECOND LANGUAGE (TOEFL)

Test: Date taken/to be taken: Score:
Test: Date taken: Score:

ACTIVITIES, HONORS, & AWARDS

List and describe briefly the most significant honors and awards you have received,
extracurricular activities you have participated in, volunteer and community service
work you have performed, special programs in which you have participated, and paid
employment you have had since the ninth grade.

HONORS OR AWARDS

Honor or award	Date received
Top Student Award in English, 1 per class per year	6/17–6/19
Top Student Award in history, 1 per class per year	6/19
Top Student Award in Spanish, 1 per class per year	6/19
1st place, District creative writing contest	4/19
Principal's honor roll	6/17– 6/20
2nd place, Talent show, dance	4/19
Junior Honor Guard, top 10% of class	6/20

EXTRACURRICULAR ACTIVITIES

Activity	Description	Years	Hours/week
Newspaper	Editor, responsible for all editorial and business activities, manage staff of 50	'17–present	10
Future Business Leaders	Treasurer. Founded and organized "Dollar-4-Dollar" charity pledge	'18–present	2
California Scholarship Federation	Secretary of academic service club	'17–present	2
National Honor Society	Member and editor of newsletter	'19–present	1

VOLUNTEER WORK AND COMMUNITY SERVICE

Organization	Description	Years	Hours/week
Reading club Founder	Student volunteer group to promote literacy to children	'17–present	5
Summer Reading Program	Staffed office for children's program	6/18, 6/19	5
Key Club	Raised money for local charities	2017–19	5

SPECIAL PROGRAM PARTICIPATION

Program name	Description	Years	Hours/week
Hometown Journalism Seminar	1 student per school selected to attend	7/20	4

EMPLOYMENT (PAID)

Position	Responsibilities	Years	Hours/week
Hometown Library Book Shelver	Sort and shelve books	'18–present	8
Peer Tutor	Tutor students in math and sciences	'17–present	2

PERSONAL STATEMENT

The personal statement is an important part of your application. The University uses the statement to learn more about you as an individual. Think of the personal statement as your opportunity to introduce yourself to the admissions officers and faculty who will be evaluating your application and to demonstrate your ability to organize thoughts and express yourself. Please write an essay (250-500 words) on a topic of your choice.

Grandma and Grandpa's Living Room

Every time I visited my grandparents' home, they sat in their own chairs—Grandpa in his cracked leather recliner flipping through the channels with the remote, Grandma in her quilted chair, cigarette dangling between her frail fingers. The recliner, worn yet comfortable from use, and the quilted chair, a mixture of fabrics and intricate stitches, were a source of security to me. They were visual monuments representative of my grandparents.

Even when his study light—which usually illuminated the room allowing him to intently fill in the answers to a crossword workbook with his sketchy yet steady scrawls—was turned off or the ashes from her cigarettes (which I truly detested but still accepted simply because they were a part of her) were cold, I still perceived their supportive presence in the room.

As I sat against one of the dark oak walls, I peered across the room to view a memorabilia of pictures. They were arranged into two sets. One, consisting of somewhat blurry black and white snapshots, held various poses of my mother, her older sister and her younger brother. In this group of dramatic photos, I was brought back to the past, a past in which my mother was a child. Youth exuding from her, dressed in cowgirl tap-dancing outfit with boots, ten-gallon hat and bandanna, or in her prom dress grinning anxiously and nervously as her date lightly held her hand or in her gleaming cap and gown peering at the world, her eyes filled with idealism and innocence. In this arrangement, I found a connection to those who meant the most to me, a link to my past and a connection to my heritage.

The other set of pictures, intermixed with the first yet easily distinguishable, consisted of color photographs. My grandmother proudly and joyously held me as a newborn, her first grandchild, her prized descendant. Laughing riotously, shrieking wildly, my grandfather bounced me lightly into the air. Comfortably seated on the couch between my two grandparents, our glowing beams were captured by the camera.

In this set of pictures lay the present, but more importantly, portended the future. Here, collected on the space of the wall, was my hope for a future of happiness. As I grew older, so my potential grew.

As I looked at these pictures, I grasped dearly onto my necessity for survival. For this, though meaningless to others, is my epitome. It is my past, my heritage. It is my future, the link that connects my family and me to the wider expanse of the world. Within this sanctity of my grandparents' living room, I gain security from my supportive family, understanding of my place and purpose in life and tranquility from the connections that it provides.

WHAT IS DEMONSTRATED INTEREST?

Imagine that you were having a birthday party, and you could only invite 25 guests. You'd probably want to invite those friends that you think would be the most likely to attend. Colleges view admissions in a similar way: They want to admit those students who will most likely accept their offer. Recently, colleges have become more sophisticated in guessing whether you'll accept through what's known as *demonstrated interest*.

Demonstrated interest is the level of interest that you show in the college. This may include the number of times that you contact the admissions office, how many information sessions you attend and how many times you visit the campus. Believe it or not, some colleges are tracking these number of contacts. They figure that the more effort you take to learn about the college, the more likely you'll attend.

The bottom line is that you need to take some initiative. Call the admissions office to ask questions or be connected with a current student, attend information sessions at your school and if possible, visit. The more interest you show in the school, the more it may show in you.

IN THIS CHAPTER

- Hunting down the best recommenders
- How to get great evaluations
- Playing the name game
- The perfect cover letter
- Story from real life: How my recommender cost me $5,000

CHAPTER 4

HOW TO GUARANTEE EXCELLENT EVALUATIONS

Find Someone to Brag About You

If there is one skill that you will hone throughout the admissions process, it will be the art of tasteful bragging. You may, for example, have already described your job flipping burgers as that of a "culinary coordinator." Or your part-time baby-sitting for the next door neighbor as training in "human education, development and discipline distribution."

The evaluations and school report are a slight modification of this bragging rite. This time you will be entrusting others, like your teachers and counselors, to sing your praises.

Evaluations are highly valued by admissions officers for the insight they provide into who you are. They rely on them to learn about your personality, skills, ambitions and weaknesses. It's not that they don't trust you, but they want proof in the form of what other people say that you really are as terrific as you say.

Your mission, which you have no choice but to accept, is to provide this proof. Although you do not have direct control over what your recommenders write, there is plenty that you can do to ensure your evaluations will present only your best points. This will hopefully be the last confirmation that the admissions officers need to offer you admission.

Start Early

Most colleges require two teacher evaluations and a school report completed by your counselor, principal or headmaster. Some schools also allow you to submit an extra evaluation. Finding recommenders and giving them the evaluation forms early should be your first priority.

Recommenders need at least three weeks, if not a month, to prepare your evaluations, especially if they are busy teachers or administrators and have a stack of other evaluations to write. Before doing anything else, work on distributing the forms to them. Refer to the *Do the Grunt Work for Your Recommenders* section in this chapter to learn how to put together a complete packet for each of your recommenders. But first, you will need to find some recommenders.

How to Hunt Down the Best Recommenders

Identifying quality recommenders is like finding star witnesses for the courtroom. You want people who can testify to your strengths, who are believable and who won't reveal anything incriminating. Essentially you want people who know your strengths and will attest to them.

For example, if your English teacher thinks that you are the next Hemingway, then you should ask him to write a letter of recommendation. Or, if biology is so easy that your teacher asks you to grade the exams, then you should ask her for her input. Obviously the teachers in whose classes you excel will be your most likely candidates.

For the school report, you may not have a choice. Many colleges specify which administrator should complete the report, usually your counselor, college advisor, principal or schoolmaster. If you are given a choice, of course pick the one who knows you and your accomplishments the best.

The Bonus Evaluation

Some colleges generously offer the opportunity to submit a third evaluation. Take them up on it. This is one more opportunity to bolster your case to the admissions officers.

You can assume that many applicants will have fairly strong evaluations from their teachers. A third evaluation can help you stand out from these students. Your two teacher evaluations will show that you have the intellectual mettle; a third evaluation can speak about your character or a special talent or interest that you have. As you know, colleges are very interested in attracting well-rounded students. In fact, the reason some colleges ask for a third evaluation is so that you can show them just how "round" you are.

Just like you did for your teacher evaluations, you should select a third recommender who knows you well. It should be someone who can describe a unique talent or interest that you have. Our suggestions are your activity advisor, work supervisor, volunteer supervisor, church leader or coach. But remember that if you don't have an extra person who can write an excellent evaluation, then it is better not to dilute your two or three terrific recommendations with a so-so extra.

Get Recommenders Who Can Write About the Intimate Details of Your Life

If you approach a teacher and ask him to write your evaluation, and he responds, "What's your name again?" that's a hint that he's not the one to write a recommendation for you.

You want recommenders who can write about the specifics of your life, providing personal anecdotes and examples if possible. Only people who know you well can refer to specific incidents and even provide vivid illustrations that not only lend genuineness to their evaluations but also make them memorable. College admissions officers will read thousands of evaluations, and for yours to stand out, it needs to be written in a way that is different from the rest.

The sad fact is that most students pick recommenders who do not know them well enough. Even if a teacher gave you an "A+," you may not necessarily want an evaluation from her, especially if you did not have the chance to get to know her. In high school many teachers may give you "A's" (we hope all), but only a few really know you well enough to be able to cite specifics.

An evaluation from a teacher who does not know you well but who gave you a good grade will certainly contain such generic compliments as "So-and-so is a fine student," or "So-and-so is great at such-and-such subject." These phrases, however, will appear in almost every other applicant's evaluation as well. Such evaluations are of little value in helping you to stand out from the pack.

Only a handful of evaluations—those from recommenders who *really* know the student—will contain such unforgettable phrases as, "So-and-so is not only the best English student I have had but has nearly doubled the readership of our literary magazine," or "So-and-so wrote an article on drug use in our school that was the talk of the town for months." These statements, which when supported by vivid details, will be the ones that admissions officers will not be able to forget.

If possible, try to select a good combination of recommenders who can praise your academic, extracurricular and leadership-motivational abilities. Let's take a look at an example.

Tom, a student who was accepted by Princeton, had two high school teachers and a student council advisor write evaluations. However, in addition to

STORY FROM REAL LIFE
THE BEST EVALUATIONS ARE FROM THE HEART

One of the most sincere evaluations we've read was written by a 9-year-old child whom Linda, a high school senior, befriended at a local shelter for battered women. —Gen and Kelly

Dear college,

My name is Patti and I am 9 years old. I am writing to tell you about my best friend Linda. When I first came to the shelter I was scared and embarrassed. My father hurt my mother. At first my mother never smiled or laughed. Linda changed that. She was very nice to me and played with me. We played tag and dolls and other games. She always made me laugh and my mother laugh, too, with her jokes.

Every time I say good-bye to her, she gives me a very big hug. She tells me that I am smart and pretty and that I am going to go to college someday. At first I didn't believe her. My family is poor. My mother didn't go to college. But Linda has told me so many times that I do believe her. I want to be just like her. I want to get good grades and become a doctor, too. And I want to make my mother laugh and smile like Linda does every time she visits us. I want to be just like Linda.

Patti

Coupled with an evaluation from the director of the shelter as well as two evaluations from her teachers, Linda's recommenders presented a vivid and heartwarming portrait of a dedicated person who is deeply involved in community service and wants to help make a difference. Since she chose to emphasize her extracurricular involvement with the shelter throughout her application (Linda's essay was about Patti's mother), the letter from Patti was both appropriate and effective. Linda successfully showed that beyond the scores and transcripts, she is a motivated, hard working and genuinely caring person who would bring such desirable qualities to any college campus.

Of course, this does not mean that you should rush out and start volunteering just so you can find an underprivileged child to write you a nice letter, but it does mean that you should consider submitting an extra evaluation from someone who can highlight and emphasize other areas of strength. This someone does not have to be a teacher.

writing about his academic achievements, his teachers were also able to comment on his involvement in groups for which they served as advisors, namely the speech team and the school newspaper. Thus, while Tom's teacher evaluations provided solid evidence of his scholastic aptitude, they also showed his other interests and abilities. A third evaluation from his student council advisor completed the picture of Tom as an all-around outstanding student by describing his contributions to the school community.

The Name Game: Bigger Isn't Always Better

You might think that the best evaluation would come from a person with high name recognition, like the President of the United States. After all, what college would reject someone recommended by the nation's leader, right?

The problem with this logic is this: Do you know the President or any other public official or famous person well enough that he or she can write about you in a personal and detailed way? If the answer is "yes," then by all means take advantage of your connection. If the answer is "no," then it really doesn't matter what title your recommender has unless he or she can write a meaningful and individual letter tailored for you.

We had a friend named David who selected people solely on the basis of their name value. He was able to get evaluations from the school principal, a district superintendent and the lieutenant governor for whom he had served as a summer intern but only met once. While the lieutenant governor's name may have initially attracted attention, the evaluation itself, David discovered, was a form letter with his name filled in the blank. And as if that were not bad enough, the letter contained numerous errors!

The only time a famous person will help is if he or she really knows you well. If you call your governor "Uncle Pete," then use your connections. But if he wouldn't recognize you walking down the street, then don't chance asking a mere acquaintance with a good name to recommend you. As David's stack of rejections proved, it's much better to get people who actually *know* you than those with impressive titles.

A Warning About Numbers

We know of an applicant who once sent 10 evaluations even though the college only asked for three. She thought the more testimonials verifying her abilities that she included with her application, the better. However, sending 10 evaluations was excessive and probably caused more annoyance than awe. When colleges specify a certain number of evaluations, you should not exceed this number.

Too many evaluations submitted under the theory that strength can be achieved in numbers will actually weaken the overall impact of your evaluations. If you have three teachers who will write great evaluations and a former boss who will write an average one, do not include the average recommendation.

Once you have identified two or three people who can write sincerely about you and your strong points, the next step is to ensure that they write good evaluations. If you have picked your recommenders well and follow the ensuing points, it should be easy.

STORY FROM REAL LIFE
MY SENATOR USED MY EVALUATION AS A PLATFORM

Chris thought that an evaluation from a recognized politician would be her ticket into college. She quickly discovered that content is more important than name recognition. —Gen and Kelly

When I was selected for a summer internship to work for my state's longest serving and most respected U.S. Senator, I had grand dreams of personally advising him about new legislation and discussing politics over business lunches. I also thought that I had just won a free ride into college. After all, what more prestigious summer job could a student have than to work for a national leader?

On the first day on the job my dreams were shattered. His secretary informed me that the Senator wouldn't even be in the state for the next two months. I spent my summer sending out photos signed not by the Senator but by one of his four automated signature machines.

Finally, I met the Senator on the last day of my internship during a luncheon for all summer interns. My only contact with him was shaking his hand as he said thank you. Still, I thought it was incredible to cross paths with such a great man and I was ecstatic when the Senator's secretary said he would write an evaluation.

I received copies of the evaluation for my applications and one for my records. Since the evaluation was not intended to be confidential I opened my copy. It was the worst evaluation that I had ever seen!

In the first paragraph it stated generically that I had been a good intern who worked hard. However, the rest of the evaluation read like a political speech and outlined how the Senator wished that more students were interested in politics, how the future of the country depended on education and how pursuing higher education was a noble cause. While this was all true and it said a lot about the Senator's stand on education and America's youth, it said almost nothing about me, which was supposed to be the point of the evaluation.

Needless to say, I quickly asked for an evaluation from my math teacher, whose platform was not political lobbying but rather lobbying to get me into college. And I was very pleased with the results.

—Chris, who has vowed not to volunteer for any more politicians

Avoid Crunch Time

When asking recommenders to write an evaluation, it is important that you approach them at an appropriate time. The best times are when they are not busy. Explain that you are applying to college and that you would like them to write an evaluation. Ask them if they think they will be able to complete the evaluation by the deadline.

If your potential recommender does not have time, don't give him or her the infamous "evil eye," fear that you have no hope of getting into college or take it personally. It is very likely that he or she is simply too busy, and an evaluation written in haste would surely not improve your chances of getting accepted anyway.

If your recommenders agree to write the evaluations, tell them that you will give them all of the necessary materials, and don't forget to thank them profusely.

Do the Grunt Work for Your Recommenders

Once you have found recommenders, prepare all the materials they will need to write detailed and complete evaluations. These will take some time to organize, but that will make your recommenders' jobs much easier and will ultimately help them to write better evaluations. Each recommender should receive a packet containing the following:

- **Cover letter.** The letter should explain what wonderful things you want your recommenders to include in their letters. Cite specific examples and accomplishments. Remember that your teachers and counselors have known many students, which means they probably won't remember what you did last semester let alone two years ago. Remind them!

  The letter should also clearly state the schools you are applying to and their deadlines. Don't forget to thank recommenders in advance for their time and effort.

- **Resume.** Include a resume that gives detailed information about your activities, jobs and academic achievements. This will be a valuable reference for your recommenders, refreshing their memories about what you have accomplished. (You can also include a copy with your applications to colleges that allow additional materials.)

  Take the time to tailor your resume for each of your recommenders so that it emphasizes the information that pertains specifically to them. For your math teacher, emphasize and list math coursework and grades as well as all of the various math awards you received before your extracurricular activities. For an advisor of a public service club, however, highlight contributions to the club and include information about other public service work, placing less emphasis on all those math awards.

- **The evaluation forms.** If the forms are to be submitted electronically, provide all the details on how to do this. Complete the waivers and basic information portions before giving the forms to your recommenders. Although you might have ideological objections to signing away your right to see these evaluations, you should do so anyway. Colleges realize that when recommenders know that their evaluations will remain confidential they write more honestly. A great evaluation in which the applicant refuses to sign away his or her right to see it does not carry as much weight as a confidential one.

- **Secret Fail-Safe Weapon for Excellent Evaluations.** This is an article at the end of the chapter that you should share with your recommenders. It will give them valuable tips on how to write an effective and personalized evaluation.

- **Evaluation/Recommendation Worksheet.** See Appendix C for this worksheet to provide your recommenders with key details about you.

- **Mailing envelopes.** If the college accepts mailed recommendations, be polite enough to attach the correct amount of postage for your recommenders to send the evaluations to the schools. Also, don't forget to address the envelopes.

These packets, while requiring some effort, will have the additional effect of showing your recommenders how organized you are and will remind them of how important you consider their evaluations to be.

The Perfect Cover Letter

Be sure that the cover letter you include in your packet to each evaluator contains the following:

- **The importance of the evaluation and what wonderful things you would like them to write about you.** Be as specific as you can about what you would like the evaluation to include, providing examples and accomplishments to which your recommenders may refer. There is nothing wrong with helping your recommenders with their letters. In fact, they will be happy that you did!

- **Instructions on what they should do after they finish their evaluations.** Provide your recommenders with envelopes already addressed to the correct office at each college if the college accepts paper recommendations. If the college accepts online recommendations, provide instructions on how your recommender should submit them.

● **The schools to which you are applying and their deadlines.** List the schools according to those that must receive the evaluations first.

● **Your heartfelt appreciation for them taking time from their busy schedule to help you.** This is always a good way to end your cover letter. Put your thank-you in the last paragraph so that it leaves the recommender with the thought that you are grateful—a thought which should make them more likely to get started right away!

Example Evaluation Cover Letter

The following is a sample cover letter to a teacher:

Dear Mrs. Chandler,

Thank you again for agreeing to write an evaluation. As you know, I am applying to eight colleges, and each of the evaluations you write is a very important part of my application. The colleges will use the evaluations to get a better idea of who I am beyond my test scores and grades so the more detailed and personal you can make the evaluation, of course, the better.

In your evaluation, I would appreciate it if you would write about my performance in your economics class, especially about the mock stock market project I led. The project gave me the opportunity to apply what we learned from our textbook and lectures toward a semester-long activity in which the entire class participated. It also made me consider pursuing a degree in economics in college.

I would also appreciate it if you would describe my tenure as President of the Business Club, especially how we worked to build membership and increase sales during our annual candy sale. You may recall my leadership in reviving the club's newsletter and in organizing our annual conference. With your evaluation and those from my history teacher, Mr. Bing, and my work supervisor at the library, I hope the colleges will get a better picture of who I am.

I am also including a copy of my resume and a short article that I found addressed to recommenders which I thought you might find interesting since I'm sure you must be flooded with requests. When you are finished with my evaluations, you can submit them directly to the colleges via the Common Application website. I will email you the details.

Thank you again for your time and effort. I am listing below the colleges to which I am applying and the deadlines for the evaluations. The colleges also recommend that you save a copy of the evaluations. If you have any questions, please do not hesitate to ask.

Harvard (deadline)	Penn State (deadline)
Stanford (deadline)	Princeton (deadline)
U. Texas (deadline)	U. Penn. (deadline)
U. Hawaii (deadline)	Washington (deadline)
Sincerely yours,	

Notice how the cover letter accomplishes a number of things in a short space. It explains the purpose of the evaluations, describes what the recommender should focus on, reminds her of past accomplishments as well as gives specific examples which she can use, clearly lays out the deadlines and thanks her profusely. All of these are essential elements of the cover letter and will result in your recommenders writing much better evaluations.

Be a Frequent Visitor to Your Recommenders

You don't have to blare a message over the school loudspeaker to remind your recommenders of their responsibility, but you do need to make sure they finish your evaluations before the deadline. You cannot assume that a recommender, regardless of how responsible he or she usually is, will finish your evaluations on time.

What this means is that you must devise some tactful ways to ask your recommenders if they have finished your evaluations before the deadline. Don't harass them, but gently check on their progress well before any due dates.

One way is to see your recommenders more often than usual. Reroute your walk home so that you pass by the restaurant where you worked last summer to say "hi" to your former boss or drop by and visit your previous science teacher once a week. Have a couple of questions for your teacher, giving you an excuse to strike up a conversation.

However you do it, ask your recommenders if they have any questions about your evaluations. Offer more biographical information or a more detailed resume if they need one.

As the deadlines approach for the evaluations, thank them again for spending the time to write them—hopefully they will tell you that they have already finished. If, however, the deadline is approaching and they still don't have their act together, ask someone else as a back-up.

Make Your Recommenders Feel Warm and Fuzzy

Another subtle way of reminding your recommenders to finish their evaluations on time is by writing them thank-you letters right before the deadlines. This way, your recommenders will get one of the best reminders possible— one that assumes that they have already done what they said they were going to do even if they haven't.

Thank your recommenders for their time and effort, and explain what an important role they have played in your pursuit of higher education. If you feel it is appropriate, give them a small thank-you gift.

Secret Fail-Safe Weapon for Excellent Evaluations

As promised in the beginning of this chapter, the following is a fail-safe weapon to insure that your recommenders write evaluations that will stand out and draw attention to your application. It is especially important when you have recommenders who do not have experience with writing college evaluations and who, while sincere in their desire to help you, may not know about the special requirements of college evaluations. All you need to do is share the following article with your recommenders. Tell your recommenders that you thought the article might be helpful in writing their evaluations.

STORY FROM REAL LIFE
HOW MY RECOMMENDER COST ME $5,000

This example of a scholarship evaluation disaster shows the importance of deadlines for evaluations of any type. —Gen and Kelly

When I was in college, I applied for a scholarship from a national journalism organization. The previous year I was a runner-up for the $5,000 prize, and the scholarship committee informed me that the only reason I didn't win was because I had only two years of experience working for non-school newspapers. They said that next year I would basically be a shoo-in for the competition.

I applied again the following year after having completed a summer internship with *The Washington Post* and a term-time internship with *Newsweek.* I was positive that I would win the competition this time. The application required an essay, clips and three evaluations. I submitted the essay and clips directly and contacted three of my previous employers to write evaluations. All three agreed.

About two weeks after the deadline, I received an email from the scholarship committee. I opened it expecting to find a congratulatory notice. Excitement quickly changed to horror as I read the email that stated that my application had been deemed incomplete and had therefore been disqualified.

I immediately emailed the scholarship committee to find out what had happened. Did I forget to submit my essay? Had I left blank a critical part of the application form? It turned out my application was complete except for one small detail: A recommender had not submitted an evaluation. I begged and pleaded with the scholarship representative to allow my delinquent recommender to email in the evaluation that day. The person, of course, said, "No." It was too late.

For several days I moped around, cursing my recommender for costing me the $5,000 prize. That was a lot of money to lose over a single evaluation! In retrospect I realize that although it was my recommender who had forgotten, it was also my fault for not having reminded her. If I had just written one simple email, I would have avoided being disqualified. It was an expensive lesson that cost me five grand.

—Jeanne, who now follows up with all of her recommenders

TIPS EVALUATING THE EVALUATION

One Teacher's Encounter With the Truth About College Recommendations

By: Dr. Dale White

As an English teacher at a rather elite private high school in New England, I could always count on two things in the fall: the stunningly beautiful changing of the leaves and the endless requests from my seniors to write evaluations for college. Since I wrote between 50 and 60 evaluations a year, I had developed a rather efficient system.

I had five types of ranked form letters stored on my computer, and each corresponded to my assessment of the student. The letters had a blank space for the student's name and a few areas where I could add specific comments about grades and performance. Most of my students got letter Type 2 or Type 3 and only a few got letter Type 1, which I reserved for my best students.

For all except my top students I spent only about 10 to 15 minutes on each evaluation, and that included changing the paper in the printer to the school's letterhead. All in all I was very satisfied with my system and never once thought about what happened to the letters once they were dropped into the mail.

Last year this self-confidence was shattered. In the fall I returned to my university to pursue an advanced degree in education. For one of my classes I had chosen to write about college admissions and made arrangements to watch the admissions process firsthand.

I was put in touch with one of the senior admissions officers whose job was to read through the second cut of applications. All of the applications that passed his desk had survived previous evaluations by other officers. This officer, whom I will call Mr. B, was a career administrator and had done his job for nearly 15 years. Needless to say he was quite the expert.

The first thing that struck me about Mr. B's office was the huge stacks of applications that he had to review. There must have been hundreds of folders, each representing one applicant—and this was after the first cut. As Mr. B opened the first folder, I was curious to see what materials he would focus on. Of course, the essay was important, and Mr. B quickly read over the ones whose applications were promising.

But what surprised me the most was the time he spent on the evaluations. He explained that more than 90 percent of the evaluations he sees are generic. Mr. B emphasized that he and his colleagues highly value evaluations that tell them something specific about the applicant. Unfortunately what he and other admissions officers end up reading are mostly canned compliments. Mr. B even recited from memory the top 10 most common phrases that he encountered. Included were some that I had used in evaluations of my own students. Phrases like "Mr. Y is a great student and highly motivated." Or, "Ms. K is a thoughtful and outgoing person." Or, "Mr. A is a highly capable student and will be an outstanding freshman at your school." How many of us teachers have used such adjectives to describe students whom we truly admired?

The plain truth is that admissions officers like Mr. B receive thousands of evaluations and after reading evaluation after evaluation, most begin to sound very similar and do nothing to help an applicant's chance of getting accepted. After talking to Mr. B and seeing which evaluations he considered to be truly effective, I decided to come up with a short list of tips which I hope will be of use. The following are four things to remember when writing a good evaluation:

1. Be Specific. The best evaluations contain specific examples of what the student has accomplished. If you say the student is a "real leader in school," then be sure to back up your statement with a solid example. Describe how he or she single-handedly organized the Culture Fair or how he or she led students in a petition to increase funding for the arts program. Now I ask students who request an evaluation from me to provide me with a resume and, if necessary, a short essay on what they have accomplished to help refresh my memory.

2. Write About the Student as an Individual. Remember that although you must comment on the student's academic accomplishments and/or extracurricular activities, the colleges also want to know what kind of person they might be getting. Mention something positive about the student's character or background. For example, if your school is in an area that is economically disadvantaged and few students even dream of going to college, then mention this fact and comment on how hard the student has worked to break free from this cycle. Such background information on the student's community will help to establish a memorable picture of him or her and will help to set his or her accomplishments in the proper context.

3. Never List. The worst evaluations simply list accomplishments, regurgitating the information on the student's resume. "Mr. A was president of his class in his sophomore year. The following year he was the band leader, etc." These evaluations are boring and redundant. The student will already have listed his or her coursework, scores, awards and extracurricular activities in the application.

While you should make reference to the student's accomplishments, try to expand and add detail from your point of view. Be sure to comment on extracurricular activities with which you are familiar. If you are the student's English teacher and journalism advisor, comment on his or her performance and involvement with the newspaper. This is the kind of evaluation that can only come from you and will help your student's chances immensely.

4. Proofread Your Evaluation. Innocent misspellings and errors in grammar not only make you look bad but also detract from the entire quality of your evaluation, which will ultimately hurt the student whom you are trying to help. Colleges expect applicants to submit near perfect applications and expect the same for the evaluations. It's surprising how many evaluations from teachers contain gross spelling and grammatical errors.

The importance of your role as evaluator cannot be emphasized enough. In fact, Mr. B showed me a copy of an evaluation from several years ago that he said was almost single-handedly responsible for getting an applicant into college. While I cannot reprint this evaluation, I can tell you that it was extremely well-written, very personal and painted a picture of the applicant so vivid that you felt as if you had already met her. While the evaluations that you write for your students are part of a larger process, they can have a tremendous effect on the chances of their being admitted.

I hope the information in this short article will be of help when you write your evaluations. As for me, I have erased all of my ready-made evaluations and now exclusively write from scratch. It takes longer, but the evaluations are much better. I also insist that students give me a list of their accomplishments and even help to refresh my memory on the specific things they have done. All of this makes for better evaluations, and the ultimate reward for me as a teacher is for my students to come to class in the spring with big smiles on their faces and letters of acceptance in their hands.

THE (SOMEWHAT) SECRET
INFLUENCE OF YOUR COUNSELOR

You may think the extent of your counselor's influence is the evaluation letter. As if this is not enough, your counselor may have even greater power in the admissions process. Counselors often provide more information about students informally and verbally. If they have a student with extenuating circumstances or a personal situation that is not easily reflected in an evaluation or if they have a student who they feel they should really lobby for, they will contact the admissions officers to let them know. In addition, admissions officers will often call counselors especially for borderline students to ask additional questions.

What does this mean for you? First, if you haven't already, get to know your counselor. A counselor can only be your ally when he or she knows something about you, your background and your achievements. Second, if you have extraordinary circumstances that the colleges should know about, let your counselor know so he or she can pass the details along.

A lot of students think that once they submit their application, the colleges have all of the information they need. The truth is that the colleges continue to gather information, and your counselor is an important source.

IN THIS CHAPTER

- Why the essay is the most important part of the application
- The 5-step workshop to writing winning essays
- Essay-writing absolute "don'ts"
- List of totally dumb topics
- Vital tips for specific questions
- Essay-writing worksheets: Academic and college goals, future career, role models, community service

CHAPTER 5

HOW TO WRITE AN IRRESISTIBLE ESSAY

The Essay: King of the Application

You can have imperfect grades and still get into Harvard. You can have less than stellar SAT scores and still get into Berkeley. You can even have mediocre teacher evaluations and still get into Princeton. But the one thing that spells rejection is a poorly written essay.

As a part of your application, you will answer one or more questions, describing an aspect of yourself beyond the dry facts of the application. The essay is one of the most important parts of your application, and as you will discover, it can also be the most difficult. Fortunately, the essay is also the area over which you have the most control and you can improve it dramatically by following the strategies and tips outlined in this chapter.

The Essay in the Eyes of the Admissions Officer

An Ivy League admissions officer once told us that of all the parts of the application, the most memorable and important is the essay. This 12-year veteran of the college admissions process explained that while each section of the application is carefully considered by the admissions committee, it is only the essay that has the potential to make or break an applicant's chance of getting accepted.

Why is the essay so important? Quite simply because it is viewed by admissions officers as their window to see the "real" you. While thousands of applicants have similar test scores, grades, evaluations and extracurricular activities, it is the essay that gives your application that all-important personal touch.

Through your essay the admissions officers hear your voice and see how you respond to questions or problems. Your essay is representative of you, and because colleges are interested in admitting interesting and thoughtful human beings—not just students with certain numerical scores—the essay is an indispensable resource for them.

The essay also shows the admissions officers your ability to analyze and effectively communicate that analysis on paper. This is one aspect of the essay that many students ignore. The admission officers are not just reading your essay and judging your writing ability, but they are also examining what you say and evaluating the quality of the ideas expressed in the essay.

Typical Essay Questions

Essay topics can be as general as, "Tell us about yourself" or as specific as, "What is your favorite book?" To give you an idea of what you will face, here are the Common Application essay questions:

- Some students have a background, identity, interest, or talent that is so meaningful they believe their application would be incomplete without it. If this sounds like you, then please share your story.

- The lessons we take from obstacles we encounter can be fundamental to later success. Recount a time when you faced a challenge, setback, or failure. How did it affect you, and what did you learn from the experience?

- Reflect on a time when you questioned or challenged a belief or idea. What prompted your thinking? What was the outcome?

- Describe a problem you've solved or a problem you'd like to solve. It can be an intellectual challenge, a research query, an ethical dilemma-anything that is of personal importance, no matter the scale. Explain its significance to you and what steps you took or could be taken to identify a solution.

- Discuss an accomplishment, event, or realization that sparked a period of personal growth and a new understanding of yourself or others.

- Describe a topic, idea, or concept you find so engaging that it makes you lose all track of time. Why does it captivate you? What or who do you turn to when you want to learn more?

● Share an essay on any topic of your choice. It can be one you've already written, one that responds to a different prompt, or one of your own design.

All Questions Can Be Answered Exactly the Same

We know of several applicants who applied to more than 25 schools. Unless you have nothing better to do with your time and money than apply to colleges, (which we hope is not the case) this is certainly overkill.

However, even if you apply to only one-third as many schools, you still may feel a little distressed at having to write two or three essays for each school. If you are applying to 10 schools, this could translate into tens of thousands of words to write. Since each school will probably ask you to write on a slightly different question, you may wonder if you will have to compose 10 or 15 different essays. The answer, thankfully, is "no." With a technique called "recycling" you should not have to write more than a few essays regardless of how many schools to which you are applying.

Recycling works because the question or topic of the essay is really only a guideline rather than a mandate. It is designed to give you something concrete about which to write. Therefore, you should not be too concerned if your essay strays slightly from the topic or if you interpret the question creatively. While you will need to stay within the boundaries of the question or topic posed, remember that these boundaries are quite flexible.

For example, one college may ask, "Evaluate a significant experience that has special meaning to you" while another may ask, "Tell us about a conversation you've had that changed your perspective." At first, these two questions seem to require two separate essays. Not true.

Say, for example, that you want to write about your father (which is the topic one of us used for the Harvard, Princeton and Yale essays), and you plan to show how his making you breakfast every morning has helped to shape your outlook on life. While this essay would certainly answer the first question about a significant experience, it could also answer the second question if you started it with the following introduction:

> Although I have had many great conversations with my father, one of the most meaningful was unspoken . . .

Thus, you could submit the essay that you wrote for the first college about how your father's actions have influenced your life for the second college's essay, even though you are not writing specifically about a spoken "conversation." It is important, of course, to make sure that you tell the reader in the introduction that you are interpreting the essay question in a less than literal way. This is the essence of "recycling." Since the first essay for Harvard was so great (it took over a month to perfect) it only makes sense to try to use it as many times as possible.

An essay on your father could also work for such topics as "Describe your saddest moment" if you began the essay by defining your saddest moment as the day you realized that you would soon be leaving home and would not be able to continue to spend every morning with your father. You could use the essay to answer a current events question by selecting the breakdown of the American family as the topic to lead into your own experience of having a strong, influential father figure.

In short, don't think of each question from each school as requiring a totally original essay. While you will have to craft three or four well-written, concise and thought-provoking essays, you will be able to use them with minor modifications for almost all of your college applications.

When selecting the topics for your essays, keep in mind their potential for being recycled. We will go into much greater detail about the strategies for recycling in the next chapter. In the meantime, concentrate on writing your essays first, since the success of recycling requires you to have at least a few good essays.

Five Step Essay-Writing Workshop

Enough talk about the theory behind the essay. It's time to get down to business with the actual writing. This workshop lays out everything you need to do from choosing a topic to performing the final spell check. Following the workshop are highly important *Essay-Writing Absolute Don'ts* as well as a list of *Totally Dumb Topics* you should read before you get started. So without further ado let's take a look at the first step.

STEP 1: Brainstorm Topics

Surprise! Here is a pop quiz for you. Is it better: a) to think of interesting topics regardless of the specific essay questions; or b) to read the questions and then think of only topics that directly address them? Answer: you need to do a little of both. (Trick question, huh?)

First, familiarize yourself with all of the essay questions. Read them over several times but don't limit your ideas yet.

While keeping the essay questions in the back of your mind, start jotting down all of the possible experiences, themes and aspects of your life about which you could write. Remember that the object of brainstorming is to reach deep into the recesses of your mental filing cabinet and pull out the greatest number of potential essay topics possible.

The only rule for brainstorming is this: Anything goes. Write down every idea that pops into your head, and do not eliminate anything. Even if some ideas lack the seed of a brilliant essay, they may lead you to think of others that do. The following questions should help you to get your list started:

- What are your favorite activities and hobbies? Why do you enjoy them?

- Do you have any special talents or skills?

- Who have been the most influential people in your life? The most memorable? The most interesting?

- What have you done during the past four summers?

- What was your best day/experience? Worst? Funniest?

- How have you changed in the past four years?

- What was the most memorable experience you have had with your parents? Brother or sister? Best friend? Teacher?

- What accomplishment are you proudest of?

- What makes you special or unique?

- What is your strongest quality?

- What is a strong belief or philosophy that you hold?

- What is the most difficult or challenging thing you have done?

- When and how have you shown leadership?

As you answer these questions, allow your mind to wander to other questions. The point is to let your imagination go free and not to do away with anything.

Also enlist the help of parents and teachers in the brainstorming process because they may remember something that has slipped your mind.

When you run out of ideas, take a break and do something else. You will be surprised at how often ideas come when you least expect them. Be sure you carry a note pad around to record any serendipitous inspirations. Ideally, you would have about a week to develop essay ideas. More realistically, try to set aside a day or at least an afternoon for brainstorming. It is well worth the time to develop topics for which you have passion.

STEP 2: Narrow the List of Possible Topics

Once you are pretty certain you have some potential winners on your list, start narrowing the field. Select topics that are important to you and reflect your personality.

If the topic or the way in which you plan to approach the topic does not seem original, put a big fat "X" through it. The best way to ensure that your topic or approach is unique is to refer to the *Essay-Writing Absolute Don'ts* and *Totally Dumb Topics* sections in this chapter. Even if your idea seems good, if it is similar to any of the topics in our *Don'ts* list, you can count on 90 percent of other applicants to write on the same "original" and "unique" topic.

Ask yourself these questions about your list of ideas:

- If your topic or subject is one that many applicants might write about (e.g., travel, parents, sports) do you have a unique approach that will ensure that your essay will not sound like everyone else's?

- Does your idea have good supporting examples or stories? Your essay needs to have concrete details about what you have done or experienced. Topics that allow you to elaborate on one or two of your activities or achievements are especially good.

- Does the topic allow you to analyze an issue? The essay is not just a writing test—it's a thinking test. The admission officers want you to learn how to analyze a topic or idea. For example, one student we know wrote about how he dislikes hugging other people. While this is admittedly a unique topic, if she had just described instances where she avoided hugging people, it would not have been a great essay. What made her essay so powerful (and ultimately successful) was that she analyzed why she hates hugging. She asked herself some hard questions and really probed into her own psyche. By the end of her essay—even if you didn't agree with her dislike of hugs—you understood why it made her so uncomfortable. Whatever you topic is, it needs to provide you the opportunity to dig below the surface and really analyze it. If it's just an entertaining story with little to no thoughtful reflection, it won't make a good essay.

- Can your idea be expressed within the limits of the essay? You should eliminate any topic that you know will require more than the given space to write. Topics that require 2,000 words to properly explain, but that are summarized in 500 words, often turn out sounding overly simplistic or are very difficult to follow since many key points and explanations have to be omitted.

- Will your essay be interesting and creative? This is a very simple question but one that is hard to answer truthfully. Take a step back when answering this question and put yourself in the place of the admissions officer who has already read 300 or so essays and has just grabbed yours, which also happens to be the last before he or she can go home. Will your essay pique the interest of this tired admissions officer? Will the topic or your approach to the question make the admissions officer want to read past the introduction? Just because a topic is original does not always guarantee that it will be interesting. Use your best judgment by constantly asking if you would be interested in reading about your topic or experience.

● Can you present the topic in a way that will appeal to a wide audience? Will the admissions officer have to have specific knowledge of the topic in order to understand it? For example, if your topic is a legal interpretation of the U.S. Tax Code or involves detailed scientific or technological terminology that can't be simplified, it may be better to choose something a little less complicated.

● Will the topic show the real you? Is it truly meaningful to you? Does your topic involve some insight into who you are, how you think or what your passions are?

● Can the topic be recycled? If you write an essay on the topic, can you use the essay in several different applications?

Hopefully after paring down your list, you will still have at least 10 to 15 ideas left. Prioritize these ideas according to their significance to you. Writing about something for which you truly feel strongly will naturally transfer onto paper and will convey your feelings and passions to the admissions officers.

STEP 3: Razzle and Dazzle! Answer the Question Uniquely

Now that you know what you want to write about, write! You will find some ideas that seemed promising do not translate well to paper while others that were lower on your list end up making great essays. Unfortunately, the only way to tell if an idea will be a good essay is to try to write it.

Many of our ideas for college essays turned out to be too difficult to write in 500 words or appeared silly or just plain boring after we started writing. We often had to return to the brainstorming process. But after many false starts a few topics began to emerge as having real potential.

Before we leave you to your writing, read a few of the tips that follow. It's also a good idea to review them from time to time as you are writing.

Be yourself. It is important to show the admissions officers the real you. Explain why you think or act the way you do, what drives you or what has moved you. Choose only the topics that are truly meaningful to you. Speak in your own voice. If you felt secretly happy that your opponent lost the quiz bowl, say so. By explaining how you really felt and not how you think the admissions committee would like for you to have felt, you will not only be truthful but will also help to insure that your essay is original.

Create some mystery at the forefront. Start your essay with an introduction that surprises the readers and makes them want to read past the first sentence. For example, you could start your essay with a description of your fear of the sounds of heavy artillery. At first blush, readers might think that you are talking about your latest trek to the firing range, and they will be surprised to find out that you are actually revealing your secret phobia of visiting the dentist. Keep in mind, however, that you have limited space and therefore your introduction will have to be fairly brief. Do not get too carried away with your own creativity.

Share something about yourself. The essay is your opportunity to impart a piece of you that can't be found anywhere else in your application. Whatever the topic may be, your essay should reveal something about your thoughts, attitudes, goals or personality. The focus should always be on you.

Razzle, dazzle and captivate your audience. When you begin writing, keep in mind that you need to write a truly memorable essay. To do this, draw the admissions officers into your essay with a quick, catchy and creative introduction. Pique their curiosity by posing questions they will want the answers to and dilemmas they too have faced. Most important, you want the admissions officers to be able to relate to your essay (not necessarily to the actual events but to the feelings involved).

How you write is just as important as what you write. Constantly ask yourself if you would be interested in your essay if you were the reader. Would you want to finish reading the essay after the first few paragraphs? Do not just rely on your opinion. Seek the opinions of others. If your essay does not compel the reader to finish the entire essay, rework it.

Raise intriguing questions or dilemmas. Ponder questions to which you think the admissions officers would be interested in finding the answers. If you raise a question or a dilemma you faced, ask yourself if the reader would be interested in knowing the results of your decision.

Use original language. Try to describe in a unique—but not awkward—style. Think of language as a toy, and play with it. Experiment with dialogue, vary the length of sentences and pose questions. If you use unfamiliar words, use them correctly. It is better to use ordinary language correctly than to use roller coaster-exciting language incorrectly.

Be witty, but only if you can. Showing your sense of humor will help to make your essay memorable. If you can make the admissions officers laugh or giggle, it will be a definite plus for your application. But, do not go overboard with the humor and remember to have someone else check to make sure that what you think is funny really is funny. Admissions officers love essays that make them laugh. However, admissions officers also dismiss essays that intentionally try to be funny but are not or that use humor that is simply silly or immature. Our advice is to forget about trying to be funny and just tell your story. If your essay is well told, conveys your thoughts and is interesting, chances are that any inherent humor in it will show through.

Highlight growth. One of the qualities admissions officers look for in essays is maturity. They want to know that you are mature enough to make the transition from high school to college. Use your essay to demonstrate how you've grown or developed over the years. Describe how you've changed or a difficulty you've overcome.

Use examples and illustrations. Don't just say that you are a strong leader. Detail an example of when you've been a leader. Describe how you felt, what you did to motivate others and what you learned from the experience. Admissions officers want details, and examples provide a way to give them what they want.

Don't just say it, show it. The best essays bring the readers into the middle of the action and help them see what the writer sees and hear what the writer hears. Appeal to the different senses. What can the reader see from your essay? Hear? Smell? (Hopefully nothing rotten.) The more you can draw the reader into your essay by using rich description, the better.

End with a bang. A powerful conclusion leaves readers with a strong impression of you. Try to end with something insightful or thought-provoking. Give the reader a memorable line or insight that will stick with them after they put the essay down.

By keeping these points in mind, you should be able to write a decent first draft. Remember that an original essay employs a unique angle, addresses a meaningful question or dilemma and is crafted with thoughtful language.

STEP 4: Write for Perfection: Rewrite, Edit, Rewrite and Edit Again, with Help from Editors

If you are like us, the first draft of your essay will be a rough skeleton at best. You will need to rewrite many times to tweak it to perfection. Throughout the editing process, keep in mind that your objectives are these: 1) to reveal something about yourself; and 2) to showcase your ability to analyze and communicate meaningful ideas on paper.

Unfortunately, spending so much time looking at the same essay can cause temporary blindness to mistakes and lapses in the ability to differentiate between what you want to say and what your essay actually says. Your enthusiasm for reading with a critical eye may wane by the 15th rewrite, and what may make perfect sense to you because you know the story intimately may not make any sense to an unfamiliar reader.

There is an old but very true saying that behind every good writer there is an even better editor. Countless literary masterpieces would not be the great works that they are if it were not for the editors who made them so. To produce the best possible essay; you must, must, must find people to read it. Your editors, you will discover, will provide you with the most valuable information and suggestions on how to improve your work. Good editors include parents, teachers, counselors, siblings and friends.

When you have found a couple of courageous volunteers to be editors, make sure that they know what to do. We have included an article you can share with your editors to help them understand the purpose of the college essay and how to edit it correctly.

When your editors are finished, heed their advice. Do not take their criticisms personally since no matter how much it may hurt your feelings, their advice is going to improve your essays. Consider each of their suggestions, even if you disagree with them. You may think a section is crystal clear, but if they are a little confused, you'd better change it.

One final note about editors. It will be to your benefit to find at least two. While some tend to look at the big picture, the overall theme and message of your essay, others will focus on details like grammar, spelling, punctuation and word usage. You want both types of editors to read your essays. So don't hold back on asking someone because of any reservations about sharing the personal feelings in your essays. This is one time when you cannot afford to let your fear of embarrassment get in the way of turning out a good essay.

Help Your Editors Learn How to Edit

College essays have a specific purpose—to convince the admissions officers that they should admit you. Your editors, while they may be excellent editors in every way, may not be familiar with this kind of writing or how to convince admissions officers that you are the greatest candidate of all time.

Thus, it is important to provide them with information about the purpose of the college essay. The following article offers a short explanation that you can share with each of your editors.

TIPS | HOW TO EDIT COLLEGE APPLICATION ESSAYS MASTERFULLY

Most college admissions officers do not hesitate to admit that the essay is one of the most important elements in the admissions process. Because of this, students need trustworthy editors to guide them in writing their essays and to offer them advice about how to make improvements. Since the college essay is a very specialized type of writing, this checklist is designed to help you masterfully edit these essays.

- The essay should focus on the student and reveal something about him or her. In a process that is oftentimes dominated by impersonal test scores and GPAs, most admissions officers view the essay as their only chance to get to know the student as an individual. Because of this expectation, make sure that the student offers some insight about who he or she is or about his or her way of thinking. This does not have to be done overtly, but when you are finished reading the essay, you should feel that you have a better understanding (as well as a mental picture) of the writer's personality.

- The essay should be creative and interesting. Admissions officers read stacks of essays each day. The ones that they remember, naturally, are those that are creative. Does the introduction draw you in? Is the essay unique or does it approach its topic in an unusual way? If not, identify where in the essay you lost interest. Does the essay start out strong but then lose its momentum? How can the essay be spiced up? How can the student take a different or more creative approach to the topic?

- The essay needs to be clear and flow smoothly with nice transitions. Are there any areas you didn't understand? Is there a gap between what the author knows and what the reader actually understands? Are the transitions smooth and does the story make sense?

- The essay should make you like the student or want to meet him or her. Since you already know the student (and presumably like him or her), imagine this essay is your first introduction. Would you like to meet the author? Is the student portrayed in a likable, interesting way? Would he or she be a valuable addition to a school?

- The essay should be flawless. Content isn't all that counts. Check the student's spelling, grammar and word usage as well. Any mistakes you find are ones that the admissions officers won't.

- Be honest. The most important thing you can do is give your honest evaluation of the student's essay. If you think that the piece needs improvement, don't be afraid to tell the student. Offer as much constructive criticism as possible and suggestions for improvement.

We hope that these tips will help you to better evaluate the college essay. Just by taking the time to read it, however, you are making a valuable contribution towards helping the student get into college.

STEP 5: Polish Your Essay

The final step is to polish and perfect your essay. Why ruin all of your hard work with a few careless errors? Review this final checklist to make sure your essay shines.

Perfect your spelling and grammar. With so much riding on your essays, you don't want something as simple as a spelling or grammar mistake to count against you.

Unfortunately, relying on your computer's spell checker is not enough. Spend the extra time to personally scrutinize your work. (This does not mean giving it the once over at 2 a.m.!) Don't think we're crazy, but one trick you might want to try is to read your essay backwards. Since your essay will be totally incomprehensible, it will force you to focus only on the words and their spelling. Also, if you are unsure of how to use a word, look it up in a dictionary.

The best way to perfect your spelling and grammar is to have as many knowledgeable editors as possible read your essay. They will often catch what you miss.

Count your words. This is another one of those little things that you do not want to count against you (no pun intended). When the application asks for a 650-word essay, you need to adhere to the limit. Limits are set to ensure that everyone has a fair chance since it would be unfair to compare a 1,000-word essay to a 400-word essay. Plus, logistically, admissions officers would never be able to finish their jobs if everybody exceeded the guidelines.

For more tips on how to lighten an overweight essay, refer to *How to Shorten a Long Essay* in Chapter 6.

The Essay-Writing Absolute Don'ts

Perhaps as important as knowing what to do is knowing what *not* to do. With this knowledge, you will be able to avoid what we call the "90 Percent Trap." You may think that writing about the jubilation you felt after you scored the winning touchdown is an original and inspiring essay bound to be your free ticket into a highly competitive college. But unless the college is recruiting you for your athletic ability, you will be sorely disappointed.

Believe it or not, 90 percent of college applicants will write identical essays. They may not write about the exact same topic, like football, but they will deal with similar topics and themes (e.g., "winning isn't everything," "we should learn to appreciate other cultures," etc.) Many of these essays will answer the stated questions in predictable ways and in nearly identical styles or tones.

Imagine that you are a college admissions officer at a large school. Each year your office receives anywhere from 20,000 to 30,000 applications. If you have to read several hundred application essays and 90 percent of them echo the themes of those you have already read, which applications will stand out when it comes time to narrow the pool? Of course, it will be those with unique and original essays. As an applicant, it is imperative that you are among this top 10 percent and avoid the common essay traps that snare the rest.

The following is a description of the most common mistakes that applicants make in their essays. Do not be surprised if some of the ideas you have for your essay show up on this list. Trust us, they are on 90 percent of other applicants' lists as well. Your advantage is that you will be able to recognize and avoid these potential disasters.

DON'T try to be someone else. The most important thing to remember when writing your essay is to be yourself. This means you should avoid portraying yourself as Mother Teresa when the closest you have ventured to philanthropy was watching 10 minutes of the Muscular Dystrophy telethon. Often applicants are tempted to create an alter-ego of what they think is the perfect student. Because the essay is a creative effort, it is very easy to stretch the truth and exaggerate feelings and opinions. One admissions officer at a small private school in the South was notorious for his critique of some essays in which he used a rubber stamp engraved with a pair of horns and the word "bull."

How can admissions officers tell a fake or forced essay? Easy. Phony essays don't match the rest of the application or the way that the student is described in the evaluations. These essays often lack details that can only come from real experiences.

Admissions officers have read thousands of essays, and if they believe your essay to be less than the truth, you will ruin not only your reputation but also any chances of getting into college. Besides, we guarantee that there is something about you that has the makings of a stellar essay. If you spend the time developing this in your essay, you will be able to blow the admissions officers off their feet in a way that no pretense or exaggeration could.

DON'T write about common experiences commonly. This is the most predominant mistake applicants make. To avoid it, resist the temptation to write about an ordinary experience in an ordinary way.

Ideally, you will be able to come up with both original topics and original ways to write about them. However, since the essay questions tend to limit *what* you can write, you need to be most concerned with how you are going to approach your topic. For example, tens of thousands of students will write about the following: a) how being class president, club founder or team captain was their greatest achievement; b) how their mother, father or teacher has been the most influential person in their lives; or c) how they were the key person in winning the "big" game, match or academic decathlon.

It is fine for you to write about an *ordinary* topic. The key is to write your essay in an *extraordinary* fashion. Ask yourself these questions: Are you presenting the material in a way that is unique to you, in a way that no one else can? What slant are you going to give to the topic or question to make your essay unusual and unique?

DON'T flex. For some strange reason, many applicants have a tendency to write about the great mysteries of the world or momentous philosophical debates in an effort to show admissions officers their intelligence and sophistication. At Harvard we called people who wrote essays that aimed to impress rather than educate "flexors," as in people who flex their intellectual muscles for all to see.

While these essays attempt to be sophisticated, they are usually entirely without substance. Often they simply parrot back the opinions of others, and unless the writer is indeed knowledgeable about the subject, such essays are completely unoriginal.

College admissions officers do not want to read an uninformed 18-year-old's diatribe on the nature of truth or the validity of Marxism. And admissions officers most certainly do not want to be lectured. Essays that try to impress with pseudo-intellectualism are definite candidates for the trash bin. Remember the goal of the essay. Admissions officers want to learn about the kind of person you are and the things that you have done.

However, if your passion is indeed sociological theory or reading Marx is your beloved pastime, then by all means write about it, but put it in perspective. Write about how you became interested in Marxism or its personal significance to you.

DON'T write in clichés. Clichés are overworked phrases like "all is well that ends well," "practice what you preach" and "don't cry over spilled milk." To you, phrases like these may seem clever. You may even use them regularly. But to admissions officers, clichés are not only trite but they also reveal a lack of sophistication and originality. If you use clichés, you will sound no better than a well-trained parrot. You want the admissions committee to know that you are a capable writer who has the imagination and skill to write without the crutch of other people's overused phrases.

DON'T over quote. Along a similar vein as clichés, quotations also tend to make essays sound parrot-like. In analytical essays, quotations are often a valuable component. However, in the limited space of the college essay, maintain your originality and don't allow quotations to distract from your voice.

Since quotations are not your own words, never use them in a critical point or in place of your own analysis. Using a very well-known quotation is especially dangerous since 90 percent of the other applicants (who have not spent the time to prepare by reading this book) will almost certainly use similar quotations in their essays. If you want your essay to be memorable, it must be kept original. Now is the time to put aside the *Bartlett's Familiar Quotations* and start writing as yourself.

DON'T cross the line between creativity and absurdity. Most of the time the problem with admission essays is that they are not creative enough. However, some applicants, in an effort to ensure their essay is one-of-a-kind, go too far on the creative side. Rather than sounding original and insightful, the essay appears trite and silly. A general rule is that you want your work to be as creative as possible but not so creative that admissions officers won't take it seriously.

If you have a question about whether your work crosses the line in the creativity department, get a second or third opinion. If one of your readers feels that the essay may be a little too off-the-wall, then tone it down or even abandon it. The college application is not the place to experiment and take radical chances. While you should write creatively, beware of the easy crossover into silliness.

DON'T go thesaurus wild. Using creative wording is one of the "Do's" of writing a good essay. However, writing your essay in the words of a thesaurus is one of the worst mistakes you can make.

First, some of the alternate words you find in a thesaurus will probably be unfamiliar. This means that if you use these alternate words, you run a high likelihood of using them awkwardly or incorrectly.

Second, admissions officers possess a keen radar for picking out essays co-authored by a thesaurus. Call the admissions officers psychic for their ability to pick out the thesaurus-aided essays, but they really are not that hard to find. Here, for example, is an excerpt from an essay that was definitely under the influence of the thesaurus:

> To recapitulate myself, I am an aesthetic and erudition-seeking personage. My superlative design in effervescence is to prospect divergent areas of the orb and to conceive these divergent cultures through the rumination of the lives of indisputable people.

This essay is the worst of its kind for using a thesaurus as a poor co-author. The author is clearly trying to be a "flexor," but has totally butchered correct word usage, not to mention simple common sense.

DON'T write a humorous essay if you are not funny. Very few people can write truly humorous essays although thousands will try. Even if it may seem funny to you, all it takes is for one admissions officer to be offended and you can kiss that letter of acceptance good-bye.

Unless you are a truly gifted humor writer—the test being that people other than you have said so—stay away from the humorous essay. If you do write a humorous essay, be very certain that it is not of the silly variety. Admissions officers don't want to feel that you are not taking the application seriously.

Of course, using small doses of humor within a serious essay is desirable, but if you are not used to using humor, then confirm the existence of real humor in your work with your editors.

DON'T resort to gimmicks. Previous applicants have written their essays in fluorescent highlighter or nail polish, sent cookies baked in the shape of the university's seal along with the essay and enclosed audio "mood" music that admissions officers were supposed to play while reading their essays to create the right "ambiance." These tricks, while entertaining, are no substitute for actual substance.

While submitting a gimmick usually does little to enhance your application, sending video files, audio files, computer programs and other multimedia is also usually a poor idea since they are often less impressive to admissions officers than applicants may think.

The exception to this rule is when your work is truly outstanding. If you have filmed a documentary that won honors at the Cannes festival or recorded a platinum-selling album, then by all means include it. But think twice about submitting an audio file of your amateur band, *Blood, Depression and Withdrawal,* that congregates in your garage every other month.

Totally Dumb Topics to Avoid

A few words should be said about plain old dumb topics. As a rule, don't write about them. What are these topics that are off limits no matter how interesting, humorous or scintillating their related tales may be? Many of these are obvious, but you would be surprised at how many students simply lose their sense of judgment when writing their essays.

STORY FROM REAL LIFE
SYNOPSIS OF TEMPORARY INSANITY IN AN ESSAY

The following is a true instance of creativity gone overboard. It's frightening that at the time it was written, the student truly felt that he had created an intellectual masterpiece. —Gen Tanabe

The author, a high school friend, wrote his essay as if he had been reborn as a cockroach. While the premise is not a bad one, the way in which it was executed was disastrous. It began with him—the cockroach—crawling out of a toilet bowl. The toilet was not your ordinary commode either, but it was also a metaphor for school where he felt he had just been running around in circles without making any progress. So having finally discovered a way out of the john, he crawled around his new environment discovering all kinds of wonderful things.

Already this essay was a little weird since it was written in the first person of an insect. At this point the admissions officer was probably wondering if my friend was just trying to be extremely creative. Unfortunately as the story progressed, it turned out that while the narrative was creative, it had crossed the line into absurdity.

I'll just highlight a few of the adventures on which my friend as a cockroach embarked. There was his encounter with the toaster where he ate some bread crumbs and pondered what a rich land—as evidenced by the sourdough and pumpernickel crumbs—he had discovered. There was the nearly fatal encounter with the roach motel. (It was a good thing my friend did not decide to get a room.) And towards the end a climactic battle occurs between good and evil where the cockroach defends his right to life and liberty when threatened by a hysterical insecticide-wielding housewife.

I have to admit that my friend's essay was very creative and would have gotten an "A" in a creative writing class. But a college admissions essay it was not. It seems that to more than a few admissions officers this essay was just too much. While acknowledging his creativity, they could not take it seriously and probably questioned his judgment in submitting such an inappropriate essay. The college essay is not a place to debut experimental writing. My friend did not get accepted at any of his top choice schools, but (I am happy to report) he did graduate top of his class from a smaller private college. His major was, as you may have guessed, creative writing.

The only exception is if you can "undumb" such topics by writing about them in an intelligent way. Unless you can do this well (and have your work checked by several editors) it is much safer simply to stay away from these subjects. These taboo topics include the following:

Sex. Answering a question about the most momentous event of her life, one student wrote about, shall we say, a very private experience. We're sure this student's essay provided something to gossip about in the college admissions office, but it certainly was not an appropriate topic.

Sex may sell in any other media, but not for college admissions. It is okay to write about your experience as a sexual abuse counselor or your volunteer work to prevent premarital sex as long as your focus is on the work that you do and not the explicit experiences of your clients.

Crimes, misdemeanors and school violations. On your application, you are required to report any serious criminal activity, suspensions or disciplinary problems. This is the one area of the application that you want to be able to leave blank. But if you are not able to, your essay is certainly not the place to highlight any trouble with the law or lack of judgment that you had as an adolescent.

While the story may be interesting and although you may think your candor will impress the admissions officers, you will actually set off warning signals. No school wants current gang members, graffiti artists or thieves.

One student we know did not follow this advice and thought that his tale of setting 200 live rats loose in his school's hallways would show the admissions officers his creative side. The admissions officers clearly didn't see the value of this type of creativity, and he was rejected from nearly every school to which he applied.

Drunkenness or getting high. One student thought it would be particularly entertaining to describe how he thought he was a chicken during his last substance-induced high. It may have been entertaining, but it did not gain him admission. No matter how humorous or memorable your alcohol or drug-induced antics may be, they are not appropriate for your essay. Like tales of criminal acts, they may make the admissions officers think you need professional help before higher education.

Your bad grades. Some schools allow a space to offer explanations for poor academic performance. If you need to, you can use this opportunity to offer reasons without sounding like you are making excuses. However, do not write about poor grades as the subject of your main essay. We strongly advise against this because it not only emphasizes that your grades have not been stellar, but it also does nothing to give the admission officers reasons to let you into their college.

Instead of trying to explain away bad grades, focus instead on what kept you busy or what kept you motivated. Such an essay will very likely convince the committee to overlook your lack of academic performance in favor of your other talents and virtues. Admissions officers know that not everyone can get straight "A's." If grades are not your strong point, show them what is.

We know of a sad but amusing story of one student who spent his entire essay explaining why he did not receive perfect grades. His reason was that he thought that he had a brain tumor, and throughout the semester he was so consumed by stress over this potential disease that he could not do his homework. At the end of his semester, he finally went to a doctor who confirmed that he did not, after all, have a brain tumor. Unfortunately, however, his explanation for his bad grades did not help him get into college, although we are sure that the admissions officers were entertained by his hypochondria.

Description of why X University is perfect. The admissions officers are already familiar with the beautiful architecture, rigorous academic courses and opportunities to meet extraordinary people at their universities. So you would only waste valuable space informing them of things they already know, especially since they probably know more about the college than you do. An exception is if you have a creative and detailed way of approaching this. This means that you do more than regurgitate the information from the website of the colleges or pile on meaningless platitudes and provide details about how specific programs, courses or other offerings are a fit for you.

The dysfunction of your family. It may be true that your family has been the most influential group of people in your life and that through your family's difficulties you have learned a lot about life. However, never criticize your family's dysfunctions too harshly. Do not complain about how you never felt that your mother loved you, how your father is essentially nonexistent or about how maladjusted your youngest sister is.

Such essays raise questions about your mental stability and your ability to deal with hardships maturely. Furthermore, nobody likes a complainer. If your father was not around much while you were growing up, then focus on how this helped you to become independent rather than how it scarred you for life. Writing about family difficulties is not taboo, but make sure you show the positive things that you have learned and how you have overcome such hardships. If you cannot in all honesty find something good to share about your family, simply do not write an essay about them.

Your mental imbalances or insecurities. The last thing that admissions officers want to read is your self-evaluation of the mental imbalances or insecurities that you have. Surprisingly, some students use the essay as their forum for revealing their deepest fears. Some even rationalize that being honest about their shortcomings is the best way to write a genuine essay.

One student focused on her belief that all the people in the world, including the admissions officers, were conspiring to her downfall. She wrote that the only way she would believe otherwise was if she were accepted by the college. It appears that there must have been some sort of conspiracy after all since she was not accepted!

While this strategy of revealing your insecurities may indeed show the admissions officers who "you" really are, this is not the "you" that you want revealed. Describing such personal issues as how you have always felt unsure about whether you will ever amount to anything, how you always view yourself as an underachiever or how you are frequently depressed will signal to the admissions officers that you may not be ready to handle the pressures of college.

Your plan to bring peace and harmony to the world or any other unrealistic dream. It is true that admissions officers like young people with dreams and determination. But when you write a whole essay about your plan to bring about world peace, stop hunger or end poverty, you sound more like a competitor in the Miss America Pageant than an intelligent high school student with a firm grasp of reality. There is nothing wrong with having ideals and dreams, just do not spend a whole essay writing about them. An essay about your dreams of doing the impossible, unless you can back it up with concrete examples of what you have done, will only make you sound unrealistic and naive.

Furthermore, such essays give nothing substantial to the admissions committee. Anybody can say they want to end world hunger. More than a few applicants will fall into this trap and will write at great lengths about what they want to do in the future, when in fact what they should be writing about is what they have already done. Resist any temptation to impress the admissions officers with your grand plans since you will end up sounding more deserving of a rhinestone-studded tiara than a mortarboard.

The Big Game. Thousands will write about the Big Game, the Big Match or the Big Tournament. Be careful with this kind of topic since it is so common. A play-by-play narration of the Big Game is not original. If you write about the Big Game, have an approach that will be different from the rest. Ask yourself when writing such an essay if others could have had the same experience and might also write about it in a similar way.

Specific Tips for Specific Questions

Besides the main essay question, colleges may also ask additional *specific* questions. Often these essays are shorter, but this does not mean they are less difficult. Since the admissions officers are reviewing your entire application, don't skimp on these essays.

In this section, we will give you some tips for answering the most common of these specific questions. Remember, the same rules apply to these shorter questions as to the general essay questions. However, because of the narrow topic guidelines, there are techniques that apply specifically to these essays. The most important thing to keep in mind is that there are no wrong answers to these questions.

The reality is that the admissions officers are *not* very interested in what your answer to any one question really is. They don't care what subject in school or which book you like best. But they do care about what your attraction to organic chemistry or Tolstoy says about you. Throughout all of your essays, the primary goal is to tell the admissions officers about you, your thoughts and opinions and your growth. Secondary is your actual answer to the question.

Here are some examples of specific questions from recent applications and some tips on answering them:

Why You Would Like to Attend Our College

Many colleges ask this question to gauge your true interest level. While these are often short answer questions, sometimes as short as a couple of sentences, they should be taken seriously. It's important to answer this question with specifics. Instead of saying that the campus is pretty or that the college has a great reputation, write about a specific class that you would like to take, a professor's research project you find interesting or a program that appeals to you. In other words, don't just repeat what you read on the college's website or brochure, but tailor your answer so it's specific to you. Also, two or three reasons are enough. You don't need to give 10 or 20. Focusing on the most important reasons will allow you enough space to write about something substantial.

Your Favorite Book

Don't write a book report. No matter how interesting it may be, the admissions officers are not interested in the plot, characters or literary analysis of your favorite book.

Instead, write about how your favorite book relates to you. Write about how you have applied the lessons from the work to your daily life, detail why it is your favorite writing or explain how it has affected you personally. Through this essay, the admissions officers want to learn less about the actual book and more about you.

Being or Meeting a Historical or Other Person and Describing the Most Influential Person in Your Life

Don't write a biography. The last thing that the admissions officers want to read is a biography of Susan B. Anthony or Dr. Martin Luther King, Jr.

While the stories of well-known personalities are often interesting, the admissions officers could just as easily have glanced through an encyclopedia. Don't waste the space.

About half the students applying to college will select their mother or father as the most influential person in their lives. Unless you are sure that you can describe the role of your parent in a way that will be unlike other students' essays, try to choose someone else. The same goes for the President of the United States, Bill Gates or any other internationally recognized figure. If you can write about these people in a creative way, do so. If you can't, pick someone whom other students won't.

Explain why you choose whom you choose. Make your reasons for your decision clear to the admissions officers. Outline why you think this person's contributions are important. Describe how they have affected your life, motivated you or inspired others. Concentrate most on how the person has made an impact on your life. After all, this essay is about you, not about the person you choose.

Your Academic or Intellectual Interests

Admissions officers don't want to hear *what* you know about Eastern philosophy; they want to know *why* you have dedicated a shrine in your room to Confucius. They want to find out *why* you are interested in certain academic or intellectual areas. Who introduced you to it? Why are you intrigued? Do you plan to pursue this interest in college? Tell them how your interest relates to or says something about you, not about the interest itself.

Your Ideal Future Roommate

Describing the person with whom you will fight over the telephone, complain to about spending too much time in the bathroom and sleep three feet above in a bunk bed leaves some room for creativity. Show your imagination.

Focus on saying something about yourself while at the same time describing your ideal roommate. Explain why you would like your roommate to enjoy late night TV or why you hope that he or she has a pet goldfish named Ned. Use the description of your ideal roommate to show what qualities you admire in a person.

Your Greatest Achievement

When colleges ask this question, the truth is that they are not solely interested in what it is that you have accomplished. Rather, colleges ask this question because they want to know how you view your own accomplishments and what has motivated you.

Don't just give facts and statistics. It is not enough to merely describe what you have done. Admissions officers are not interested in reading an expanded form of your resume. These details are in your application form anyway.

They will be interested, however, in what the description of your accomplishment says about you. They want to know why you think it was your most outstanding achievement, what standard you measure it by, what your motivations were, and how you felt. They want to understand not only *what* you did but *why* you did it. They also want to know how your accomplishment has affected your life and how it has changed your perspectives.

Hobbies

Don't just describe your hobby, write what your hobby is or how long you've done it. This tells the admissions officers nothing about you. They will be more interested in why you find enjoyment in creating knitted Barbie doll dresses than in actually how to knit.

Show yourself through your hobby. Explain why you have a passion for it, what inspired you to begin it or what it has taught you. If you have excelled at the hobby, by all means, now is the time to mention it.

A Page of Your Autobiography

Lucky you. Chances are that you can easily recycle one of your essays for this question. Because of the open-endedness of this question, almost anything you have written is suitable. You can describe your favorite hobby, your greatest accomplishment, your family or anything else of significance in your life because all of these topics would be a page in your autobiography.

The key is to make sure that you know how to recycle this material. Don't make it obvious that you are using an essay that you wrote to answer a different question. To learn more about how to recycle your essays, see Chapter 6. Remember that your goal is to tell the admissions officers something important about you.

Your Future Career Plans

Colleges may ask about your future career plans to get a better idea of where you are headed. Here again, colleges aren't interested in how final your decision is or exactly what you see yourself doing. Rather, they want to know what is motivating you to choose this career path. And don't worry, they won't hold you to your answer.

Don't write a job description. Unless the job you wish to have is so uncommon that the admissions officers will not know what it is—which is highly unlikely—don't simply provide a description of your future career. You also need not mention how much money you want to earn. Even if you are absolutely positive that your future career will result in your becoming the first 20-year-old self-made gazillionaire, don't share your financial dreams with the admissions officers. You don't want to present yourself as a greedy, dollar-track-minded individual, even if that's where you lean.

Is There Anything Else You Would Like to Add?

The short answer to this question should almost always be, "yes." This is your opportunity to address an aspect of you that hasn't been addressed elsewhere. Use this opportunity to raise extenuating circumstances, discuss a disability that you have or explain why you didn't perform as well as you could have in classes or on standardized tests. It's better to answer the questions the admissions officers may have (even if they are a touchy subject) than to leave them wondering. The caveat is that this is not the place for excuses. Instead of making excuses for bad grades, explain the reason and then state how you have since improved your grades or now have a stronger focus on your classes. Or, instead of just describing a learning disability, discuss what you have done to overcome the disability. In other words, acknowledge the negative but focus on the positive.

Next Up: The Magic of Recycling and Examples of the Good, Bad and Ugly . . . Essays that Is

Now that you know how to write a winning essay, it's time to lean how to use the art of recycling to save your time and sanity. Plus, you'll also get to see all of the strategies and tips put into action in our chapter filled with sample essays that worked as well as some that bombed. So before you start writing, glance over chapters 6 and 7. Happy writing!

ESSAY-WRITING WORKSHEET
Academic and College Goals

Colleges are curious about what you hope to gain by going to college. Sharing what you want to study and how your education fits into your future makes an impressive essay. Even if you are not completely sure what you will major in, you can still write about the subject areas that interest you. As much as possible, try to show how your college education will help you to achieve your own personal goals.

STEP 1: Brainstorm Your Academic Goals

Think about why you are going to college and what you want to accomplish. To help you brainstorm, answer a few of these questions:

1. What will be your major in college? If undecided, what majors sound interesting enough to be a possible choice? _____

_____

_____

_____

2. How will college studies prepare you for your future career? What do you expect to do or learn? _____

_____

_____

_____

3. What are you most excited about studying in college? Any new things you are especially looking forward to? _____

_____

_____

_____

4. Which subjects and activities have you enjoyed and excelled at in high school? _____

_____

- Which of the above questions was the easiest to answer?   _____

- Which question gets you started on the best stories you can tell? _____

Choose one to two main points to use in STEP 2 of this worksheet. Also, weave in some of the rest of your answers into your essay in STEP 3.

STEP 2: Uncover Your Main Point

Your essay needs to have a strong main point. You need to tell your reader: "THIS is what I'm going to tell you about." Here are three examples of how to start your essay with a strong main point:

I have always been good at languages. This is one of the reasons why I want to be a Chinese language major in college. I am excited about studying Chinese at the college level and I hope to someday use my skills in international business.

In high school, my favorite class is history. I plan to continue to study it by becoming a history major with a focus on early European history.

I've always been fascinated with the stars but my school does not offer any astronomy classes. This is one reason why I want to study astronomy in college and learn more about the universe and how planets are formed.

What will be one or two main points of your essay?

_____
_____
_____
_____
_____
_____

STEP 3: Construct Your Story

Your essay needs stories and details to support your main point. Good examples also bring your main point to life and make your essay memorable. Notice how the following example builds up the essay:

Focus of essay:

I have three goals for college. First, I want to earn my degree in accounting. Second, I want to learn more about business. Finally, I'd like to improve my math skills.

Details:

I've always loved business and math. In high school I was a member of the business club as well as the math team.

Although I enjoy math, it is not my strongest subject. I want to take more math classes so that I can improve my skills.

I may want to become an accountant in the future, so I want to major in accounting and possibly minor in business.

I have read that the college also has a business club for students. I'm looking forward to joining it.

STEP 4: End Strong

End your essay by shining a new light on the main point you started with, or leave the reader with something interesting to think about. Here are four examples:

Although some people think physics is boring, I find it extremely interesting because you can use the principles in physics to explain much of the world. I don't know of any other subject that promises to explain the mysteries of the universe.

After earning my business degree, I plan to return to my hometown and start my own business. The skills that I learn in college will be extremely useful in helping me to establish my business.

I am really looking forward to going to college to be able to learn how to think critically and express my opinions better. One of the things that I have enjoyed in high school has been the debates that we've had in our social studies class. I know that these debates will continue in college with my classmates.

My dream to become an architect begins with college. By majoring in architecture and design I will be fulfilling a lifelong dream.

ESSAY-WRITING WORKSHEET
Future Career

Writing about your future career is an astute way to show colleges how you will use your education. College is, after all, not your final destination, but a springboard that will help you reach larger goals in life. Don't worry, colleges do not expect you to be 100 percent certain about what your future job will be. Don't be afraid to aim high and write about your dream job.

STEP 1: Brainstorm Your Future Career

Start by answering these questions to help you decide what to focus on in your essay:

1. What is your dream job? _____

_____

_____

_____

2. What attracts you to this job? _____

_____

_____

_____

3. How did you first get interested in this type of work? Did someone in this career inspire you? How? _____

_____

_____

_____

4. What do you hope to accomplish in this career?_____

_____

_____

_____

5. Have you prepared yourself for this career in any way? (e.g., talked to someone in the field, read a book about what it's like to have such a career or tried a workshop or class?) _____

_____

_____

_____

6. What will you do in college to help prepare you for this career? (You might list a major, classes or activities you'll pursue.) _____

_____

_____

_____

7. Have you had any experiences that have helped you learn about this career? (e.g., summer job, internship, job shadowing, etc.) _____

_____

_____

_____

- Which of the above questions was the easiest to answer? _____

- Which question gets you started on the best stories you can tell? _____

Choose one to two main points to use in STEP 2 of this worksheet. Also, weave in some of your other answers into your essay in STEP 3.

STEP 2: Uncover Your Main Point

Your essay needs to have a strong main point. You need to tell your reader, "THIS is what I'm going to tell you about." Here are four examples of how to start your essay with a strong main point:

My dream is to become a civil engineer. Ever since I was a child with a Lego set, I have enjoyed building things. Engineering would let me express my love for creating things, and allow me to apply my science and math skills.

In the future, I would like to become a teacher. Teaching seems like the perfect match for me because I enjoy working with children and teaching them new skills. Also, my own teachers have played an important role in my life, and I hope to do the same for other students in the future.

I want to become a chef just like Emeril. To me, cooking is very creative and although it can look easy from the outside, it is often very difficult to do well. Plus, I love to eat!

Although I'm not sure what job I will have, I do know that it will be in the field of medicine. I have learned a lot about nursing from my aunt, who has inspired me to consider a career in medicine.

What will be one or two main points of your essay?

_____

_____

_____

_____

_____

_____

STEP 3: Construct Your Story

The heart of your essay will be the stories and details you use to support your main point. Good examples also bring your main point to life and make your essay memorable. Notice how the essay is built up in the example:

Focus of essay:

> My dream job is to be a crime scene investigator. This job would combine my love of science with the challenge of solving a real life mystery.

Details:

> I have always enjoyed science. This year I am taking chemistry and have learned how various chemicals react and how you can test for the presence of different chemicals.

> Reading detective novels is a favorite pastime. It's a challenge to figure out "who did it." Real life detective work would be much more exciting.

> I watch CSI: Cyber every week. It's amazing how the simplest clue can lead to the arrest of a criminal. Just one tiny fiber from the assailant's jacket can lead to his capture.

> Law enforcement helps to keep the community safe. CSI detectives make sure that criminals do not get away with their crimes.

STEP 4: End Strong

End your essay by shining a new light on the main point you started with, or leave the reader with something interesting to think about. Here are three examples:

> Medicine is a very honorable profession since it seeks to help those who need it the most. I am looking forward to becoming a pre-med major in college and taking the first step toward becoming a doctor.

> Seeing people enjoy my cooking is one of the best feelings in the world. Becoming a chef is one way I can spread this joy to many more. Hopefully someday I will even have my own restaurant named after me!

> Becoming a mechanical engineer like my father has always seemed like a dream. Going to college will not only make this dream possible, but it will also help me to reach my lifelong goal.

ESSAY-WRITING WORKSHEET
Role Models

There's no question that some people play a significant role in your life. Essays about how others have shaped who you are in positive ways can tell a lot about how you learn and how you relate to others. It's important to remember that even though you are writing about an influential person, your essay must still be about you. Connect the lessons and influences from your role model back to your own life. The essay is always about you.

STEP 1: Identify Your Role Model's Impact on You

To jumpstart your essay, answer at least three of the following questions to figure out how you can write about your role model's influence on your own life.

1. Who has been an influential person or role model in your life? _____
_____
_____
_____

2. What do you admire the most about this person? Why? _____
_____
_____
_____

3. What specific things have you learned from this person? _____
_____
_____
_____

4. How have you used teachings from your role model in your own life? _____
_____
_____
_____

5. Which of your role model's traits (e.g., special talents, skills, way of treating others) do you hope to one day have yourself? _____
_____
_____
_____

6. Can you think of specific examples of what this person did or said that made a
lasting impact? _____

_____
_____
_____

7. How is your life different since meeting your role model? _____

_____
_____
_____

- Which of the above questions was the easiest to answer? _____

- Which question gets you started on the best stories you can tell? _____

Choose one to two main points to use in STEP 2 of this worksheet. Also, weave
in some of your other answers into your essay in STEP 3.

STEP 2: Focus Your Essay

You want your essay to have a clear and focused main point. The reader should
know exactly what you're trying to say. Here are three examples of how to start:

*My grandfather is my role model. The things that I admire the most and
have tried to apply to my own life are a strong work ethic, unwavering honesty and a love of family.*

*My English teacher has inspired me to pursue a career in education. She
has also taught me how important it is to be patient with students and to
always encourage them to live up to their potential.*

*My judo sensei is the most influential person in my life because he has
shown me how making small gains each day will eventually lead to huge
progress and that I need to believe in myself even when I don't feel like it.*

What will be one or two main points of your essay?

_____
_____
_____
_____
_____
_____

STEP 3: Find Some Examples

To illustrate your main point and to make your essay memorable you need to provide examples. Just remember that the essay needs to be about you so find examples from your role model and then try to connect them back to you.

Focus of essay:

My uncle is my role model. He has taught me a lot about life, especially how to take responsibility for my actions and to always think about my family and community.

Details:

For the past 20 years my uncle has held the same job – waking up each morning to go to work at 5 a.m. without complaint. I try to do the same thing with my part-time job at Zippy's. Even though I don't always feel like going to work I try to remember that it's part of my responsibility and commitment to my boss.

Every third Sunday, my uncle invites the whole family to his house for dinner. I try to do the same with my friends. Even when I am busy with work and school, I always try to make time to get together. For the past two years during Labor Day weekend I have hosted a potluck barbeque at the beach for both my friends and family.

My uncle is always willing to help out a neighbor. I also believe it's important to contribute to my community and have been involved with a lot of public service projects including an effort to help the homeless.

STEP 4: End with a Bang!

There's a reason Hollywood movies end with a big finale—it makes them memorable. Do the same thing by leaving your reader with one last thought in your essay. Here are three examples:

When my grandfather passed away, I was devastated, but I also realized his influence was something that I would carry with me for the rest of my life. He has taught me so much about working hard and enjoying life. In this way I know that his spirit will always be a part of me.

I know I will face many new challenges in college, but I also know that if I apply the lessons from my coach, I will be able to overcome any obstacle. Whenever things get really tough, I'll just repeat his words, "It's not about failing but about rising back up every time we fall."

There is one last lesson that I have learned from my mother: time makes everything better. Even when I have what seems like the worst experience and things are falling apart, I know if I take it one day at a time, things always get better.

ESSAY-WRITING WORKSHEET
Community Service

Community service is a great topic for essays. Admissions officers want to know how you are involved in your school or neighborhood. They want to see that you do more than study and look for students with a variety of experiences, skills and interests. When writing keep in mind that it is important to not only share how you've been involved with community service but also what kind of impact you've made.

STEP 1: Think Before You Write

Before you begin writing, answer at least three of the following questions to figure out what to share in your essay:

1. Which community service activity has meant the most to you? _____
_____
_____
_____

2. When and how did you first get involved with this activity? _____
_____
_____
_____

3. Who have you helped, and in what way, through community service? _____
_____
_____
_____

4. What types of skills have you used or developed through community service?
_____
_____
_____

5. How has your community service experience made you think differently about others or yourself? _____
_____
_____
_____

6. How has your community service influenced your plans for college or work in the future? _____

_____

_____

- Which of the above questions was the easiest to answer? _____

- Which question gets you started on the best stories you can tell? _____

Choose one to two main points to use in STEP 2 of this worksheet. Also, weave in some of your other answers into your essay in STEP 3.

STEP 2: Start Your Essay with a Clear Focus

Your essay needs to be focused like a laser beam, so begin by telling your reader, "THIS is what I'm going to tell you about." Here are three examples of how to start an essay:

I became involved in collecting toiletries for the homeless after seeing a TV news special that made me realize how even the smallest items that we take for granted can really help homeless families.

I learned from organizing a Key Club car wash to raise money for hurricane victims how important it is to communicate effectively to increase aware-ness and get the community involved.

Volunteering as a Little League assistant coach has taught me a lot about training boys to work as a team. This experience has also made me decide to pursue a career in youth sports.

What will be one or two main points of your essay?

_____

_____

_____

_____

_____

_____

STEP 3: Build Your Story

The heart of your essay will be the stories and details you use to support your main point. Good examples also bring your main point to life and make your essay memorable. Notice how the example builds up the essay:

Focus of essay:

Tutoring third graders in math has been a rewarding experience because it has taught me to be creative and has helped me to decide to become a math teacher in the future.

Details:

Kids have a hard time understanding why they should learn about numbers and math. I need to show them how math helps in the real world.

Kids like the idea of having money to spend, especially in places like candy stores, so I came up with a shopping game that gets students to add and subtract while they pretend to shop.

It feels great to see a student who has struggled with a problem finally get it. This is what I love most about teaching kids.

I have decided to become a math teacher and want to go to college to major in education and minor in math.

I used to think that math would be the most boring subject to teach, but through my work as a tutor, I discovered how much fun it can be.

STEP 4: End Strong

End your essay by shining a new light on the main point you started with, or leave the reader with something interesting to think about. Here are three examples:

Since getting involved in helping the homeless, I learned that for a time one of my relatives was homeless. When you have a house it's easy to take it for granted, but all it takes is some bad luck for you to lose it. This is why I feel it's so important that we all try to help those who have no home to go to.

As hard as it was to motivate others to volunteer and help out with our fundraiser, it was worth it in the end. We raised more than $1,000 for the hurricane victims. Now when we see news coverage of that terrible disaster at least we know that we have done our small part to help.

The reward for being a coach has nothing to do with winning games. The reward is seeing everyone working as a team and enjoying the game. Win or lose, as coach you're always proud after each game.

IN THIS CHAPTER

- How to answer any question with only one essay
- Interpreting the questions to fit your essay
- Recycling in action
- How to make a long essay short or a short essay long

CHAPTER 6

RECYCLE YOUR ESSAYS WHEN APPLYING TO MANY COLLEGES

Presto-Chango! Turn One Essay Into Two

Writing one essay can take weeks or even months. What if you plan to apply to 5 or 10 or more colleges? Yikes! Does this mean you will have to skip school just so you have enough time to write dozens of perfectly crafted and individual essays? Thankfully, despite how tempting playing hooky can be, the answer is "no."

Why go through the difficult and time-consuming essay-writing process again and again to answer each school's questions when you can modify a few essays to answer all of them? In fact, if you write three or four good essays, you will have enough to apply to an almost unlimited number of schools. Sound too good to be true? It's all made possible through the magical technique we call "recycling."

In this chapter you will learn some of the finer techniques of recycling and see how to change a single essay so that it answers a variety of seemingly unrelated questions. Essay recycling does require some effort to pull off successfully. But as you will see, doing so will shed weeks off the essay-writing process.

The Common Application: The Easiest Way to Recycle

The ultimate in recycling is to submit the exact same essay word for word to all of the colleges to which you are applying. While a fantasy for past applicants, this is increasingly becoming a reality through the growing acceptance of the Common Application and Coalition Application.

These are a single application that several hundred schools accept in place of their own application. This means that if you are applying to more than one school that accepts the Common Application or Coalition Application, you can send the same exact application to each of these schools.

But for those schools that do not accept these applications, which unfortunately are still the majority, you will need to learn the art of recycling.

How to Answer Any Question With Only One Essay

There are two secrets you need to know to understand how recycling can work for you:

- **Secret #1:** You don't have to answer the question the college asks, *at least not literally.*

- **Secret #2:** For most recycled essays, the only major modifications needed are to the essay's introduction and conclusion.

As we mentioned in the last chapter, the particular essay questions posed by the colleges are not important in and of themselves. Think of them as suggested topics that help you to focus your essays. What the admissions officers are really seeking is more than your actual answers. They want to read an essay that contains your thoughts and opinions to help them gauge what kind of person you are and to show them your thinking and writing skills.

Therefore, while you need to stay within the bounds of the question, the boundaries themselves are quite flexible.

Let's look at an example of how this might work. A typical essay question is, "Evaluate a significant experience or achievement that has special meaning to you." Since you are a smart applicant who has read this book, you would of course follow all of the tips in the last chapter and after several weeks have a perfect essay describing, for example, a hike in the Grand Canyon that changed your outlook on the meaning of life. This essay directly addresses the significant experience question and could be submitted as is.

However, for another school, you might think you need to write an entirely new essay to answer their question, "Describe a book, class, project or person that you find intellectually exciting."

Before you begin brainstorming, wait a minute. If you have read any books along the lines of *Robinson Crusoe, Tom Sawyer, Huckleberry Finn* or *The Heart of Darkness*, you could in your introduction begin by referring to one of these books, describing the importance of nature and adventure in the book and then show how these same themes have affected your life.

With a good transition, you could then attach word for word the main body of your first essay describing your own adventure in the Grand Canyon and how it changed you. In the conclusion you could again juxtapose your adventure with that of one of the characters or themes in the novel and reemphasize the significance of both the book and adventure in your life.

The result would be another perfect essay that only took a fraction of the time to write. The major requirement for recycling to be successful is that you have at least one good essay with which to begin. Remember that as powerful as recycling is, it will not improve a bad essay. In fact, a bad essay recycled and sent to 100 schools will still only yield 100 rejections.

Recycling in Action: A Case Study

Now that you understand the usefulness of recycling, let's turn to a real example. In this case, Anita, known as the "Queen of Recycling," was able to answer six different questions using only one essay. Anita's original essay illustrated how other people's prejudices about her have made her stronger. The power of her essay lies in her gripping introduction and in her mature confrontation with a difficult problem in this country.

The original question Anita answered was for Columbia, "Write an essay which conveys to the reader a sense of who you are." This is a very common question, and Anita sent the same essay to several schools that asked similar questions with almost no changes. However, some of the schools that Anita applied to asked more specific questions. With some thoughtful editing, however, Anita was able to modify her original essay to answer five additional questions.

The following is Anita's original essay, which answers Columbia's very broad question. After the original essay are examples of some of the major changes Anita made when she used the same essay to answer the additional questions. You will see that by just adding a few sentences to the introduction or conclusion she was able to shift the focus of the essay to address the specific question posed while leaving the bulk of the essay untouched.

"Yo Soy" (Original Essay)

I am a Latina, but don't hold it against me. Please don't equate my last name, Rodriguez, with low intelligence or motivation. Don't look at my brown eyes and see an illegal immigrant who refuses to speak English preferring incomprehensible Español instead. Don't view my dark skin and black hair as exotic. Don't stereotype me as a Latin lover. Please don't judge me so readily. Others have done so too many times already.

On the first day of kindergarten my mother drove me to school. Before letting me out of the front seat of our old station wagon, she pulled me close, clasping her hands around my face for emphasis. "Take care of yourself," she said with a face so expressionless that I knew she meant it. As my feet hit the ground I heard her say, "You are a Latina. Be proud." At the time I didn't know what she meant but for some reason it stuck in my memory.

It was only as I grew older that I came to understand the meaning of her words. Throughout my education, I have been a minority at my schools. Instead of attending the schools in my neighborhood where 95 percent of the children are Latino, my mother arranged for me to be transferred to schools where 95 percent of the children are white, telling me I would receive a better education that way. At first, as with all innocent children, I did not notice any differences between my classmates and me. The first time I realized a difference, it was pointed out to me.

In sixth grade we had a dance. My four girl friends and I lined up against one wall while the boys were against the opposite. After our teacher realized that the lines would remain that way all afternoon unless he did something, he guided five hesitant boys to our side of the room. Each of them chose one of my four friends to dance with, but the last boy, Bobby, did not choose me.

"Mr. Henshaw, I don't want to dance with a Mexican," he said, pulling back toward our teacher. Mr. Henshaw pulled Bobby to the side, and I could tell that he was scolding him. When he was finished, Bobby came up to me again and sullenly asked me to dance.

Although I had noticed that my hair did not fall down straight like the blonde and brunette hair of the other girls and that when we studied skin coloring in health class mine was darker than the rest, Bobby was the first to actually show me how being a Latina was different from being white.

Unfortunately, he was the first of many to remind me that I could be looked down on for who I was. Since the sixth grade dance, I have been told to return to Mexico, to stop stealing money through the welfare system and to speak America's language. I was even threatened with having my Green Card revoked even though I don't have one, having been born here.

In spite of these bad experiences, I have been fortunate enough to rise through the education system to where I am now at a well-known high school that has a reputation for sending a large number of students to college. The atmosphere at my high school often enforces the idea that we must compete for the limited number of positions at each top-ranked college. I have tried to stay out of this competition, but have become involuntarily involved.

Other students frequently mention to me, "Anita, you have it made. You're going to get into the college of your choice. What I wouldn't do to have the advantage of being Mexican, too." Or, "Anita, you are so lucky. Affirmative action really makes this whole college admissions process a piece of cake for you, doesn't it?"

At first the questions and comments of my fellow students really crushed, frustrated and angered me. I wondered, do these students think that I should be flattered by their comments? Do they think that it is so easy to be a Latina and that I have not worked hard to achieve everything that I have? Would they really elect to be a Latina if they had the choice? If America's supposed best students in pursuit of higher education hold such beliefs, what hope was there at all for me?

As my fellow students continued to make such thoughtless comments, I came to realize that some of the people in this world would always judge me more by my last name than by my abilities, more by the hue of my skin than by my personality. It would be wonderful of course to live in a world where race didn't make a difference, but the sad fact is that such a world does not yet exist.

Although it has been difficult, I have come to face those who doubt me without getting angry. I have accepted that I will have to live and work with them and that they will continue to make assumptions about me. But, the difference now is that I have decided to fight against their cruel assumptions, not by feeling belittled, but by proving them wrong.

Today I do more than complain about the misguided attitudes that people have. I show them to be in error. Through my achievements and work I challenge anyone who has doubts about my abilities. I will continue to work hard to achieve the good grades and accomplishments that I already have. I finally know what my mother meant in the front seat of our station wagon. If other people choose to stereotype me, so be it. It won't change anything for me. I am a Latina and I am proud of who I am. Yo soy Latina.

Changes to Introduction for Stanford's Question: "Discuss an accomplishment, event, or realization that sparked a period of personal growth and a new understanding of yourself or others." *Changes are noted in italics.*

(2nd Paragraph)   On the first day of kindergarten my mother drove me to school. Before letting me out of the front seat of our old station wagon, she pulled me close, clasping her hands around my face for emphasis. "Take care of yourself," she said with a face so expressionless that I knew she meant it. As my feet hit the ground I heard her say, "You are a Latina. Be proud." [*Although I didn't know it at the time, those simple words, that one-way conversation with my mother, would remain forever etched in my mind. At the time I had no idea what the significance of that conversation would be. But through the*

12 years that it has taken me to learn the meaning of that exchange, it has always remained, perhaps subconsciously, the foundation of a strength which has helped me to deal with one of the greatest sources of frustration in my life.]

Changes to Conclusion for Harvard's Question: "How you hope to use your college education." *Changes are noted in italics.*

(Last Paragraph)   Today I do more than complain about the misguided attitudes that people have. I show them to be in error. Through my achievements and work I challenge anyone who has doubts about my abilities. [*What I truly hope to gain from a Harvard education is the chance to acquire the skills and experience to continue to do this. I want to continue to work hard by challenging myself with the best education possible.*] I finally know what my mother meant in the front seat of our station wagon. If other people choose to stereotype me, so be it. It won't change anything for me. I am a Latina and I am proud of who I am. Yo soy Latina.

Changes to Introduction for Princeton's Question: "Tell us about a person who has influenced you in a significant way." *Changes are noted in italics.*

(2nd Paragraph)   On the first day of kindergarten my mother drove me to school. Before letting me out of the front seat of our old station wagon, she pulled me close, clasping her hands around my face for emphasis. "Take care of yourself," she said with a face so expressionless that I knew she meant it. As my feet hit the ground I heard her say, "You are a Latina. Be proud." [*Although I didn't know it at the time, those simple words from my mother would remain forever etched in my mind. I had no idea how significant this moment would be. But in the 12 years that it has taken me to discover what my mother meant on that morning so many years ago, I believe that her words have helped me to come to terms with what has been a constant source of frustration in my life.*]

Changes to Introduction for Yale's Question: "The lessons we take from obstacles we encounter can be fundamental to later success. Recount a time when you faced a challenge, setback, or failure. How did it affect you, and what did you learn from the experience?" *Changes are noted in italics.*

(First Paragraph)   I am a Latina, but don't hold it against me. Please don't equate my last name, Rodriguez, with low intelligence or motivation. Don't look at my brown eyes and see an illegal immigrant who refuses to speak English preferring incomprehensible Español instead. Don't view my dark skin and black hair as exotic. Don't stereotype me as a Latin lover. Please don't judge me so readily. Others have done so too many times already. [*Although for many people racism and discrimination are well-known but abstract issues, for me they have been a very personal challenge that I have had to confront on a daily basis.*]

Changes to Conclusion for Dartmouth's Question: "While arguing a Dartmouth-related case before the U.S. Supreme Court in 1818, Daniel Webster, Class of 1801, uttered this memorable line: "It is, Sir…a small college. And yet, there are those who love it!" As you seek admission to the Class of 2022, what aspects of the College's program, community, or campus environment attract your interest?" *Changes are noted in italics.*

(Last Paragraph)   Today I do more than complain about the misguided attitudes that people have. I show them to be in error. Through my achievements and work I challenge anyone who has doubts about my abilities. I will continue to work hard to achieve the good grades and accomplishments that I already have. [*In an environment as diverse as at Dartmouth, I know that there will be others who will join me in my mission. I hope to learn from the ways in which they have dealt with similar problems and also that they will gain something from my experiences. Discrimination will not go away on its own, but that does not mean that we who are its victims must sit still.*] I finally know what my mother meant in the front seat of our station wagon. If other people choose to stereotype me, so be it. It won't change anything for me. I am a Latina and I am proud of who I am. Yo soy Latina.

From Anita's examples, you can see that it is possible to use the same essay to answer a number of questions. Anita's original essay was easy to adapt to the various questions. Chances are that your essay will need a little more editing to make it fit. Also, since we don't have the space to reprint her essay five times, keep in mind that we could only show you the *major* changes that Anita made.

When you begin to recycle, keep in mind that more important than *where* you add is *what* you add. Some essays are easy to recycle while others require more work. But whenever you modify an existing essay to answer another school's question, you are saving a tremendous amount of time. Even if you have to tinker with a few sentences in each paragraph, it sure beats writing a whole new essay.

How to Shorten a Long Essay

There is nothing more frustrating than cutting, clipping and reworking your essay for the 14th time only to find that it is still 126 words too long. When you are trying to trim a too-long essay, word or page restrictions can be an insufferable burden. You can cut a word here or scrap a word there, but it always seems that you need to do more.

In this section, you will learn some techniques for reducing a too-long essay. The key is that it is too slow and painstaking to clip word by word. To truly downsize an essay, you must delete whole sentences and even paragraphs.

The first step to heavy-duty slimming down is to read through your over-weight essay and mark the key segments that are absolutely, without a doubt necessary. Among what's left, look for parts of the essay that are not essential but merely add detail. (Do not try to eliminate single words—although if you find a word that you don't need, don't be afraid to give it the ax.)

Your goal is to divide your essay into sections that are essential and sections that can be discarded if necessary. To help separate the icing from the cake, ask yourself the following questions:

- What are the main ideas that you are trying to convey?

- If you delete this sentence, will your idea still be coherent?

- Are the details in this sentence absolutely essential to the overall point? Can a phrase or two be eliminated?

- Is there a way to shorten the sentence and present the same information in fewer words?

When you have finished categorizing your essay, start eliminating the unnecessary parts. Keep asking yourself if the reader really needs the extra information.

It may be hard to accept, but some of the best-written sentences in your essay may only add details that are not really necessary to advance the point. You may be very proud of creating such wonderful prose, but remember that pride is one of the seven deadly sins. Eliminate these sentences, no matter how personally attached you feel to them, since they really are only overburdening your essay.

After you finish cutting, read the essay again (or better yet have someone else read the essay) to make sure that it does not sound choppy and that you have not inadvertently removed a critical piece of information. You may need to alter or add transitions between paragraphs.

The following essay was a very detail-heavy one. It was written in response to the question, "Tell us about a significant or meaningful experience in your life." While the college allowed the author, Kyle, to add extra papers as necessary, the scholarship application for another school (which also asked about a significant experience) provided much less space. Note that to trim this essay, much of the detail was removed but the main ideas and emotional power were retained.

Ozzie Without Harriet (Condensed Version)

Note: Stricken sentences are those that Kyle deleted.

I was eight years old when they told me. At the time I was wearing my Superman pajamas and was lying in bed waiting for my kiss good night. I could tell that something was wrong when my parents came into my room together. ~~They looked like they were on parade, marching in one after the other. Only this parade had no music or cotton candy.~~

"Your father and I have something to tell you, Kyle," my mother said. ~~For the first time she did not look at me as she spoke.~~ "Your father is going to have to go away, and you are going to stay with me. We're getting a divorce."

Until that moment my concept of marriage and family had been based upon my favorite daytime rerun: Ozzie and Harriet. ~~I looked forward with great anticipation to each Saturday's episode.~~ Part of the show's appeal was that I would unconsciously impose the qualities of this ~~black and white~~ TV family upon my own and viewed them as a mirror of my parents and me.

Now with my whole world threatened (with destruction) I did not know how to react. I still recall, ~~even to this day,~~ that my first spontaneous thought when my parents made the announcement was: What's Ozzie going to do without Harriet?

~~"When will Daddy come back?" I asked my mother, who still did not look at me.~~

~~"Kyle, he's not coming back. You will still see him on the weekends, but he's going to move away for good."~~

From that night on I vowed never to forgive my parents and I promised myself that I would never again watch another episode of Ozzie and Harriet—~~feeling somehow that my TV family too had betrayed me.~~ Life was not simple and families were no longer defined by two parents, children and a house surrounded by a white picket fence.

It's amazing how the human mind deals with trauma and how quickly it recovers. Although initially shocked, sad and angry, I found, ~~to my great displeasure,~~ that I could not continue to be mad ~~at my parents. Even though I felt that they were making a great mistake and were entirely insensitive to the wishes and desires of their only son, I could not maintain my depression.~~

A couple of weeks after my father moved out I visited him for the first time. I was amazed to see all of his belongings gathered in the small space of his new apartment. ~~His electric shaver I used to pretend to shave with was on a tiny sink in an unfamiliar bathroom; the beat up fuzzy yellow chair I used to jump on was in a strange new living room on the tenth floor and the picture of me in the macaroni frame I made in the first grade sat next to a bed in which my mother~~

did not also sleep. I knew that these were his belongings, but I was not convinced that this was his home. I still imagined that his place was with my mother and me. With each visit, however, I came to realize that this was his new home.

As I grew older I learned the sad fact that divorce is not such an uncommon experience. More than a few of my friends had parents who were separated. However, I noticed that they often retained their anger and bitterness for far longer than I had. Certainly none said that divorce had been good for them.

Was I odd? Not only did my bitterness wane after a few months but I also learned some things that made me realize that my parents' divorce was not necessarily such a bad thing.

This revelation came while talking to my mother over dinner one night. I had just entered high school and was brimming full of a premature sense of adulthood. We almost never talked about the divorce but for some reason on this particular night I asked my mother why she and my dad decided to end their marriage. I was amazed at how clearly my mother was able to lay out the reasons for their growing unhappiness with each other and how they mutually agreed after a long discussion that separation was the best option. Their reasons for divorce were not unusual—my parents just discovered things about each other that they did not like and as time went on their arguments became more frequent and their disenchantment grew deeper. As I was going to sleep, in the same bed I had been in when I was told of their divorce, I had a strange feeling in which a part of me was glad that my parents had separated rather than stayed in a situation where both were unhappy.

My father has since remarried and seems to have a full life with his new family. He is still an important part of my life and I try to see him at least once a week—although my ever-increasing commitments to the tennis team and debate club have often made it difficult to find the time. My mother has not remarried but seems very content with her life and still stays in touch with my father and his family.

Perhaps I was lucky that my parents' divorce was amicable. I am sure others have experienced more bitter separations and therefore have not been able to overcome their animosity as easily. But I for one am glad to have been able to come to terms with the situation and see that all was not for the worst. With the talk these days of America's high divorce rate I wonder sometimes if we can say unequivocally that such is always lamentable. After all, divorce can mean the end to a union which is in a state of unhappiness. If this means two people have realized that they have made a mistake and need to seek fulfillment elsewhere, then what is so wrong? Is it not better for people to admit

~~their mistakes and move on rather than stay locked in a situation of perpetual unhappiness?~~

Children of the divorced, like me, are of course the hardest hit. And it's not easy to see the good behind what seems to be so obviously a mistake. ~~Even I still harbor, deep down inside, a wholly unrealistic fantasy that someday my parents will reunite.~~ I may not be as happy as I could have been had my parents had a good marriage. But they didn't have a good marriage and they are vastly happier now than before.

I have broken all of the vows I made on the night I learned of my parents' divorce. I no longer hate them. I no longer feel betrayed. And I have even watched Ozzie and Harriet since then. But this has only been possible since I now know that Ozzie without Harriet can be for the better.

To slim down his essay, Kyle eliminated a number of descriptive passages. However, he kept his key points: how he overcame the trauma of his parents' divorce and even found some good in it. By removing the extras, Kyle's essay loses some of its color, but it still has enough detail for the reader to be able to visualize and feel what he has experienced. This is the kind of balance that you want to achieve between over and under trimming.

How to Build a Longer Essay

It's a toss-up about which is more difficult—slimming down an essay or adding to one. Chances are you won't even encounter the second problem because, with the limited amount of space you have, it's just too easy to use it all up.

However, occasionally you may find that you have not written enough. If so, don't worry. Admissions officers have a reputation for preferring less to more. Case in point, Princeton's instructions for writing the essay contain this note: "Remember, Lincoln's Gettysburg Address was only 272 words."

If you only have 400 words for a 500-word essay and have nothing left to say, leave it. It's better to submit 400 quality words than to add an additional 100 words of fluff.

Still, if you have a phobia of too much white space on paper or feel that there is something missing in your condensed work, there are a number of ways you can expand an essay.

One of the first things to do is add more detail. Try to include information that aptly portrays your physical environment: What can you see, smell, touch, or hear? What is the weather like? Is it hot? Humid? Freezing? What time is it? What are the people around you doing?

Try to also include more information about how you feel and why: What factors are influencing your emotions? What mood are you in? How do your emotions change throughout the essay? What is the history behind how you are feeling?

Another strategy is to take simple sentences and expand on them to create depth. Instead of saying, "I had never felt so sad in my life" you can change the sentence to read, "I had never felt so sad in my life but it was not because I lost the game; it was because I had done so in such a poor manner." In this case you not only double the length of the sentence but you also add more meaning and clarity. You don't want to do this for every sentence, but read through your work and find places where you can create depth of meaning.

When you do this, it is important that your main idea does not get lost in the added details and descriptions. Don't "pad" an essay with useless words. Still, almost every essay can be skillfully lengthened by adding relevant descriptions and detail.

A Final Warning About Recycling

The greatest danger of recycling is that in the process of clipping and reworking, the original focus of your essay may become lost. To make sure that this does not happen, reread the question and your essay several times. Ask yourself: Does this essay truly answer the question? Remember that while you have the freedom to interpret the question in your own way, you do not want the admissions officers to wonder if you misunderstood it because your essay lacks focus and does not clearly state at the beginning how you intend to answer the question given.

Here are some other important questions to ask yourself:

- Does the introduction set up the essay so that it is clear that you are trying to answer the stated question?

- Have you given too much or too little information or detail?

- Do the sentences and paragraphs flow together well?

- Are the transitions smooth and the connections between your ideas apparent?

- Is the logic of the essay preserved?

If you are unsure about your recycled work, get a second opinion. Have someone who has not read the original essay read the recycled essay to see if it is still clear and understandable.

Although recycling can produce an essay in a fraction of the time, careful attention still needs to be exercised, especially when writing the introduction and conclusion. Your recycled work needs to be just as polished as the original essay. When you are done, congratulate yourself on having saved valuable time and effort.

IN THIS CHAPTER

● An opportunity to learn from essays that worked

● The magnum opuses: 15 essays that opened college doors

● Seven disastrous essays that spelled rejection

CHAPTER 7

EXAMPLE ESSAYS: THE GOOD, BAD AND UGLY

The College Essay in the Real World

After the last two chapters you probably have so many writing strategies, tips, *Do's* and *Don'ts* swimming around in your head that you must be wondering just how it all comes together in a real essay.

Your wish is our command! In this chapter we will look at real-life essays. Since this is an exercise in learning by example, pay attention to how each student has used the techniques in the previous chapters to craft his or her essay. When you write your essays, use these examples as models with which to compare your own work.

We also have included some essays that were not so successful. While a few of these disasters might have gotten "A's" in English class, all failed to make the grade with admissions officers. We hope that by reading these essays you will understand better what doesn't work and will not repeat these errors in your own essays.

Violating our own essay-writing rule of not using clichés, we must emphasize that college essays are like snowflakes: No two are alike. Each essay reflects the personality and character of the individual writer. Therefore, when considering how to use these essays in your own writing, it is important that you only try to emulate the quality, enthusiasm and creativity of the writers, but *not* their specific style, word choice, topic or approach. Besides being plagiarism, it is very unlikely that your personality and writing style matches precisely those of the authors.

Some years ago a student found a fantastic essay in an out-of-print book on admissions. Thinking that no one would remember this essay, he copied it virtually word for word. A few months later he received what he thought was an acceptance letter. Instead, it was a letter from an admissions officer informing him that he had been the editor of that long out-of-print book. The letter promised that the student's plagiarism would be made known to other colleges. The admissions officer made good on his promise since this student was rejected by every school to which he applied.

Each one of us has unique experiences, philosophies, outlooks and styles. If you can convey some of yours on paper, you will have an essay that is far superior to that of anyone else.

Do not take these essays as absolute paragons of perfection. Although they are superbly written and were critical to each student's admission into a top school, they still have areas that could use improvement. One week after I (Gen) submitted my Harvard essay, I realized that one section could have been made infinitely better with a few minor changes. As with all writing, no essay is ever completely finished.

Please also keep in mind that there are many ways to write a good essay, but unfortunately we only have space to print 15 samples. If the essay you are writing does not look like any of these essays, that's fine! If you followed the rules and advice in Chapter 5, then you probably have a winning essay that is 100 percent original. Don't let these examples limit your imagination.

After each essay is a short analysis that highlights its strengths or weaknesses from the point of view of an admissions officer—which really is the only point of view that matters.

One last note: Some essays were submitted for a general "tell us something about you," topic while others were directed at more specific questions. Also, some colleges allowed the applicant to use several pages, while others only let them use one. Remember to follow the guidelines when writing your essay.

Magnum Opuses: Essays that Opened College Doors

These are the essays that worked to help their authors open the gates to America's elite colleges. As you read them, it will be apparent why they worked. All captured a part of the writers' personalities, thoughts and emotions. Seductively and creatively, they captivate the readers, creating in them a desire to learn more and to get to know the authors better. The writers carefully crafted their words, virtually constructing original pieces of art. Again keep in mind that your goal is to emulate their quality (not their words). We hope that these examples are an inspiration for your own writing.

My Two Dads

By: Gregory Y.

I have two fathers. My first and biological father is the one who taught me how to drive a car, throw a baseball and find the area under a curve using integral calculus, among the innumerable other common duties of a good dad. He has been there for me through the ups of my successful piano career and the downs of my first breakup, and has always offered his insightful hand of guidance. My second father is who I connect with on a different level; he is the only person I know who thinks like I do. My second dad is my music composition teacher, Tony Fox, and he shares the one passion that has been a part of my life since the age of two: music.

Tony is a hardworking professor who can spend hours illustrating the meaning of a particular chord in a famous classical composition or ease an extraordinarily stressful situation with his colorful wit. He may appear intimidating to a new student at USC as the Assistant Band Director, but once someone mentions music, there is no one more adept, more creative or more dedicated to making music for the world to hear than Tony.

Tony has touched my life in a way few people have experienced. At my lessons with him, I bring compositions I am in the progress of perfecting, and with a few words of his guidance, I can almost see the changes needed before he mentions them. Almost instantly after I ask a question - such as which chord progression works best at a certain point in the music or why a certain counter melody sounds so beautiful – we agree on what is best for the music. It is almost as if we know what the other is thinking and merely state aloud our thoughts just in case one or the other is caught off guard. It is truly rare to find two people who agree with each other on what it is exactly that makes compositions aesthetically pleasing.

Last year when I was working on a composition, I ran into a discouraging roadblock that could have delayed my progress significantly. No one in my family and none of my friends could help. However, as soon as I shared the piece with Tony, he made some suggestions and together we made the necessary amendments to the music. The result was a finished project, a beautiful mosaic of our collective design, and it was debuted last year by my high school wind ensemble. When I first heard my music performed, I thought back to the hours I had spent tinkering at my piano and Tony's thoughtful guidance. This is how Tony and I relate. It's a common frequency upon which the most advanced radio cannot even begin to comprehend.

Tony has filled in areas of my life where few people, including my real father, could understand. He is the teacher of lessons big and small, from looking into the eyes of those whose hands I shake to recognizing that time is the most valuable gift one can give or receive. Whereas many of my peers have only *one* father, I have been fortunate enough to have two of them.

Comments on "My Two Dads"

An accomplished musician, Gregory could have written an essay about all of the competitions he has won and musical awards he has received. Boring! Instead, Gregory does some self-analysis to tell us what music means to him. We get to go inside his head to see the creative process at work. Writing about what he goes through to create a composition allows even those of us who are tone deaf to experience what it is like to create music.

Gregory uses powerful imagery to show us how he interacts with his music teacher and overcomes difficulties while composing. Gregory also subtly works in some of his most important musical accomplishments. But notice that he does this within the context of the essay and not by hitting us over the head with a list. This essay allows us to see the person behind the music.

Laughter Is What I Like to Hear

By: Laurie C.

It happens the same way every time. It begins with her head tilted at a slight angle, her hands resting on each hip and her slightly abundant belly thrust forward. The first thing you notice is a shake beginning to run through her body. There is no audible counterpart until a fraction of a second later. Then, the sound follows. And what a glorious sound it is. It is hearty and natural and fills up every empty space in the room. It is full and beautiful, a melody to my ears. For as long as I can remember, I have been bathed in my mother's laughter.

One of my first recollections of my mother's laughter was when I brought home my first-grade report card. As my mother looked it over she began her ritual movement; tilted head, hands on hips, belly thrust forward. "All A's! It's time to celebrate!" she shouted, with the sound of her laughter shortly following. She whisked me off the ground and held me close as we danced around our kitchen cheek to cheek with both of our laughter thick in the air.

Since that first report card, every achievement has been celebrated with my mother's laughter. From my second all "A" report card to winning the potato sack race at the Girl Scout Jamboree to my first-place prize in the high school science fair to finally beating my rival from Smith High at the district track meet, my mother's laughter has been my most rewarding congratulations.

Although I am about to venture out into the world by myself, I still expect to share my mother's laughter. In the sunny Harvard Yard during commencement, above the pews of my church at my wedding and by my hospital bedside after giving birth to her first grandchild. There is so much laughter that I have heard already in my short lifetime and so much more that I have left to hear.

My mother's laughter will always be a source of comfort and inspiration. Hearing it, I know that I have done well. When others who know my family tell me that I am just like my mother, I grow happy indeed. And then, I laugh just a little bit louder.

Comments on "Laughter Is What I Like to Hear"

A well-written and solid essay, Laurie takes a common subject and presents it in an original way. She displays her writing skill through her thoughtful use of rich detail and creative language when describing her mother's laughter. You can almost hear it echo as you read her words.

Most important, Laurie's approach and style show that she's mature and sensitive. We learn about her through the moments in her life that she shares and by the fact that she hopes to carry on her mother's laugh. Laurie does not try to use fancy writing or embellish her narrative with unnecessary events. She writes an honest piece that says a lot about herself. Finally, Laurie's essay has the added advantage of being upbeat and positive as she shares with us her obviously strong relationship with her mother. This kind of positive attitude always reflects well on students.

Visiting Grandfather

By: Jacob K.

Worse than movies about overgrown, blood-thirsty sharks; worse than ghost stories of night marchers coming to steal my soul; worse even than trips to a six-inch-long needle wielding doctor were my childhood visits to see grandfather. There was nothing that caused a greater amount of fear or consternation in my eight-year-old psyche than those simple words, "Jacob, we're going to visit Grandfather." Not even, "Jacob, it's time to take a bath" could come close.

Visits to see Grandfather were so dreadful because they meant going to his nursing home. For me there was something wholly terrifying about nursing homes and hospitals. Maybe it was the musty, mediciney odors that wafted through the halls. Or the wheelchair-bound people with eyes glazed over and bodies contorted in strange positions. Or maybe it was the sounds of ignored mumbling, crying and moaning that echoed throughout the building. As a child, these were the scents, sights and sounds that I remembered most poignantly.

My grandfather's room offered little safety. I knew that the man lying motionless in the hospital bed was family. But his frail body—I remember that his skin was so thin that every contour of his face was visible—and his inability to communicate more than a nod or unintelligible mumble made me look at him as if I were viewing an Egyptian mummy at a museum.

Since my grandfather passed away while I was still young, this was my lasting image of him—the frail, nearly petrified man lying on that horrible hospital bed in that terrible nursing home. But last Christmas this all changed because of a decision to make a book tracing the family tree as a gift to my mother.

As part of this project I found my grandfather's photo album. I started from the back. The last page of pictures was of my grandfather in the hospital—just as I remembered him. As I flipped through the book from back to front, however, he grew younger. A picture of him posing with my mother when she was 16. Another of him in a crisp Navy uniform after returning from the Pacific. And finally, as a young man in his senior year wearing the jersey of an offensive lineman for Wilshire High. On his chest was printed boldly the number 28, his number—which was, coincidentally, now also mine.

As I looked at the pictures, I no longer envisioned the frail, motionless skeleton of a man who I thought of as my grandfather. Instead, I imagined the handsome young man posing with his baby daughter in front of his first house. I saw the confidence-inspiring face of a destroyer captain who coolly commanded his crew as they pursued enemy submarines. I imagined the high school senior with thick forearms that at one time had plowed through countless defensive lines. The man who I remember in the bed who never walked and hardly talked faded and was replaced by this new image.

Like my grandfather's life I hope to pass through time with something to be proud of at each moment. And I hope that when I am confined to a bed, my grandson will see me not for what I have become but for what I once was.

Comments on "Visiting Grandfather"

A super essay for a jock! Jacob was an All-American football player but you wouldn't have known it from this essay. He is modest and reflective—hardly the stereotypical arrogant athlete that you might expect. Plus, you'd better believe that the admissions officers were happy they did not have to read another essay about how Jacob won the Big Game or how important football had been to his life. Instead, the admissions officers were treated to a side of his character that was nuanced, sensitive and thoughtful, not to mention the essay also demonstrates that Jacob can write some decent prose.

Jacob begins his essay with a strong introduction that piques the reader's curiosity about why he hated to visit his own grandfather. In his explanation he does not try to minimize or justify his childhood fears and anyone who has ever been to a nursing home would probably empathize with his feelings. The main body of the essay takes a depressing situation and shows how it was transformed through Jacob's discovery of his younger grandfather. The only weakness of the essay is in the conclusion, which is somewhat disjointed and abrupt. It would have been better if Jacob had developed it a little further. Nevertheless, this is a solid, honest essay that makes no pretensions and is a pleasure to read.

A Family Expedition

By: Samantha C.

Driving along the Columbia River gorge, moving 65 miles per hour toward Eastern Oregon from Portland I imagined we were the brave explorers Lewis and Clark. Only we were following their trail in reverse and in the comfort of an air conditioned mini-van chauffeured by my father.

It was summer and we were on our "family road trip." While I always add "family" before "road trip" I really should say "my father's road trip." He is the one who insists on driving, enjoys mapping out our route in great detail and loves stopping at all the fast food pit-stops along the way. (I think he secretly looks forward to the greasy hamburgers and steaks that his health-conscious wife and three daughters rarely let him eat at home.) This year although the rest of us had wanted to fly to Orlando we nevertheless agreed, after our customary complaints, to once again go by car.

I wonder how often Lewis and Clark got lost? Probably quite often but then without a map and charting heretofore unexplored territory (at least by Europeans) they had a pretty good excuse.

My father, on the other hand, despite the numerous improvements in cartography that have occurred since the Lewis and Clark expedition, never fails to let us experience what it is like to be totally lost. This often happens on what he calls a "scenic route."

On this trip it occurred after we had passed the small town of Pendleton in Eastern Oregon. My father as usual had his USGS map on his phone, which for those of you who do not know stands for U.S. Geological Survey and are highly detailed maps often used by forestry rangers, mountaineers and my father. My mother, on the other hand, always relies on the more user-friendly GPS on her phone. So as we neared the designated point which my father had duly marked on his

USGS map as our place of departure from the main road my mother, out of years of experience, pulled out her phone to confirm my father's "scenic route" plans.

"I don't see a road on this map," she announced.

"Sure, there is. I have it marked right here on the map," my father replied.

Of course, we in the back seat knew that they were looking at two different maps.

"No. Listen to mom!" we three sisters shouted just as our dad turned the van off the highway and on to a very unimproved gravel road.

I wonder how often Lewis fought with Clark over which way to go?

"Look at how beautiful the countryside is," my father exclaimed. Unfortunately there was so much dust being kicked up that everything looked hazy. My father tried to spray some water onto the windshield but only succeeded in creating mud.

Our narrow gravel road eventually turned into an even narrower dirt road.

"Sure is a bad road," my father said after the umpteenth bump had jarred us out of our seats causing my little sister to scream. Now when my father says something even remotely negative I start to worry.

"Turn around, turn around," we all shouted from the back seat.

Did Lewis ever tell Clark that he wanted to turn around?

My father is not one to concede easily. He shifted the van into its lowest gear. In the back we were already shifted around like popcorn as each rock, rut and bump sent us and our luggage into the air. I was growing dizzy and my little sister appeared to be turning green. In the front my mother was trying to reason with my father, "The road is only going to get worse." "That map of yours is out of date." "We're going to get stuck out here." But to no avail.

My father has that pioneer spirit. However, things were going from bad to worse. The road was barely distinguishable from the surrounding prairie grass and the van was beginning to strain from climbing the hills. The back seat was total chaos. The cloud of dust in which we were traveling was quickly infiltrating the interior, causing my allergy sensitive sister to sneeze. My mother was now yelling at my father to turn around. My little sister was crying. My other sister was adding to my mom's admonitions between violent fits of sneezing. And me? I could only wonder what Lewis and Clark would have done if their wagon was in the same predicament.

Then all of a sudden the van stopped.

"Look," my father said softly. As we slowly turned our attention away from him and looked out the window we realized we were on a plateau overlooking a lush valley with not a single man-made structure in sight. And stretched out before us was no longer a road but un-trampled, virgin prairie grass. The last trace of the road was 50 yards behind.

"Well, I guess this is the end of the road," my father laughed. We got out and huddled around each other taking in the view. It was absolutely gorgeous.

When we finally returned to the main highway it was late and we decided to stop at a local motel. After taking a shower and eating our standard greasy fare for dinner we all lay in our beds while my father peered over his maps planning our next "scenic" detour. Before I fell asleep my mind wandered upon Lewis and Clark one last time and I knew that for a few special moments I had known what it must have been like to discover an unspoiled vista.

Comments on "A Family Expedition"

Travel is a very popular topic for college essays. However, most applicants try to tell too much. They try to compress a two-month tour of Eastern Europe into a single 500-word essay. It just doesn't work. Samantha has focused on just one small part of her family's summer trip, and it works very well. It is interesting and humorous. Notice that Samantha adds levity by simply drawing attention to what was naturally comical about the incident. Best of all, Samantha gives us a peek into her family. She shows us their idiosyncrasies and how this created a memorable, and stressful, situation. Samantha also approaches the chaos of her family's road trip compassionately. No one is put down or lampooned and there is no uncalled-for sarcasm, which does not usually appeal to admissions officers.

Playing With Play-Doh

By: Cynthia M.

I must confess. My hobby is playing with Play-Doh. I love to squish the malleable dough between my fingers forming little neon people and animals. I am addicted to that plastic fragrance which comes from a freshly opened yellow jar. And the bright, wonderfully artificial colors excite my imagination to create.

Now while my hobby might not seem to be an issue of international concern, it really is.

The truth is that I think the world could use a little more Play-Doh. Naturally as we grow older we lose interest in what fascinated us as children. For me, this was dressing Barbie in her latest high fashion, screaming across the playground in a lively game of freeze tag or creating works of art worthy of being hung on the finest of refrigerators.

However, with this loss of interest in childhood games, we lose a whole lot more.

I've noticed that as we grow older we lose much of our childlike creativity. We no longer use our imagination to create new things and develop new ideas as we did when we were children. In the first grade we had an assignment to invent something. Mine was a car with brake lights that got brighter the harder you stepped on the brake pedal. Of course my car also had a button that when pressed ejected the passenger 50 feet into the air through the sun roof. But minus the ejection seat, why can't we, young- and full-adults, continue to come up with such fantastic ideas? Imagine if General Motors gave everyone the day off and told them to invent something. The wonders that would be produced in that single day would probably eclipse all other inventions.

Growing older also makes us lose our tolerance of differences. When we were kindergarten students, we drew self portraits. Our skin was a rainbow of purples, greens, browns and yellows. It didn't matter to us then what hue our real skin was, whether we were girls or boys, or even that some of us came from richer or poorer families. We overlooked these kinds of differences as children. Why do we now divide ourselves by these differences? I've had the pleasure to work with a Brownie Troop for the past two years and it always amazes me how well these young girls cooperate and play together in spite of their different backgrounds. And it saddens me to think of the day when these girls will grow up and no longer associate with each other—choosing to belong to groups more homogeneous.

As children we viewed the world with a sense of wonder and excitement. A field of grass could keep us occupied for hours. An ice cream cone could make our day splendid. A puppy could be our best friend. But as adults we are such cynics and simple things no longer make us happy.

We can blame a number of sources for our abandonment of our childhood creativity, tolerance and optimism. We are taught to color in the lines, to connect with those who are most like us and to not be satisfied with what we have. I think it would be better sometimes if we reversed these life lessons.

Other students may write about homelessness, world peace and racial harmony, and while these are critical international concerns, I believe the loss of our childhood qualities is one equally important. Sometimes I wish we could revert—if only for a moment—back to our childhood innocence, untainted by society's expectations and unspoken rules.

A little bit of playtime with Play-Doh would certainly go a long way.

Comments on "Playing With Play-Doh"

Cynthia cleverly uses Play-Doh to illustrate the creativity and tolerance that children lose as they grow older. The points that she makes about being open-minded could have easily been conveyed as naive. However, she discusses them intelligently and without sounding like she is preaching. She shows that she is a person with conviction and ideals and sounds like she would dedicate herself to making the improvements she suggests.

Wimbledon Champ

By: Angela B.

I am standing in center court. As my name thunders over the loud-speaker, my followers erupt uncontrollably awarding me with a standing ovation. Dressed in their tidy uniforms, the judges hand me my silver trophy. It is almost as big as I am. Still, triumphantly I heave it over my head, holding it proudly as the victor at the same time that I am blinded by the flash of the cameras.

In my dreams I am the next Wimbledon champion, one of the greatest athletes in the world and a symbol of strength, talent and endurance. In reality, however, I am lucky to have my racket meet the speeding blur of yellow fuzz which my coach persists in trying to convince me is an actual tennis ball.

I began taking tennis lessons six months ago. Unfortunately, I can't say that I have discovered any latent talent, but I can say that I love the sport. Twice each week I join a dozen other younger and better tennis aspirants in learning the mysteries of connecting the racket to the ball. Equipped with my feather light shoes for bouncing, colorful polo shirt for athletic appearance and logoed cap for good luck; I am a giant towering above my dozen elementary school aged classmates. Unfortunately, neither size nor style is an indication of mastery.

Take for instance a recent lesson. It consisted of learning how the different angles at which we grip our rackets change the direction of the ball. Not surprisingly, the theory behind which direction the ball should go and the reality of where my balls actually went did not coincide perfectly. That is assuming that my racket actually made contact with the ball in the first place, which was often not the case.

Needless to say, it was frustrating to watch as the 8- and 11-year-olds in my class effortlessly met the fuzzy yellow thing with their rackets creating that satisfying "pop." I often wonder if there has been a genetic mutation in the past 10 years that enhances children's natural racket swinging ability which I somehow missed out on.

Still, despite my lack of coordination at times, the desperation I feel when my classmates easily master the strokes I only dream of attempting and the sympathetic looks that my coach gives me, I love playing. I have felt no greater satisfaction than the first time I hit the ball across the net or the first time the ball actually remained within the confines of the court. And I have felt no greater pride than when my coach said, "Good job," and actually meant it or when my classmates selected me second to last instead of my standard last place for a round robin rally. I may not be the best tennis player, but I am proud of myself because I am trying. Wimbledon cup or not, this to me is the true essence of victory.

Comments on "Wimbledon Champ"

Most essays on sports showcase the mastery that the writer has achieved. Angela, however, writes about something she is not good at—in fact she sounds absolutely terrible at tennis. But being bad at tennis does not mean that she is a failure. In fact, the inner strength that she shows by persisting with the sport even though her lessons are a humbling experience demonstrates an incredible tenacity. This essay works because it is positive, expresses Angela's feelings honestly and without affected histrionics and amuses readers with a story they want to finish.

Kidney

By: Noah A.

Would you like to buy one of my kidneys? How about a piece of my liver? I'd offer you my heart if I could. What? You don't want them? You are appalled that I would even consider selling a few of my organs? Would it make a difference if I told you that I need the money to put myself through school? No? Well, what is wrong with selling a few of my not so "vital" organs? They are, after all, mine.

Disgusting? Degrading? Well, who are you to tell me what I can do with my body? Unless maybe you are an advocate of some form of slavery where one human being is able to own another. That is what you are implying, right? That you (or your laws) can forbid me to dispose of my body (or at least a part of it) as I please is tantamount to claiming some right to it, is it not? If I truly am free and if I do "own" myself—and everything inside—then why can't I choose what to do with it?

Human decency? I've heard that argument before. You think that by affixing a price to myself and placing my body parts on the open market that I am devaluating all human beings. That's just not true!

How much is a human being? What kind of question is that? I don't know. You can't put a price on human life. But I'm not selling my life just some organs. I suppose that by offering to sell a piece of me I might be contributing to the commodification of the human body. But I still don't see how what I am doing is so harmful.

Ok. So maybe you're right in saying that if many people did what I am doing there would arise a market for human body parts. Yes, I suppose some sort of trading would occur with a fluctuating price determined by supply and demand. But that's capitalism.

Yes. Brokers in body parts would probably emerge. And you might not be wrong in predicting that newspaper business sections would start to print the price of lungs and kidneys along side the day's exchange rates and price of pork bellies. I suppose that would be somewhat degrading.

I guess my actions do contribute to making our bodies more objectified. Certainly if everyone were like I am there would be no such thing as organ donation—only organ sales. Ok. I've heard enough. You sure do talk a lot. I guess I won't sell some of my organs. But say, do you have any ideas on how I can pay for my tuition?

Comments on "Kidney"

This is an offbeat and slightly risky essay that paid off. It was not the only essay that Noah submitted and was designed to complement another essay he wrote in which he talked about his work with Amnesty International (a human rights organization) and a suicide hotline. Since that essay was very serious, Noah wanted to show a little of his creative side by addressing the real issue of a person's right to sell his or her organs through a fictional dialogue. The first few lines of this essay certainly capture your attention. Noah also clearly demonstrates that he knows the positions for and against the sale of organs. A creative essay like this is not easy to write, but if you can do it, then your essay will certainly stand out.

Dad's Pancakes

By: Gen Tanabe

In spite of the various extracurricular activities I've done and interesting people I've met, not one event or person has been more meaningful to me than my father's preparation of breakfast.

Every morning I wake up to the sounds of my father cooking breakfast. While lying in bed, I try to guess if the clank of a pan means scrambled eggs or maybe his specialty, banana pancakes. Waking up to nearly 7,000 such mornings, I have grown to admire my father's dedication, a dedication which never falters even after hours of late night work.

I readily applied this value of dedication when I was elected Vice-Chairman of the State Student Council. With the tremendous amount of work related to this position, there were numerous occasions when I found myself having to choose between reviewing Board of Education policies and going to the beach with friends. And whenever I felt myself beginning to vacillate, I was always reminded of my father's unwavering dedication. I knew that the students who elected me depended on my dedication, and like my father's daily commitment, I would not let them down.

Whenever I hear my father making breakfast I always hope that he is preparing his piece dé résistance, banana pancakes. My father's pancakes are not generic "Bisquickies," but one-of-a-kind masterpieces. He uses scratch ingredients from hand sifted flour to homegrown bananas. As I grew older I noticed that I also began to assume the same ambition toward life as my father has toward his pursuit of the perfect pancake.

In my freshman year I took an interest in film making and soon my goal was to own a high definition camcorder. To accomplish this goal I could either wait six months until Christmas and hope Santa could afford a new camcorder, or I could earn the money and buy it myself. My ambitious yearning took over and for the next three months of summer vacation I held a brush in one hand and a can of latex in the other as the hired painter of my grandmother's house. Although the work was hard and tiring, by the end of the summer, I was able to earn the money to fulfill my goal. Having learned from my father to strive for success, I have since worked fervently but patiently to attain my goals in life.

After my father has flipped the last pancake, the best part of breakfast has arrived—consumption. As I devour the stack of scrumptious pancakes, I notice that my father has a bright smile across his face; I am not the only one to savor this moment. My father truly enjoys making my breakfast. My father's joy from even the simplest things has been the model that I have tried to apply to my life every single day.

Failure to heed my father's lesson was disastrous in my sophomore year when I decided it would be impressive to become a cross country runner. As I was running the three-mile course, I began to realize around the second mile that I did not particularly enjoy running. In fact I hated running. This painful experience reminded me of my father's overarching aim to enjoy what he is doing. Since then I have chosen to excel in tennis and other activities, not for the prestige or status, but simply because I enjoy them.

My father completes the tradition of preparing breakfast by soaking the dirty pans in the sink. As he does, I think of how fortunate I am. Some people only have one meaningful event in their lives, but I have one every single morning.

Comments on "Dad's Pancakes"

The "My Dad Is My Hero" essay is very popular. For it to work, you need to ensure it is unlike any of the thousands of others which will be written. Many essays will talk about a father's commitment to his child's happiness by always "being there." But how many will explain how a father's making of breakfast has changed a life? Finding an original angle takes a lot of time, but if you can do it, you will have won half the battle. This essay is also effective because it weaves the events of Gen's life into the narrative. We learn some very interesting things about him, and while this essay is ostensibly about his father, we come away knowing more about Gen. Remember, it is always to your advantage to make sure your essay says something about you even if your topic is about someone else.

Hawaii

By: Andrew B.

When I sat down to write this essay about what individual has influenced me the most, a long list of potential candidates came to mind. I'm sure many applicants will write (and with good reason) that their parents or teachers or coaches were very influential in their lives. But, for me, after thinking long and hard I have come to the conclusion that no living individual has affected my life more than the island on which I live.

Growing up on this remote speck in the Pacific I came to think that the longest it took to get anywhere by car was an hour and a half. I assumed that summer, winter, spring and fall denoted only minor changes of a few degrees in the daily temperature. And I certainly believed that Santa Claus arrived by boat and entered my chimney-less home through our unlocked window.

But more than these circumstantial influences of living on a 60 mile-wide island is the effect (directly and indirectly) that it has had on shaping who I am. I would like to share with you three of the most significant factors: the sun, ocean and rocks.

The sun. One constant in Hawaii is the sun. Never allowing a change of more than a few degrees throughout the year, the sun seems to moderate any attempt by nature to cause a sudden seasonal change. I do not know if science would support my belief, but I am convinced that this lack of temperamental weather and drastic seasonal change has unconsciously seeped into my own nature. Rarely do I suddenly swing from calm to upset, happy to angry. Like the steady rays of the sun my personality is rarely jarred.

Testing such a hypothesis has been easy. Last year, for instance, I spent over a month constructing a cardboard model of turn of the century San Francisco as part of my final project in AP history. Building the model actually took longer than writing the report, but when I was finished I had what must have been the most realistic and accurate 3D scale model of downtown San Francisco ever produced by a high school junior. The day before I was to turn in my project I came home from school and was greeted at the door by my mother. "I'm really sorry but something terrible has happened," she said seriously. She led me into the den where I saw my so recently finished project sitting on the floor in shambles.

Apparently my four-year-old brother had decided to pit GI Joe against Cobra for control of the city. In the fracas, many of the buildings got bent, a few were torn in half and I think he even stepped on one section of the model flattening an entire block. I was stunned but right away realized that getting mad would not fix what had been done and that I had to think of some way to save my project. So I called my brother down from his room and had him help me destroy the rest of the buildings that were still standing. After we were done I printed out a new label for the model that simply said, "San Francisco After the Great Earthquake." Not only did my project get an "A" but I was complimented for such a dramatic presentation of the effect of nature's destructive force.

Of course, I hope this doesn't leave the impression that I am emotionless. I do sometimes get angry, just as even Hawaii suffers an occasional hurricane.

The ocean. From a very early age I have been enthralled by the beauty of the Pacific. Who would not want to explore its rich depths teeming with life of unimaginable form and beauty? Yet the perils— riptides, sharks and moray eels—kept me away from descending beneath its surface. Although I often swam in the protective shallows near the shore, the thought of heading past the boundary of the reef terrified me.

But it seems even the ocean itself was out to tempt me. One day I went to an exhibit on undersea exploration and as luck (or fate) would have it won a special drawing for free scuba lessons. So, on the appointed day I donned a loaned wet-suit and strapped on my tank. I only realized after I had spent one of the most exciting hours of my life observing some of nature's most spectacular sights that I had also just conquered one of my greatest fears. Now I enjoy being a modern day Magellan as I probe the reefs in search of hidden passages or sneak up on a school of a thousand stick fish, their long, slender bodies motionless until through some intuitive sense the whole group decides to take a collective pulse forward. This is something that had I let my fears control me I would never have been able to witness. The ocean has shown me that my fears can be overcome.

The rocks. It may be hard to imagine that rocks can have any influence on a person's life, unless they want to be a geologist, but for me the rocks of Hawaii have helped create a special bond with my father. One day while my father and I were driving along a sugar cane field, we noticed a pile of rocks. It came from a turn of the century irrigation ditch and was originally used as a lining for a water flume. But the most amazing thing was that the rocks had been carefully cut into precise squares. The time and skill it must have taken to cut each stone was remarkable.

Since these stones had been abandoned to make way for a newer concrete irrigation ditch, my father and I decided that to leave them would be a tragic waste. Since each rock weighed between 75 and 100 pounds, we could only load a few into the car at a time. Each day for a whole month my father and I would drive up after he came home from work and load a few stones into the car. It was a kind of bonding experience for my father and me. As we drove the half-hour to get the rocks we would talk about the day's happenings and once there we would admire the craftsmanship of the unknown stonecutters.

That event marked the beginning of other father-son projects. The next was to do something with all the rocks that were now piled in our yard. We decided to make a patio. Now each time I step out onto the patio I am reminded of how many ways the rocks have made my relationship with my father richer.

I don't suppose many of the essays you have read today have thanked an island for the influence it has had on someone's life. But for me the island of Oahu has certainly influenced who I am in countless ways. The sun, ocean and rocks have left their indelible marks on my life, and it will be with a lot of sadness and a little trepidation that I leave my island home. When I do I will be sure to take some things with me as a reminder of where I came from: the multi-colored shell which I found on my very first dive and a piece from the rocks that my father and I used to make our family's patio. As for the warm rays of the sun that last throughout winter, I make no promises but I'll try to bring them along too.

Comments on "Hawaii"

This is a powerful essay because it describes important interactions in Andrew's life and uses illustrations so vivid you can almost picture them in your head. If you read carefully the chapter on recycling, you may have noticed that this is a recycled essay. The introduction and conclusion were tailored to fit the question, but the body was lifted almost word for word from another college essay that Andrew wrote. Ironically, part of what makes the essay interesting is that it answers the question in an unusual and certainly unique way. Andrew was lucky that this college gave him an unlimited amount of space. Ordinarily an essay like this should be shortened.

Nerd

By: Dave B.

I am a computer nerd. I have a subscription to PC Magazine and I stay up all night reading online about UI, data architecture and data modeling. I can scan your picture and with a few clicks of the mouse give you a totally new hair style or create a custom database that will automatically compose and print personalized Christmas cards in December and thank-you cards in January. Yet, in spite of my love for computers and technology and all that is high-tech, my most passionate hobby may surprise you.

I love to sew.

In particular I make men's neck ties. I learned to sew from my grandmother while I was still in elementary school. At that age I was not yet immature enough to think that sewing was only for girls. I was fascinated at the way in which my grandmother worked her machine, taking various shapes of cloth and adeptly assembling them into beautiful shirts and pants and, once in awhile, a cowboy vest or two. One day my grandmother let me use her machine to connect two pieces of fabric. I was hooked. Every weekend I practiced sewing—usually making little bags to hold my toys.

I was learning how to make shirts when I entered junior high school and finally gained the immaturity that led me to quit sewing for a while. But, during the summer before 10th grade I found myself in need of money to fund my burgeoning interest in computers. When I told my grandmother my dilemma she suggested that I try making neck ties.

And so began a period of research and development that two months later resulted in the founding of my own tie making company as well as taught me the power of economics to overcome stereotypical roles. Financed by a $100 no-interest loan from my parents, Pacman Ties began operation. Our first line was, not surprisingly, blue cotton ties upon which I had silk-screened yellow Pacmen and multicolored ghosts. They were an instant success—at least among my relatives. Their enthusiasm and my satisfaction from actually producing a useful product with my own hands led me to expand.

First production was systemized like an Intel assembly line to promote worker efficiency. This meant that my brother Brad got assigned the job of cutting all of the material for the ties using a state-of-the-art plastic pattern and fabric knife. Next, my sister Cynthia folded and ironed the fabric into the rough shape of the tie around another advanced tool: a pattern made from a pizza box. Finally, I took the shaped material and sewed the points and basted the back by hand.

During its first year Pacman Ties produced a variety of styles using exotic fabrics from around Seattle. But I was most proud of our video game inspired collection. Each tie was hand screened with images closely but not exactly resembling some of the year's most popular video games. They were not the most outstanding sellers, but they were certainly my favorite for their artistry. Pacman Ties sold mostly at craft fairs and swap meets and we built up a fairly loyal clientele. A year from when my grandmother suggested the idea of making ties I had made enough of a profit to buy my first computer.

As I was walking through the mall on my way to the Apple store I had to pause in front of a display. For a long moment I seriously reconsidered purchasing the computer for in the window of a fabric store stood a gleaming new Singer sewing machine.

Comments on "Nerd"

The strength of this essay lies in the interesting story that Dave has to tell. While Dave might have mentioned in his application that he was the founder of Pacman Ties, he certainly would not have had room for an explanation. Thus, Dave wisely uses the essay to showcase this unique personal accomplishment. If you have started a business, founded a club or have an unusual hobby, the essay is a perfect place to highlight that accomplishment. But don't focus on the dry details of what you have done. Instead, explain what motivated you to do it and how it has affected you. This will help to convey your personality along with the details of your accomplishment.

Since Dave was applying to an elite technical school, it helped that he was able to display another (non-science) side of his personality. It would not be unimaginable that after reading his essay the admissions officers started to refer to Dave as "the tie man," making him unforgettable.

Dear Roomie

By: Charissa Y.

Dear Future Roomie,
    I am very eager to meet you, and knowing that we will be spending the year together, I thought that you should know a little more about the person with whom you are going to share a bunkbed and bathroom. But instead of writing a traditional, perhaps boring, letter I'd like to share with you what I consider to be the perfect illustration of my personality—the contents of my wallet. So let me take you on an adventure-filled guided tour of my wallet.

Safely protected between two strips of lamination is my Rhino Club Card, a cheesy remnant of a student leadership conference. Boldly printed on the front of the card is the Rhino Creed: "I am a Rhinoceros. I am full of Rhino energy and I can't wait to get up in the morning to start charging." Please don't think that your new roommate is a lunatic, but every morning I have stood in front of the bathroom mirror and recited the Rhino Creed. Not only have I used the Rhino Creed to energize my tired body, but I have also used it in times of stress.

I remember one of my most trying days, when in strict accordance with Murphy's Law everything that could go wrong did. That day was so stressful that I almost called my mother to take me home, but instead of succumbing to the pressure, I went to the bathroom, whipped out my Rhino card and repeated the Creed three times. Understandably, I got a few strange looks from other students, who were perhaps not as well versed in the Rhino creed, but when I left the bathroom, I felt like I was in control again. I got through that day thanks to my Rhino card, which is always safely secured in my wallet. As my roommate you are of course welcome to borrow it at any time!

Folded evenly in half behind my Rhino card I keep my blood donor's certificate. Although donating blood for most people is not a big deal, for me it was a test of will power in overcoming a great fear. Since childhood I have had an extremely weak stomach for the sight of blood. In my freshman year I had to watch a movie about facial reconstruction. When it reached the actual surgery, I had to leave the classroom quickly and spend the next 20 minutes regaining my composure with my head between my knees. (I am certainly not going to become a pre-med.)

So, when the Red Cross came to set up our school's blood drive, I was faced with the challenge of confronting my psychological fear of blood. I decided to confront my fear and was ironically placed first in line. As I lay on the cot, I began to envision myself losing consciousness, rolling off the bed, ripping the needle out of my arm and spraying blood across the school library. I blocked these thoughts and started to concentrate on something a little less gory, what I had just learned in math class. I had barely finished recounting logarithms when the nurse leaned over and said I was through. Although she told me that I might feel a little fatigued, I felt energized from my accomplishment. I have since kept my blood donor's certificate as a reminder of my personal victory over fear.

Hidden behind my driver's license and library card is a 1905 Buffalo nickel that I found when I was a child. When I found the nickel I was fascinated that something from so long ago could last so long. I then began to imagine the history behind the nickel. How many hands had it passed through and how many products had it purchased? I suppose that was the beginning of my interest in history.

Since then I have taken as many history classes as I could possibly fit into my schedule. I am now more intrigued not so much by the physical aspects of the past but by the social, political and economic ideas of the time. I sometimes dream about what it must have been like to live during the American Revolution, Industrial Revolution or

Civil War. I have kept my buffalo nickel as a reminder of where my interest started.

I hope that you now know a little more about me (and still want to live together). Although there are many more facets to my personality as you will discover, I have shared what I thought were some of the most significant. I'd like to close with just one warning: Although my wallet is always filled with a lot of mementos, the one thing it always lacks is money.

Comments on "Dear Roomie"

Who wouldn't want to have a roommate this personable? Charissa takes a fresh approach to what can be a tired letter to a future roommate. Instead of merely describing who she is, she creatively uses the objects in her wallet to segue into the personal stories of her life. She is also honest and not afraid to expose some of her most private idiosyncrasies.

My Voice

By: Kelly Tanabe

I have a soft voice. When I was younger, I did not like to present oral reports to my class because my voice did not carry. I have always desired a powerful voice, a voice that beckoned others to listen, that captivated them and provoked them into absorbing the thoughts which I expressed.

I was not born with this voice.

For this reason, I have turned to writing. For me, my voice is projected through the words I write. Since I wrote my first article for my elementary school newspaper at the age of eight, I have had a passion for journalism.

Through my school newspaper, Aspects, I grew acquainted with the field of journalism. As the Editor of this self-funded work, I learned the steps necessary to produce a publication—from the conception of articles to the distribution of the paper.

This background with Aspects developed in me the desire to continue my growth as a journalist. For this reason, I plan to develop my communications abilities in college as well as to write for a publication upon my graduation. With this education at Harvard and Radcliffe, I hope that my writing skills will progress in order to prepare for my future in the field.

With this education, I hope to hone my voice. I want others to listen, to hear my ideas, to have their lives affected by the articles that I write. For while the words that I speak are heard only once, the words that I write will be heard many times. Now, I have a powerful voice.

Comments on "My Voice"

This essay works because it not only explains the ambitious career goals of the author but also reveals something about her personality. The reader learns that while Kelly is not a vocally aggressive person, she is a strong voice through her writing. It takes a lot of courage and self-confidence to admit to an Ivy League college that you are soft spoken—an attribute not usually seen as positive. However, after reading Kelly's essay you certainly don't feel that she is a passive person. This essay also illustrates that when writing an essay about your career goals, you should focus not only on those goals but also on yourself.

Why I Like Postage Stamps

By: Jeremy M.

On the last day of every month I have the bland job of adhering an entire roll of stamps, and even though this assignment is without much excitement I am never happier. Adhering stamps is just one of the many tasks I do as founder, editor, writer and publisher of "Vermont Sporting News," a statewide monthly newsletter dedicated to promoting outdoor activities such as hunting, fishing and wildlife conservation.

Starting my own business was probably the most difficult thing I have ever attempted. Initially I had to deal with skepticism from my friends and family, who thought that this was too big of a project for a mere high school student. Then I had to formulate a plan to attract subscribers and manage the financial aspects of the business. Even after I successfully accomplished these tasks, my problems were not over, for I still had to find time to research, write and publish each month's newsletter with a staff of one.

Looking in retrospect at all the lessons I have learned, I feel that there is one that underscores the rest: the importance of enjoying my work. "Vermont Sporting News" is a success because it allows me to combine my interest in outdoor activities with my love of writing. Because of this interest and love, I am able to make time to complete each month's issue. In fact the greatest reward for my efforts came not when I first turned a small profit, but when I received a letter from a subscriber that began with "Dear Staff..." and ended with "Keep up the good work." I had to chuckle to myself; after all, I am the staff and for me this job is as much pleasure as it is work.

Comments on "Why I Like Postage Stamps"

In the limited space that many colleges allow for describing an extracurricular activity, Jeremy does a good job of engaging the reader with his creative introduction and then explaining the reasons why he has devoted a lot of time to his business. Notice also that his business is not successful in terms of money, but this is precisely what makes Jeremy all the more impressive. He clearly holds an alternative meaning of success that is far nobler than just making money.

Let It Snow

By: Kelly Tanabe

With so little snow, it was difficult to sculpt a snow creature in our backyard. Still, it was the first time that I, at the age of three, and my sister Steffany, at the age of three months, experienced a "white Christmas" or even snow at all.

Because I have lived in California for most of my life, snow is an unfamiliar phenomenon to my siblings and to me. For this reason, I would like to pursue photography while at Harvard and Radcliffe.

I was 10 years old when I received my first camera, a simple yet reliable Canon. With this camera, I photographed my father opening the water gun he received for his birthday, Uncle Ronnie's new dogs—McGoo and McGrowlski—and my friend Dalila frolicking in the water after our elementary school graduation.

At the age of 14, I received a second, more advanced camera as a present. With this, I continued recording the events of my life. In the pictures that I took, my friendships grew stronger, my sister taller, my parents a bit older. With my pictures I traveled—to the beaches of Hawaii, the Mall of Washington, D.C. and Seattle's Space Needle.

Photography is truly a gift. It enables me to record events on film that would have become blurred images in my mind. At Harvard and Radcliffe, I would like to pursue photography in order to share this present with my family. For although my parents have seen snow maybe once or twice in their lives, my sister has only seen it at the age of three months and my brother never has. I would like to share with my family the scenery of the East, the people around me and the school that I attend.

Although my family will be unable to be with me at college, I would like to be able to bring to them through photographs a bit of my way of life and as the Christmas song goes, "Let it snow, let it snow, let it snow."

Comments on "Let It Snow"

The mistake that most students make when describing their favorite extra-curricular activity is that they *only* describe the activity, forgetting to describe themselves. This essay on photography works because Kelly chooses to focus (no pun intended) on herself. The writing is sophisticated and the reader can easily envision all of the moments that Kelly has captured on film. This gives the admissions officers a more complete picture of who she is (pun intended this time).

Losing a Bet Can Be Good

By: Chris K.

To an 11-year-old boy, The Boy Scout's Handbook is like a bible. Inside this half workbook half textbook are 20-something different areas of study. Each area has several requirements that must be completed before earning a merit badge for that discipline. A parent's signature on the last page of each section signifies proof of completion. The average scout will finish one or two badges a month. As a young and already overambitious scout, I was intent on earning five. Also, I had the added incentive of a wager with my best friend.

As the month progressed, I passed the requirements for an Engineering badge, Fitness badge, Swimming badge and Drama badge. All I needed was one more to complete my goal, but time was running out. On the night before our troop meeting I still had one requirement to fulfill before I could earn a Citizenship badge: I had to memorize not only the National Anthem but also the preamble to the Constitution.

As the night grew later and my eyes heavier, I realized that I was not going to be able to finish. I was then faced with a choice: succumb to failure and lose the bet or forge my mother's signature and earn what I would have rightfully earned if given only one more day. The choice was not easy, after all I was just a pen mark away from fulfilling my goal. But then I began to think about how much the badge and bet were really worth. I grudgingly concluded that lying, which was counter to everything the Boy Scouts represented, was not worth a silly medal or a stupid bet.

I did not achieve my goal of five badges and consequently lost the bet with my friend. But I maintained my honesty. Although I cannot say that The Boy Scout's Handbook has been the only thing that has tested my honesty, it forced me to make a decision about my integrity at an early age. Although I have long quit scouting I can still recite the scout pledge that begins with, "To be honest..."

Comments on "Losing a Bet Can Be Good"

Chris utilizes a short space wisely by presenting a dilemma that he faced as a child, the outcome of which still influences him today. It helps that he is honest in his essay, admitting that naturally he was tempted to do the wrong thing. Surely many of the admissions officers could relate to similar situations in which they had to make a choice between what they wanted to do and what they knew they should do. It also helps that although Chris writes about a moral issue, he does not preach. This is not a story about how "everyone should be honest" or how "honesty would make the world a better place." Chris tells a simple story about one event in his life where he made the right choice. He stays focused on the story and resists making general morality statements that would only detract from the narrative and give him an air of self-righteousness.

Seven Disastrous Essays That Spelled Rejection

Here's a pop quiz: If we are trying to show you how to write a successful college essay, why would we print essays that failed? One answer: It's great entertainment during what can be an ugly and stressful time. The real answer: These essays demonstrate what does *not* work. By reading them, you will know better what sorts of essays turn admissions officers off, cause their eyes to glaze over and send them into a deep slumber. In this way, the essays that did not work can be even more illustrative than those that did.

To give you a taste of what to expect, here are some of what we like to call "Dumbo Leads." These are real-life openings written by students. Right away you can tell that the essay is going to be boring or worse.

- **My name is . . .**

- **The other day my probation officer said . . .**

- **Please let me into your school!**

- **I want to go to Harvard because . . .** (written on a Yale application)

- **Pee Wee Herman is one of our nation's greatest political heroes.**

- **I think applying to college is like sitting on a big toilet . . .**

And now, ladies and gentlemen, boys and girls, for your further entertainment and education, the essays that failed. Warning: Some of these essays are truly painful to read.

My Wish to End Homelessness

By: William M.

If I had only one wish in life, I would wish to end homelessness in the world. In America, homelessness is one of our biggest problems. There are simply too many people without a place to live, without food to eat and without clothes to ward off the winter wind. It is to help these huddled masses that I would like to fulfill my wish.

I first learned of the plight of the homeless last Thanksgiving when my Social Studies class took a trip to our city's homeless shelter to help serve meals. It was one of the most eye-opening experiences I ever had. Before, I had never been to a homeless shelter. I had never touched a homeless person or even talked to one. The only homeless people I knew were the ones who held the signs at the side of the freeway saying "Will Work for Food" or who asked if I could spare a quarter. But here I was confronted with the stark reality of the evils in our country. Seeing how these people really lived changed my life completely.

After going to the homeless shelter last year, I realized that homeless people are human beings. They have feelings and they have dreams. They need to eat and sleep and deserve to at least have a roof over their weary heads.

It is my greatest dream to solve the homeless problem. I think that there are many things that we can do to address this issue if only every person in American would take just a moment to realize the depth of this problem. Together we can work to find a solution.

Homeless people need food, clothes, shelter and work. If only we can meet these simple, basic human needs we could, in a single day, wipe out the problem of homelessness.

We truly need to work together as human beings on our shared Planet Earth to make sure that every person has a home.

Comments on "My Wish to End Homelessness"

William writes what we call the "Miss America" essay. Like contestants in the Miss America pageant, William professes in a melodramatic and overly emotional tone a desire to solve a serious social problem that clearly cannot be easily resolved. Notice that William never mentions what he has done since discovering the plight of the homeless nor does he even try to expound on his vague idea of a solution. This essay reveals either his naivete or simply a lack of effort to consider his topic carefully.

At all costs, avoid writing a "Miss America" essay. Do not write about your plan to personally end worldwide problems such as war, hunger or poverty. Do not write about your lifelong dream to hug every child, stop gang warfare or quell the drug trade. These are the unrealistic and trite wishes that Miss America wannabes robotically repeat. While these can be excellent topics, remember that if you choose them, you should keep your essay focused and centered on what you personally have done. It's okay to mention your dream for a better tomorrow, just don't make it your whole essay. Also note that William shamelessly steals well-worn phrases from such places as the Statue of Liberty. Get some originality!

My Achievements

By: Kevin W.

There are many things that I have done that I am proud of. Throughout high school I have done well academically and socially. I think that my achievements portend what I will accomplish in college. Please allow me to describe some of my successes.

First, when it comes to academics, I have excelled. Throughout high school, I have maintained a 4.0 grade point average while taking challenging classes such as Advanced Placement biology and Advanced Placement English. I also studied Latin for two years and math for all four years. My teachers have always said that I am an excellent student, and I will work hard to get good grades in college, too. I also scored in the top 10 percent on the SAT.

I have participated in a number of enjoyable activities in high school. I played the clarinet in the school band for three years. I volunteered at the local hospital for one summer. I also was a member of the Tennis Club and the tennis team for two years. In college, I plan to join many clubs and organizations as well. I will probably join the band and would like to play on the tennis team.

In high school I have also won numerous awards. For example, I won first place in the science fair last year. I won an Outstanding Writing Award from my ninth grade English teacher. I also earned a varsity letter by being on the tennis team.

During the past two years I have also worked part-time at a clothing store in the shopping mall. This experience has taught me much about what it is like to work hard and long hours. While I certainly do not want to make this a career, I am glad to have had the experience.

Last, I have a very nice personality. Many people say I am thoughtful and kind. I enjoy being nice to others, especially those who are less fortunate than I am. I think I would be a great addition to your college. I have achieved a lot, and I plan to achieve a lot more in the future.

Comments on "My Achievements"

Instead of writing an essay, Kevin writes an expanded resume. Although he is rightfully proud of his accomplishments, his essay tells us little more about him than what we already would have known from his application. Kevin also seems to be concerned with bragging about his accomplishments and making sure that the admissions officers will not overlook all the wonderful things that he has done. It's too bad, however, that this is not what the admissions officers want to see in the essay.

Never offer a laundry list of your achievements, no matter how incredible they may be. Also, don't write about information that is found elsewhere in your application, unless you plan to elaborate on an interesting aspect about it. Finally, notice that Kevin's essay looks like it could have been written in an hour. There is no originality or even an attempt to correct obvious mistakes.

Harvard Is Perfect for Me

By: Missy S.

I have dreamed all of my life of going to Harvard. I think that it is the perfect college for me and that I would fit in wonderfully.

First of all, the environment of your college is incredible. Harvard Square that surrounds the campus is always alive with a mix of interesting people. Last summer I visited Harvard and enjoyed watching a magician, juggler and other street performers. Harvard is also close to Boston, one of the most charming and historical cities in America. I love walking the Freedom Trail and seeing the sites of our country's important historical events.

In addition to the surroundings of Harvard, the campus itself is beautiful. Last summer the trees were full with leaves, and students peacefully relaxed in the Yard. Some tossed frisbees while others read or sunbathed. I have heard that the falls are beautiful with gold, red and orange leaves and that winter is gorgeous as well with snow-capped trees. I also love the old architecture of the red brick buildings.

Of course I would not spend all of my time gazing at the trees and watching street performers in Harvard Square. Harvard also offers so many interesting courses. The Freshman Expository Writing course sounds difficult yet intriguing. I would love to take the macroeconomics course, the introduction to psychology course and the history course on China. Looking through the course catalog, I think that there are more courses that I would like to take than I could ever possibly fit in my four-year schedule.

Outside of academics, Harvard offers such a variety of extracurricular activities as well. I would love to volunteer with a public service organization. I would also like to star in one of the student theater productions and maybe even play intramural soccer.

My dream has always been to go to Harvard. The student body is so diverse and talented. The activities are innumerable, and the academic requirements are rigorous. The environment is truly indescribable. I know I would be a good addition to the next entering freshman class.

Comments on "Harvard Is Perfect for Me"

Missy's essay is little more than a simplified regurgitation of Harvard's website. Does she really need to tell an admissions officer who has been working for years at Harvard that nearby Boston is a "historical city?" Would he or she even care? Missy lists a lot of information about what the reader already knows— the college—and little information about what they know nothing—her. This essay says very little about the author except that she can read an information packet and course book.

Greed Is Good

By: Tony A.

My greatest hero is Gordon Gecko. In the movie "Wall Street," Gecko, played by Michael Douglas, gave the most inspiring speech ever, his "Greed is good" speech. There is no other phrase that so accurately represents my goal in life. Some in this world may want to work to feed the hungry, enter the realm of politics or travel around the world. But my sole goal in life is to earn as much money as I can. Of course, I do not want money just so that I can buy things for myself. Once I accumulate enough money, I will donate at least 10 percent of it to charities such as the United Way and homeless shelters. I am a firm believer in philanthropy.

My college education will be the first step toward attaining this goal. I will study business during my four years. After graduating, I will work for a financial institution in investment banking. While I know that my hours will be rigorous, it will be worth the time. After spending two years in investment banking working for a prestigious firm, I will enter one of the top five business schools in the country. After that, I will start my own financial institution. I want my company to be worth millions within three years, and I want my salary to be either six or seven digits. This way, I will be a millionaire before my 30th birthday.

I have been told that I have a one-track mind, and I guess that I would agree. I do see almost everything in terms of profits and losses. However, I think that I am justified. I think that I can best help improve the world by earning as much money as I can. Once I earn enough money, I will donate a tax-deductible percentage to charities. If I didn't have that money in the first place, I wouldn't be able to donate it. By attending your college, I will be well on my way toward achieving this goal.

Comments on "Greed Is Good"

It would have helped if Tony had the money now. At least he could have offered a large donation to the college, although even then we doubt that it would have made any difference on his admittance standing. Never write about how much money you have now or how much money you want to have in the future. This is a turn-off for admissions officers and now you see why. Colleges don't want to be flooded with heartless, egocentric money-mongers whose sole focus is on their own well-being. Colleges want students with integrity who will contribute in positive ways.

Education Is the Key to Success

By: Ethan C.

To me the pursuit of education has always been of the highest importance. Ever since I was a little boy, my father and mother told me, "Ethan, education is the most important thing in life. It is the key to your future." In my youthful ignorance at the time, I was skeptical and did not believe them. However, today I know the truth of my parents' words of wisdom imparted to me so long ago.

Throughout school I have always given 100 percent. I have elected to take difficult classes when I could have taken easy ones. I have always completed my homework. I have always studied hard for every test. My hard work has paid off—I've earned all "A's" and "B's" in high school. This has made my parents proud. They say to me, "Ethan, we are so proud of you. Education really is the key to success."

When I say the pursuit of education is important, I am taking into account that in this world there is a lot to learn. We can learn about nature, science, cultures, mathematics and history to name a few subjects. I think that every person should try to learn as much as possible about as many things as possible.

For example, I want to learn as much as I can about other cultures. By doing this, I can expand my knowledge of the world. I can cross racial, ethnic and cultural boundaries. I also want to learn about nature. I want to appreciate the beauty of the outdoors and learn about animals, plants and our environment. I also want to learn about history. I think history teaches us lessons about the past that are very important to our future.

In this way, education is the most important thing in life. Education expands our minds. It exposes us to new information. It takes us to a higher level. Education makes people better. It provides them with knowledge about the world, nature and other people. It exposes them to new ideas and new thoughts. It is what places us at the top of the evolutionary chain. These are the reasons why education is so important in life. This is my purpose for going to college. I want to become truly educated. I want to raise my mind to a higher level, to be exposed to new ideas and to learn as much as I possibly can.

Comments on "Education Is the Key to Success"

In this essay, Ethan writes about the merits of higher education, an appropriate topic, but one that he treats too generally. All students who apply to college are implicitly making the same statement—that they value education. Otherwise, they wouldn't bother to apply, right? Ethan should have explained why education is significant to him as an individual, what exact subjects he wants to learn more about and why certain topics excite his intellect more than others. He should have focused on specific experiences rather than ramble about general principles.

When comparing many of these essays that failed to the essays that were successful, you probably have noticed one consistent difference. The essays that worked were all focused directly on their objectives and did not try to say everything about a topic. So, keep your focus narrow and make every sentence interesting.

We Can Learn a Lot From the Japanese

By: Angela L.

Last summer I traveled out of the country for the first time. I spent the summer in Japan living with a host family as an exchange student. Even though my stay was a short three months, I still learned a lot about the Japanese way of life. While both the United States and Japan are advanced countries and have some commonalities, I discovered many differences between our two nations.

The Japanese people have such a rich culture that is shared among everyone. In America, of course, we have little culture that is shared by everyone. There are so many people with such diverse backgrounds. We celebrate Christmas, Hanukkah and the Winter Solstice, to name a few American winter holidays. Each of these holidays has an entirely different background and way of being celebrated. In Japan, however, everyone celebrates the same holidays. Even though we have more diversity in America, there is something special about knowing that on a given day nearly every person in the country is celebrating in a similar way. There is something harmonious about such unity.

The Japanese also have a different way of life. For example, they remove their shoes before entering their homes to keep their straw mat floors clean. They oftentimes sleep on futons on the floor that they fold up and tuck away in the morning. They eat with chopsticks, and their diet mainstays are white rice, a variety of noodles and vegetables. On the other hand, we usually wear our shoes inside carelessly tracking in mud and dirt. We sleep in beds that we do not have to move in order to make needed space. We oftentimes eat meals made up of the McDonald's or Pizza Hut food group.

In our countries, we also have different work ethics. Japanese businessmen leave their homes before the sun rises to commute an hour to two hours to their offices. They spend much of their lives there because work is everything. When they socialize, it is usually with their business partners. In flocks, they head to bars for late night drinks and business talks. They vacation with their co-workers, too. Much of their lives revolves around their work. In America, work is also an integral part of life, but for most Americans it is not the only part. American workers enjoy socializing with their friends from outside of the company as well. Americans also enjoy vacationing with their families. For most American people, their lives do not revolve around work as is oftentimes true for Japanese businessmen.

Another difference between America and Japan is the educational system. Japan's educational system is based on examinations. After every level of school—elementary, junior high and high school—students take an examination. The results of these examinations determine the quality of school that the students may attend. Within this system, students oftentimes as young as elementary school spend months and even years in advance preparing for the exams. They know that their test scores will determine not only what schools they are accepted to but eventually what level job they will hold and what incomes they will receive. While many students in the United States try to do well, this kind of pressure on students as early as elementary school does not exist.

Thus, after living in Japan last summer, I came to realize that there are many differences between the two countries. There is much that each could learn from exposure to the other.

Comments on "We Can Learn a Lot From the Japanese"

Although Angela's essay is marginally interesting, it still failed to get her into a top college. The reason: Angela's essay says little about Angela. She has written an essay that sounds like it came from a tour book. Instead of reporting the differences in a provocative and enlightening way, Angela merely catalogs the contrasts. How much more interesting would it have been had she engaged the reader with a comparison of her host mother's life with her own mother's life? Angela tries to cover too much and ends up with an essay that is totally boring. It is impossible to write about all of the differences between two cultures in the limited space of a college essay. She would have had a much better essay if she had focused on a single difference. Angela's generic introduction and point-by-point structure leave nothing to the imagination.

No memorable examples are given or vivid images created. This is a forgettable essay.

Power of Poetry

By: Joseph L.

If poetry be the wine then I the drunkard. If poetry be the rifle then I the marksman. Nothing has so profoundly altered my mortal existence than the discovery of the poetic word.

Poetry offers such penetration into the human condition with a passion and propensity that is unmatched by any other endeavor since it has the ability to capture the essence of the emotional spirit and combine it with discursive attributes which stimulate our acknowledgment of the human condition and privilege our understanding of our innate value vis a vis the syndrome of mortality.

My own work in the construction, deconstruction and reconstruction of the poetic has blossomed from a fleeting fascination with rhythm and rhyme to an intense desire to hone my sense of utterance so that it is neither myopic in its treatment of the sensual predications of modern existence nor ignorant to the monster of nativism. I hope that my constructs do not descend into the ephemeral but solidify as monumental testaments to the intellect of man and his thorough understanding of what can only be called the "floating world."

If offered admission into your school I will employ my time and energy into further developing my talents to effect an impact which would have repercussions throughout our metaphysical conception of being. It is to this mission and the leveraging of poetry that I dedicate my existence and consider my sacrament.

Comments on "Power of Poetry"

Too bad no one can understand this essay. We doubt even Joseph could explain exactly what he meant to say. Notice the ridiculously long sentences and hyperbolic words that add confusion rather than clarity. Nothing will hurt your chances more than an unintelligible essay. Admissions officers are a well-educated bunch, but no one wants to read an essay that is so inflated with thesaurus-pumped words.

A Final Note on the Essays That Bombed

It should be obvious that one major problem with the last seven essays is that the students did not spend enough time developing their ideas and crafting their works. In all likelihood none were edited by anyone other than the writer. All of these essays could have been winners if the students had spent more time, followed the suggestions in Chapter 5 and found editors to read their work. No essay is ever perfect the first time it is written. It takes a lot of rewriting and editing to make it a winning college essay. These essays bombed because they were first drafts submitted as final copy.

Do yourself a favor and get an early start. Don't worry about what your essay looks like after you write the initial draft. Keep working. Get someone to look it over and make suggestions. Re-read Chapter 5. The only essay that counts is the one you ultimately turn in to the admissions office.

Do You Have a Good Essay?

We are always looking for examples of successful college essays. If you have an essay that you're willing to share, why not send it to us? If we use it in our next book, we will give you full credit, making you a full-fledged published author. Mail your essays to this address:

Gen and Kelly Tanabe
SuperCollege, LLC
2713 Newlands Avenue
Belmont, CA 94002
gen_kelly@supercollege.com

CHAPTER 8

THE SECRETS TO CRUSHING THE INTERVIEW

The Interview Nightmare

Your essays may take more time to write and your grades more effort to earn, but for many students there is nothing more nerve-racking, stomach-churning and downright intimidating than the college interview. Unlike the rest of your application, which will be evaluated in the private offices of the admissions officers, the interview will put you face to face with an actual person who appears to have the almighty power to get you in or keep you out of the school of your dreams.

Before you consider forging a letter from your doctor saying that you have a rare disease that prevents you from taking part in live conversations, read this chapter. In it you will discover numerous ways to prepare yourself for the interview to make it more of a friendly chat than a scary interrogation.

Plus, if this is not enough to allay your fears, we'll let you in on a little secret that the colleges do not want you to know: The interview is really not as important as you may think. Surprised? Read on.

In the grand scheme of the application process, the interview will most likely not make or break your chances. In fact, many schools use the interview as a check in the process rather than a major determinant of admission. Usually the colleges will already have enough information to decide whether to admit you or not.

There are cases, however, when an applicant who looked good on paper turned out to be a total dimwit in person. Weeding out these few deceptive applicants is the interview's main purpose. If colleges get reports back saying that the applicant showed up in a T-shirt and shorts and had trouble composing a coherent sentence, they will certainly think twice about offering admission regardless of how stellar that student's application appears.

Although the main role of the interview is to confirm the preliminary decisions of the admissions board, it is of course still a good idea to prepare for the interview. If you are in the borderline group, your interview may, in rare instances, be that extra something that pushes you into the admit group.

If an interviewer is particularly impressed by one of the borderline students, he or she will write a strong letter of support. Admissions officers have been known on a few occasions to change their minds based on an interviewer's passionate appeal. While this is not typical, it is still a possibility, which gives you a good reason to prepare.

Secrets of the Interview

Now that you know the interview is not as important as you thought, you can relax a little. No amount of reassurance (and even practice for that matter) will totally eliminate the stress of the actual interview. However, if you adhere to the following advice, you will not only possess a much higher level of confidence, but you will also make a strong, positive impression that could cement your acceptance to the school.

Make the Most of Your Sweaty Palms

Not that this will provide you with any solace, but with nerves on edge and not knowing exactly what to expect, your first interview may seem like a total disaster. Many of the questions will be unexpected and some may even stump you. This, however awful it may seem, is normal.

Your last interview, by contrast, will probably be your best. An experienced veteran, you will no longer be as nervous, you will be able to anticipate what questions your interviewer will ask and you will have developed a repertoire of answers that you can apply to almost any question.

Take advantage of the fact that your palms will become less sweaty as you do more interviews. Schedule your interviews strategically. Arrange to have your second- or third-choice school interviews first, and save your first-choice schools for last. By arranging to have your least-important interviews first, you will minimize the impact of your early interview nervousness while gaining confidence and experience to perform better in the interviews that really count.

Interviewers Are Real People Too

Remember when we were in elementary school, and we thought that our teachers were somehow above ordinary adults, that their sole purpose in life was to educate and discipline us and that 24 hours a day they were at school doing who-knows-what kind of alien teacher rituals? Perhaps you still remember, like we do, the moment of revelation when you suddenly realized that your teachers actually had lives outside of school.

STORY FROM REAL LIFE: WHY THE INTERVIEW MATTERS LESS THAN YOU THINK

The interview is probably not as important as you think it is and here's proof. —Gen and Kelly

My interview for a well-known Ivy League college was relatively stress-free. My interviewer was very nice and seemed more interested in answering my questions about student life than pounding me with tough questions about my academic performance or interests. In fact, by the end of the interview, I felt as if I had already been accepted and my interviewer was trying to convince me to choose his school over other colleges.

A few months later I got an acceptance letter from this school. After accepting, I called my interviewer to inform him of my decision and to thank him for the interview. We ended up having lunch together where I heard more praise for my decision.

Near the end of our lunch, I innocently asked my interviewer how important the interview had been and if it may have made the difference in my acceptance. He looked around as if to see if anyone was eavesdropping on our conversation. He took a sip of coffee and told me the little-known secret about the real role of the interview. He said that when he received his assignments of people to interview, the list separated the applicants into three categories: those who the college strongly wanted to admit, those who they strongly wanted to reject and those who fell in the middle.

Before my interview took place, he knew that I had a good chance of getting accepted. In fact, he admitted that he had been so worried that I might accept an offer from another school that he felt he had to push the college as much as possible.

This explained why I felt my interview was more like a sales pitch. I wish I had known this before the interview. It would have saved me from some unnecessary nervous butterflies.

—Robert, who still keeps in touch with his interviewer, now friend

It is easy to view college interviewers, like our elementary school teachers, as something more than human. What you must realize is that interviewers, no matter which college they represent, are real people with real lives. Many interviewers are alumni who have volunteered through their alumni club to conduct the interviews; they are not high-ranking college officials.

Keep reminding yourself that the interviewer sitting across from you is an ordinary human being since this will help you to relax and view your interviewer in the right context. Think of him or her as a good adult friend or relative. If you can view your interviewer as a real person who enjoys interesting conversations, you will be able to establish an easy rapport, which will help make your interview both pleasant and memorable.

Going in too stiff and intent only on reciting your accomplishments and your memorized list of the benefits of going to college is a sure recipe for disaster. As the next strategy explains, try to engage the real person sitting across from you in dynamic conversation rather than stiff Q&A.

Don't Just Talk About You

Since the interviewers are real people, they value real conversations. What would you prefer: Listening to a one-hour soliloquy, with Socratic references, on the merits of academia as perceived through the eyes of an 18-year-old or participating in an intriguing conversation about current events, life experiences and personal opinions? Needless to say, interviewers prefer the latter.

Throughout your interviews, remind yourself that your goal is to achieve two-way conversation. Be careful of any interview where the subject is *you* and *you* dominate the interview talking about *your* accomplishments. Don't worry about trying to mention all of your achievements—your interviewer will ask about them. At the same time, however, this is not the only thing the interview is about.

Common sense tells us that most people enjoy talking about themselves, and college interviewers are no different. They volunteered for this job because they enjoyed their college experience and they like talking to potential students. Interviewers are usually the kind of people who love to give advice to young prospects. Think of this as a time not only for your interviewers to learn about you but for you to find out as much as you can about them and their experiences.

Creative Digressions and Connecting: How to Become Bosom Buddies With Your Interviewers

The more you know about your interviewers, the better. At the beginning of the interview after greetings are exchanged, take a few moments to get to know your interviewers. Ask them about their current professions, their college majors and where they were born and raised. Be friendly but don't be ingratiating.

Another big hint for the interview: Look on the walls. The first thing you should do when you walk into the interviewer's office is search your surroundings for clues. Clues can be anything: a diploma on the wall, picture of your interviewer receiving an award from a politician, Museum of Fine Arts calendar or a Mr. Potato Head on the desk. Clues are invaluable sources about whom you are meeting, what he or she enjoys and what makes him or her proud.

Throughout the interview, ask your interviewers questions about themselves and their experiences during and after college. Of course, do not go

---

STORY FROM REAL LIFE
HOW I GOT IN BY JABBERING ABOUT KARATE

A friend of ours named Rob used to brag that he got into college simply by acing his interview. From the very first question Rob said he hit it off with his interviewer, with whom he shared a passion for karate. Rob's claim that he got in simply by bonding with his interviewer is questionable—in addition to a dynamite interview, he also had remarkable grades and held several leadership positions. Still, his experience shows how connecting with interviewers can make the time much more enjoyable and provide you with strong support from them. —Gen and Kelly

Before my interview my college guidance counselor advised me to have a list of possible topics to speak about including such fascinating things as current events, my favorite book and a philosophical debate. When I arrived at the law office of Jill Stevens and saw the pictures of her in a karate uniform on the wall, I knew our conversation would take a different turn.

Jill's first question was about my interests, and I immediately seized on the opportunity to talk about my involvement with karate at school and the local YMCA. I learned that Jill had been taking karate lessons for just over a year and was very interested in progressing through the ranks. She asked me question after question about my technique, training and instructor. We had a great conversation about the benefits of karate in disciplining the mind and improving concentration. I commended her on her achievement in such a short time and even recommended a dojo where her five-year-old son could try karate.

Instead of the usual stuff about my academic achievements and interests in school, we spent two hours talking about our mutual love of karate. It worked out for me. I was accepted by the school with, as Jill later told me, an enthusiastic letter of support from her. Plus, I really didn't want to talk about current events anyway.

—Rob, who is now a volunteer interviewer himself

overboard by barraging them with an unending stream of questions, but make sure that the conversation is engaging for them as well as for you.

Let's say that your interviewer asks what you enjoy most about school and you respond, "The math team." If while you are answering the question, the interviewer makes a remark like, "Oh, I enjoyed that too" or "Yes, I understand, it was like that for me also" or any other comment that indicates you have something in common, take advantage of it. Ask your interviewer a follow-up question. "Were you in your school's math club?" or "What do you think about Princeton's math department?" may spark an interesting two-way conversation with your interviewer and you may even discover that you have some mutual interests.

Don't follow every question your interviewer asks with your own question, but when the opportunity presents itself, take it. Again, the goal is to try to engage your interviewer in a two-way, dynamic dialogue.

Listen, Too

It really is true that the best conversationalists are also the best listeners. If you happen to get interviewers (and the chances are high) who really love to talk, let them. One student told us that in his Princeton interview his interviewer spoke 90 percent of the time. He thought the interview had been a disaster since he hardly got a chance to speak about himself and his accomplishments. This applicant was very surprised when at the end of the interview his interviewer shook his hand and said very sincerely, "This was one of the best conversations I have had all week. Thank you."

Although the applicant's interviewer did all of the talking, consider the conversation from the interviewer's point of view. Since the applicant had been a good listener and had asked a few appropriate questions from time to time, the conversation was great. Had this student tried to wrest control of the interview, the interviewer would have felt like the student was uninterested or even pushy and rude. This was an extreme case, and most interviews are not as one-sided. Our point is that the goal of the interview is to establish a good two-way conversation. The worst thing you can do in an interview is to do all the talking.

Your Interview Homework

Remember those college brochures filled with pictures, statistics and text cultivating dust balls under your bed? Dig them out before your interview and do something terribly, horrifyingly radical—read them! It is not necessary to read them cover to cover, but knowing such basic facts as where the school is located, what kind of environment it has, some of the courses it offers and some of the activities you may choose to participate in is a good idea. It does not impress interviewers when they discover that students who are applying to their beloved alma mater do not even know what state it is located in or that the college is single sex. (There was an applicant who actually made it to the interview before he learned that the college he was applying to was an all-women school!)

Try to talk to relatives or friends who now attend or have attended the college. They can give you insights into the college that are not found in the glossy brochures or on the website. The more you know, the better.

Doing your homework will allow you to ask intelligent questions. You are making the most important decision in your life so far. It makes sense that you would have a question or two about it. Having prepared questions not only helps create that prized two-way conversation, but it also demonstrates that you are serious about attending the college.

Not all questions are good questions, and in particular, avoid asking those obvious questions with answers that are on the first page of the college's glossy brochures. Instead, the best questions to ask your interviewers are those that make them reflect on their own experiences, require them to do a little thinking and elicit an opinion. Making your interviewers think or express their opinions makes the interviews more interesting for them and makes your question seem insightful and probing. Some examples:

- What do you think about the X department?

- How did the small/large class size affect your education?

- How did X college prepare you for your career?

- What was the best opportunity you felt X university provided?

- What is the best/worst aspect of X university or X city?

- If you had to do it again, what would you do differently?

Think of more questions and write them on a list with the most interesting ones at the top. Take this list into the interviews and refer to them when the conversation begins to stall or when your interviewers ask you if you have any questions.

Cheat Sheet of the Most Commonly Asked Questions

In addition to doing your homework on the school, do homework on yourself. In other words, know how to speak about your background, talents, interests, goals and accomplishments intelligently and coherently. The best way to do this is to get a preview of what your interviewers will ask before the big event actually takes place.

Throughout the history of interviewing, some interviewers have been known to pitch a couple of curve balls. Unpleasant ones that we've heard include the following: "Please estimate right now how many quarters it would take to build a column as tall as the Empire State building;" "Give us three convincing reasons for *not* admitting you" and "I want you to do this interview without using the word 'I.'" Fortunately, however, most interviewers choose from your standard fare of non-lethal questions. The following is a list of the most common questions that you should be prepared to answer. You can use these questions for your mock interviews, which are discussed later in this chapter.

- Why do you want to attend X university?

- What is your strongest/weakest character trait?

- What have you done to prepare for college?

- What has been your greatest experience in high school?

- What do you want to do in the future?

- Tell me about yourself. (You should focus on about three things.)

- Tell me about your interests.

- Tell me about your involvement in extracurricular activities.

- Tell me about your family.

- What do you think about [current event]?

- What is your favorite book? Who is your favorite author?

- Which of your accomplishments are you the most proud of?

- What is the most challenging thing you have done?

- If you could meet any important figure in the past or present, whom would it be and what would you talk about?

- If you could be any animal, what would you be? Why?

The "No-No" Topics

It should be pretty obvious that your college interview is not the place to share your addiction to inhaling paint thinner or that you have a collection of traffic tickets from all 50 states.

There are some topics that you just should not bring up. While these topics may seem self-evident, they are topics that students have actually used in their interviews. The "no-no" topics include these:

- Your membership in a cult or any unorthodox or extreme beliefs.

- How you want to single-handedly instill world peace or end hunger or any other dream that would be viewed as unrealistic or overly idealistic.

- Your membership in the Anarchy of America Association or any other very radical or conservative political beliefs.

- Your passion for vodka or any other alcohol or drug use.

- How you drove the bank getaway car or other illegal acts.

- Sex and your personal sexual history or experience.

- Why your parents think they are the King and Queen of England or any other sort of severe family dysfunction.

Of course you will have to be the ultimate judge of your interviewers and of what is an appropriate topic. If you have very strong religious beliefs, and you see that there are numerous religious icons in your interviewer's office, or if you are applying to a religious institution, talk about your dedication to the church. If your interviewer seems turned off by a shift in the conversation, change the topic.

Throughout your interviews, note your interviewers' reactions to the topics you discuss. If they appear uncomfortable, change the subject.

Know the World Around You

If you are already knowledgeable about current events around the world, you will be very well prepared for the interview. If not, start reading news websites as frequently as possible so that you will have a basic knowledge of current events and issues.

Many interviewers ask applicants about current events since they are good conversation starters. They do not expect you to be an expert on the current political, economic and social upheavals of the world, but they want to know if you occasionally pick up a newspaper. Interviewers also want to see how you analyze issues such as, for example, a heated political election. It is difficult to demonstrate your analytical skills if you do not have the basic facts.

If you are surprised with a question that you know nothing about, admit your lack of knowledge and try to give as much information as possible about those things with which you *are* acquainted. It is better to concede what you don't know than risk embarrassing yourself by pretending you are familiar with a subject when you clearly are not.

You may also want to keep extremely conservative, liberal or radical views to yourself. While your idea to cure the world's ills through a global day of nakedness may be revolutionary, you probably do not want to make such an idea public—at least not until after you are accepted. Show your interviewers your thoughtful and opinionated side, not your lunatic fringe side.

As your interviewers are "normal" people, they too have opinions. If yours are the polar opposites of theirs and you engage in debate, they may appreciate you for expressing your views but may also dislike you for disagreeing with them. Once you enter the college of your dreams, you can take center stage and extol any and all opinions (including your proposed day of nakedness). Before then, however, it is better to keep extreme opinions to yourself.

Is Religion a Taboo Topic?

No. Although religion is a personal and perhaps controversial topic for some, it is not a taboo topic in the interview. You do need to be sensitive to the beliefs of your interviewer and keep in mind that nobody likes to be preached to or made to feel like their own beliefs are inferior to someone else's. So while it is totally legitimate to speak about your involvement in the church, you should focus on concrete actions and accomplishments rather than the details of your specific religious beliefs. For example, describing your responsibilities as a Sunday school teacher or how you helped with your church's hurricane relief effort are all actions that your interviewer—regardless of his or her own feelings toward religion—will understand and be impressed by.

No Snoozing Allowed

A simple mistake that many students make during their interviews is simply not showing interest in what their interviewers have to say. Throughout your conversation with your interviewers, always appear as interested as you can. Ask questions. Respond to what they say. Take a notebook and a pen to write down any information your interviewers provide. This will visibly show them that you value their opinions and that you are serious about your desire to attend their alma mater. If you start to feel sleepy, start taking notes on your conversation or ask for a second cup of coffee. The best cure for a sudden attack of drowsiness is to keep the conversation lively and interesting.

The Mock Interview

The best way to prepare for the interviews is to do them. Ask a friend or family member to act as the interviewer and do a mock interview at home. If you cannot find someone who will play interviewer, you can play the part yourself by asking and then answering your own questions. (Warning: If you do this in public people *will* think you are crazy.)

To make the mock interview a learning experience, make a video of it. Use the questions provided in this chapter and any others that you think might be asked. Find a quiet place with two chairs. Sit face to face with your interviewer and go for it.

Try as much as possible to act like you are at a real interview. Practice creating two-way conversation, talking about meaningful topics and expressing your opinions. You can even instruct your mock interviewer to purposefully create dead time where he or she does not say anything so you can practice jump-starting the conversation with a question or comment.

When you are finished, ask your interviewer for his or her opinion. Did you come across as intelligent and mature? Did you speak clearly and slowly enough? Was the conversation interesting? Were the topics you chose appropriate? Did your personality come across well? Ask for suggestions for improvement.

Review the video and try to locate weak areas. Did a question throw you off? Rework your answers in your head or on paper and try the interview again. Doing as many mock interviews as possible with as many interviewers as you can find will greatly reduce the stress and improve your performance when it comes time for the real thing.

During one of your mock interviews make sure that you wear your actual interview clothes. You may find that the collar of your favorite shirt is just a little too tight to speak comfortably for an extended period. Check that your slacks, dress or skirt feels comfortable when you sit.

Leave the Halter Top and Short Shorts Behind

Speaking of clothes—they do a lot in establishing a first impression. Since your appearance will provide your interviewers with their first idea of who you are, dress appropriately. This means leaving the sexy cutoff T-shirt that reveals your pierced belly button, super baggy jeans 40 sizes too large and the mini-mini-mini patent leather skirt in the closet.

For men, dressing your part means a dress shirt and slacks or even tie and sports coat. For women, a dress, pants and a nice shirt or a skirt and a nice shirt are appropriate. We hear your groans, but by dressing well, you will appear professional and mature, which will be remembered. If you are not sure about a particular outfit, it is better not to wear it.

More important than what you actually choose to wear, however, is that you are comfortable in what you wear. You could be wearing a design straight from the pages of the latest fashion magazine, but if it pinches, your squirming and uneasiness will do more damage than if you had worn a simple hand-me-down suit from your older brother.

At least a day before your interview, put on your most comfortable outfits and make sure they are stain and wrinkle free. If you cannot choose between two outfits, go with the more conservative one. Don't forget to make sure that your footwear is clean and polished. Before your interviews, examine yourself in a mirror to check for any runs, rips or other grooming faux pas.

A Safety Pin, Aspirin and Other Emergency Supplies

By emergency supplies, we do not mean a first aid kit or canned goods in case of an earthquake (although in certain areas of the country that would not be such a bad idea). We are referring to all of the supplies you may need in case of a mini-emergency such as a missing button or a sudden pang of nausea.

Pack in your car, purse or briefcase anything you think you could reasonably need in case of a mishap. For example: sewing kit, aspirin, stomach medicine, mouthwash, hairbrush, cosmetics, safety pin, mirror, candy bar.

Remember that Murphy's Law will be in effect and what you least want or expect to happen, will. With these supplies, at least you will be prepared. Glance at yourself in a mirror before you walk in and check that your hair is combed, tie straight, zipper up and a piece of today's lunch is not still between your teeth.

STORY FROM REAL LIFE
MY FISHNET STOCKINGS SPELLED REJECTION

The following is a hard to believe but true story. The student admits it is the truth but is, understandably, very embarrassed and cannot imagine that she was ever so naive. In order to protect her identity (and pride) she has assumed the pseudonym Helen. —Gen and Kelly

I had heard from a friend that with the hundreds or even thousands of applicants admissions officers meet each year, it was best to wear clothes that stood out so that the interviewer would remember you most. This made sense, I thought. I definitely wanted to be remembered by the admissions officer, so I selected the flashiest getup in my closet, believing that the flashier the outfit, the more likely I would be remembered.

Decked out in a hot red satin top, black leather skirt, fishnet stockings, and thigh high boots, I entered the admissions office. I ignored the stares of the other students, dressed in suits and loafers, and took their surprise as evidence that my outfit would certainly be remembered.

When it was my turn, I walked confidently into the interviewer's office. I was prepared to explain how I was a leader at my school and how I was eager to begin college when the admissions officer stopped my train of thought. With her arms crossed and her eyes narrowed at me glaringly she snorted, "Do you think this is a night club, dear? Please come back again when you are dressed appropriately for a college interview." I was so embarrassed from her reaction that I never even went back for my interview, which probably sealed my rejection to the school.

For my next interview, I learned my lesson. Wearing a simple skirt and blouse sans the fishnet stockings, I was actually given the chance to complete my interview.

Note: Although Helen's outfit blew her first interview, she learned her lesson early. For the rest of her interviews, she dressed appropriately and was rewarded with several acceptances.

Show Time! Psyche Yourself Up for the Real Thing

When it comes time for the Big Event, the most important thing to remember is to be yourself. When you are yourself, you are the most comfortable, the most natural and the most likable. Interviewers can detect when you are faking it by trying to be someone you are not.

Remember that interviewers are *real people* and that you are going to have real conversations with these real people about your and their real lives. Try to think of this as a wonderful chance to meet interesting people and learn a little more about the colleges to which you have applied. And do not forget that while you want to put on your best performance, world peace does not hang in the balance. Relax!

Why Blowing It Is Not Blowing It

If after your interview you feel that you did not do as well as you wanted, you are not the only one. Everyone has doubts after their interviews—especially the first one—and regrets not having asked a particular question or made such-and-such insightful comment. All of this is apparent only after the interview is over.

As you replay the interview in your head, all kinds of clever responses that you could have made will come to mind, and your few mistakes and stumbles will appear glaringly large. This is perfectly normal. Fortunately, unlike you, your interviewers were not placing your every gesture and word under a microscope. While you may remember that you accidentally ended a sentence with a preposition, your interviewers will not.

Interviewers are not looking for details, but for an *overall* impression of you. If you engaged in two-way conversation, connected with them and followed the other suggestions outlined in this chapter, you will have made a good impression. But since nothing will keep you from thinking about what you should have done, take advantage of this, and try to remember some of your better ideas. You may use them in your next interview.

CHAPTER 9

CRITICAL FINAL STEPS BEFORE SUBMITTING THE APPLICATION

You Are Done! (Well Almost...)

Congratulations! You have survived the most difficult part of the college admissions process. You have written a spectacular essay, filled out every blank on the application form and had glowing reviews of yourself written by teachers and others. Whew! What an accomplishment. Before you start to party, there are still some easy, but nevertheless important, finishing touches you need to do before pressing submit.

Do a Once, Twice and Thrice Over

At the risk of sounding like a nagging parent, you should check, double check and even triple check to make sure that you have submitted everything required for your applications. Forgetting something will not spell instant rejection, but it may slow down the admissions process. Here are some frequently overlooked items:

Application. Every blank and question should be completed. And don't forget to sign (or e-sign) the application!

Transcript. Forget about any schemes like Photoshopping less than perfect grades; colleges require an official copy. As a side note, one student recently attempted to electronically remove all of the minuses on her report card. Suspecting foul play, the college requested an official transcript from the school. When the college confirmed the difference, the high school was informed, the student was punished and she was promptly rejected from the college. It was a shame, especially since the minuses the student whited out belonged

STORY FROM REAL LIFE
I MISSED THE DEADLINE AND WAS STILL ACCEPTED

Never miss deadlines. It could cost you stress, money and embarrassment and affect your chances of admission. Just don't do it. With that said, we have included this Story From Real Life not because we condone missing deadlines—in case you missed the point of our diatribe, we don't—but if for reasons out of your control you find time creeping to the last minute, you shouldn't lose hope. —Gen and Kelly

I promised myself again and again that this time I would not procrastinate, but nevertheless, I did. So on the night before three of my applications were due, I had an incredible amount of work left. I still had to add introductions to my essays as well as finish all three of the application forms. I planned to go to sleep early and then wake up early to finish everything.

You can probably guess what happened. After I slept through my alarm and finally stumbled out of bed at 11 a.m., I still had so much to do that by the time 11 p.m. rolled around I realized that I had much more to do. I was able to submit two of the applications before the deadline, but I submitted the third one at 12:04 a.m., five minutes late.

As I waited for the colleges to make their decisions, I had nightmares that the college I submitted late to would reject my application without even reviewing it. I began to wonder if I should write asking that my application fees be refunded. When the decision letters began to arrive, I cringed each time I approached the mailbox, expecting a rejection from the school. To my amazement, I was accepted at all three schools, and two even offered scholarships!

I was very lucky that things worked out. My advice is to do everything you can to prevent submitting an application late. If you absolutely, positively cannot finish an application by the deadline, I think it is better to submit it a few minutes late and take a chance than to submit an incomplete application or to not apply at all. Some colleges are more lenient than others, but you never can predict which ones will give you a break.

—Emma, who no longer procrastinates (too much)

mostly to "A's" and she would have been a strong candidate with such a record.

Signatures. Yours, in all the right places. Especially on the application form certifying that what you have written is true.

Check or credit card payment. No free rides here. If you do not send the money, the colleges will not process your application.

Financial aid forms. These are usually due a few months later, but remember that every blank and question should be completed. Include tax forms and any other relevant forms. Take a look at Chapter 11 for more information on these special forms.

Also, do not forget to check the following:

Evaluations. Follow up with your teachers, counselors and other recommenders to make sure that they submit your evaluations before the deadline.

Score reports. Even if you'd rather keep your scores to yourself, don't forget to have the College Board and ACT send the reports for your SAT, SAT Subject Tests, ACT, APs and any other scores to the colleges.

No mix-ups. If you apply to more than one college (and who doesn't these days) it is very easy to get things mixed up. Make sure that you are submitting the right essay to the right school, especially if all of your essays are similar. One student we know didn't check and discovered only after he had submitted his applications that he had accidentally sent all 14 schools the same essay in which he had declared his desire to attend Duke!

The Big Send-Off

Most college deadlines are based on the postmark or time of online submission. In other words, as long as the postmark or online submission is on or before the due date, the application is considered to be on time. If you are the type who waits until the last possible moment to do anything, then you must gather every morsel of energy and self-discipline you have to combat this urge when submitting your applications. While we don't expect you to finish your applications six months before they are due—although that would certainly be nice—you should complete and mail or submit your applications as early as possible.

At the very least, designate the day before they are due as your deadline for submitting them. Sure, you will miss the excitement of racing off to the post office at 4:59 and getting down on your knees to beg the postal worker to accept just one more letter or trying to submit at midnight and having the website crash, but you will ensure that your application is received by the admissions office on time.

Having preached the virtue of finishing early and submitting on time, we must confess that sometimes application forms need to be submitted late. As you will see from the accompanying Story From Real Life, submitting your application past the deadline, while definitely not a smart move, does not necessarily mean instant rejection. But we should warn you that even though the story has a happy ending, we definitely do not recommend that you try this!

Thank All of Your Helpers

Make Miss Manners proud by writing thank you letters to everyone who helped you along the way. Not only is it the polite thing to do, but it will also make those who have helped you feel appreciated and useful. Include letters to your teachers and other recommenders, interviewers, editors, advisors and anyone else who deserves a thank you. Do not forget to also tell them where you have been accepted and where you have decided to attend.

We welcome you to send us a letter telling us where you will be going to school and how our book may have helped you get there. We'd love to hear from you! Send your letters or email to:

Gen and Kelly Tanabe
SuperCollege, LLC
2713 Newlands Avenue
Belmont, CA 94002
gen_kelly@supercollege.com

CHAPTER 10

HOW TO ACE THE SAT AND ACT

How to Survive the SAT and ACT

One of the most detested aspects of applying to college is the fact that you will spend no less than three excruciating hours on one or more early Saturday mornings taking tedious tests that pit you against every other college-bound high school senior in the country.

Because colleges recognize that high schools have different levels of difficulty and grading systems, they need a standard way of comparing the academic readiness of students from across the country. These standardized tests include the SAT, ACT and SAT Subject Test.

The results of this stressful experience will be a set of numbers that you can use to compare yourself to your friends to see who really is smarter! That wouldn't be so bad if were not for the fact that you also have to submit these scores to the colleges, and they will use them to help decide if you are worthy of admission. It's no wonder that some students have been attending after-school test prep courses practically since they were in pre-school. But how important are these tests anyway?

You may find it hard to believe, but there was a time when students didn't worry about these tests. On the appointed day they got up, went to school, took the test and that was it. Those days are no more. Now, most students (and parents) subscribe to the myth that these tests are the only things that count. Just go to the bookstore and see how many books there are on how to master, crack or outsmart these tests. Conduct a search online, and see how many test prep centers are listed in the vicinity around your home.

How this hype surrounding college tests has come to be, we do not know. But it sure is enough to scare any college-bound senior. So, before you fall into this stricken state of mind, let us try to clear up some of the misunderstandings.

MYTH #1: Standardized tests make or break your chances.

Absolutely not true! While it is true that standardized tests are important in the admissions process, they are certainly not the only determinant of your admission into college. A friend of ours who got a near perfect score on the SAT was passed over by Harvard, while another friend who barely got half as high was accepted.

The reality is that admissions officers are interested in more than just the numbers. When they evaluate students' applications, they take into consideration all of the components including the application, evaluation letters, essay, academic record, awards, work experience, leadership, extracurricular activities and interview.

To think that test scores top all these factors is simply wrong. In fact, between a) your grades and the types of classes you took; and b) your SAT scores, the former is much more useful in predicting how successful you will be in college. Admissions officers lean toward accepting academically motivated but low-testing students rather than the opposite.

In fact, there are more than 1,000 colleges that admit all or a "substantial portion" of their freshmen students without requiring SAT or ACT scores. The list of colleges is available at www.fairtest.org.

MYTH #2: You have to score in the top 90 percent to get into a selective college.

Less than perfect test scores will not doom you to rejection. Thus, when you are looking at the profiles of colleges in the guidebooks, don't get worked up because your scores are lower than a certain median or percentile.

Many guidebooks and websites provide a median score for each school. This indicates the score at which half the students scored higher and half scored lower. Some schools list ranges between which most of their students who are admitted have scored. Although these numbers can give you a good target to aim for, keep in mind that every year thousands of students with good high school records, but lower than average test scores, are admitted to top schools.

If your scores are lower than the scores in the guidebooks or on the websites, remember that admissions officers recognize that even well-qualified and motivated students do not always perform well on standardized tests. A student with a high GPA but an average SAT score is just as competitive (if not more so) than someone with an average GPA but a high SAT score. Plus, there are many other factors that admissions officers evaluate when making their decisions. Academic performance, teacher evaluations and the essay can be much more important than any single test score.

In short: The scores count, but they are not the most important factor in admissions decisions. Don't take yourself out of the running if you don't get a "high" score.

MYTH #3: There is nothing you can do to prepare for the tests.

The test makers would like you to believe that you cannot prepare for their tests. They are wrong. To score well, you must practice and study. Fortunately, there are many ways to study the material you will be tested on as well as to improve your test-taking skills. The tips given in this chapter will help you prepare for these tests effectively.

Now that we have dispelled some of the myths that surround these tests, let's take a look at each test in more detail and see how you can improve your scores.

The Ingredients of the Alphabet Soup of Tests

The name of each college test is an acronym, and when you put them together, there are enough letters for an alphabet soup. Here are the ingredients of the alphabet soup of tests: the SAT, SAT Subject Tests, ACT, PSAT, AP, IB exams and for non-native English speakers, the TOEFL. In case you are not yet familiar with these tests, it's time to get acquainted. After all, you can't start studying for a test unless you know what will be on it. For more information on how to register for each test, refer to the Appendix.

The SAT

The SAT is the granddaddy of all the tests, the one to which most preparatory manuals and courses are devoted and the one that often creates the most anxiety. The SAT covers two general areas in three hours—math and evidence-based reading and writing. There is an optional essay test that is 50 minutes. The math section and reading and writing section are each scored between 200 and 800 for a combined possible score of 1600. There are insight scores from 10 to 40 in three areas: reading, writing and language and math. The optional essay test has three subscores between two and eight in reading, analysis and writing.

The Math Test

Arithmetic, algebra I and II, geometry and some trigonometry are tested. This sounds simple, but under the pressure of the clock and knowing the importance of the exam, it can be a challenge. The Math Test is a total of 80 minutes, broken down into one 55-minute section of 38 questions with a calculator and one 25-minute section of 20 questions without a calculator.

The key is to go into the exam with an intimate knowledge of the different types of questions. Later in this chapter, we will give you specific strategies on how to attack the math questions; but first, here is a sample of each type of question:

Multiple Choice With Four Possible Answers. For example, JoJo, Junior and Jiji got in a fight over x number of jelly beans. If JoJo ended up with three times as many jelly beans as Junior and if Jiji ended up with twice as many jelly beans as JoJo, how many jelly beans did Junior end up with, in relation to x?

   (A) x/3   (B) x/5   (C) x/6   (D) x/10

(*Answer:* JoJo had three times as many jelly beans as Junior. If Junior had n jelly beans, then JoJo had 3n jelly beans. JiJi had two times as many jelly beans as JoJo, which is 6n jelly beans. All of their jelly beans added together equal x, meaning n + 3n + 6n =x or 10n=x. We are trying to figure out how many jelly beans Junior had. Since he had n jelly beans, we could divide 10n=x by 10. This would result in n=x/10. Answer: D.)

Student-Produced Response or Grid-in. You will provide your own answer to a question like this one: A poll was conducted at a high school with 1,000 students to see who the "super popular" kids were. The rules stated that the students must first be rated "popular" in order to be judged "super popular." If 30 percent of the students were rated "popular," and 70 percent of the "popular" students were voted "super popular," how many students were "super popular"?

(*Answer:* 1,000 students x .30 = 300 "popular" students. 300 x .70 = 210 "super popular" students. Answer: 210 students.)

That's it for the Math Test. Did you get the right answers? If not, it's time to pull out those old math books!

In keeping with the movement toward machines over human thought, you may now use a calculator on part of the Math Test. Don't start celebrating yet, thinking that your friend the calculator will do all the work for you. None of the problems on the exam can be solved with a simple click of a few keys; you have to invest some brain power as well. In fact, the SAT gurus recommend that you don't use your calculator on every problem. Some are still faster to solve the archaic pencil and paper way.

The Evidence-Based Reading and Writing Test

There are two sections in the Evidence-Based Reading and Writing Test: a 65-minute reading section and a 35-minute language and writing section.

Reading. All 52 questions on this part of the test are multiple-choice with four choices. There are reading passages, pairs of passages and informational graphics, which are tables, graphs or charts. On each test, there will be:

- One passage from U.S. or world literature

- One passage or a pair of passages from either a U.S. founding document or related document such as the U.S. Constitution or a speech by a prominent world leader

- One passage about economics, psychology, sociology or another social science

- Two passages or one passage and a pair of passages about science

The Reading Test measures your ability to use evidence in a passage, understand the context of words and analyze passages in history/social science and science.

Writing and Language. This 44-question test is all multiple-choice and requires you to read 400- to 450-word passages and improve them. The passages are non-fiction and cover careers, history, social science, the humanities and science. During this part of the exam, analysis of evidence, word context, analysis of ideas and standard English are tested.

The Essay Test

The Essay Test is optional, although some colleges require it. During the 50-minute exam, you will read a 650- to 750-word passage, describe the author's argument in the passage and use evidence as support. The test is designed to measure reading comprehension, ability to analyze and writing skills. The purpose of the essay is to demonstrate how you organize your thoughts and support a main idea. Many students worry about the subjectivity of an essay on the SAT, but the College Board has a team of trained high school and college teachers who read the essays and evaluate them on a scale of one to four.

SAT Scoring

The SAT has a complex scoring structure:

- Total score (400-1600): Sum of math and evidence-based reading and writing scores

- Two section scores (200-800): Evidence-based reading and writing and math

- Three test scores (10-40): Reading, writing and language and math

- Seven sub-scores (1-15): Reading and writing and language: command of evidence and words in context. Writing and language: expression of ideas and standard English conventions. Math: heart of algebra, problem solving and data analysis and passport to advanced math

- Two cross-test scores (10-40): Analysis in history/social studies and analysis in science

- Three SAT Essay scores (2-8): Reading, analysis and writing

The PSAT/NMSQT, PSAT 10 and PSAT 8/9

Don't think that before senior year you will miss out on all the fun of taking the alphabet soup of tests. You have the opportunity to take the PSAT/NMSQT (Preliminary Scholastic Assessment Test/National Merit Scholarship Qualifying Test), PSAT 10 or PSAT 8/9 as practice for the real thing, the SAT. Typically, juniors take the PSAT/NMSQT exam and sophomores take the PSAT 10, although sophomores may also take the PSAT. The PSAT 8/9 is administered to eighth and ninth grade students.

The format is similar to the SAT although the test is shorter, clocking in at two hours and 45 minutes for the PSAT and PSAT 10 and 2 hours and 25 minutes for the PSAT 8/9. For all exams, there is an Evidence-Based Reading and Writing Test and a Math Test.

Scoring for the PSAT and PSAT 10 has a common scale with the SAT although the scale is slightly modified with a total score of 320 to 1520, two section scores of 160 to 760 and test scores of 8 to 38. The PSAT 8/9 has a total score range of 240 to 1440, two section scores of 120 to 720 and test scores of 6 to 36. There are subscores as well for each test.

For the PSAT and PSAT 10, there are 47 questions in 60 minutes for the Reading Test, 44 questions in 35 minutes for the Writing and Language Test and 48 questions in 70 minutes for the Math Test. For the PSAT 8/9, there are 42 questions in 55 minutes for the Reading Test, 40 questions in 30 minutes for the Writing and Language Test and 38 questions in 60 minutes for the Math Test. There is no Essay Test.

While your PSAT scores will not affect your admission into college, taking the exam will make you eligible for scholarship and special programs, including the following:

National Merit Scholarship or National Achievement Scholarship: The National Merit Scholarship Corporation identifies students who score high on the PSAT as Semifinalists. Based on additional achievements, scholarships are awarded by the Merit program and businesses.

National Hispanic Recognition Program: Assists academically qualified Hispanic or Latino students by identifying them to colleges to recruit them and offer financial aid to them.

National Scholarship Service: Assists African-American students with an advisory service and by referring them to colleges.

The Telluride Association: Offers academically talented juniors summer programs in the humanities and social sciences.

In addition, you can choose to participate in the Student Search Service, which provides your contact information to colleges. If you take part, you will receive informational brochures on colleges and their financial aid programs. If you score well, expect your mailbox to be full!

It's not required, but it's a good idea to take the PSAT during your junior year. You will get an idea of how you might perform on the SAT, gain valuable practice for the SAT and you may also win some money for college.

The SAT Subject Tests

The SAT subject tests consist of 20 exams in five subject areas: English, Math, History, Science and Language. Thankfully, you don't have to take all of them.

Individual schools may have different requirements for the tests, but most colleges and universities require that students take three exams. Colleges use your scores on the SAT exams as an additional measure of your academic ability, a way to assess your performance in specific subjects and sometimes as a method for determining which level courses you should take in college.

The SAT tests are based on an 800-point scale, with subscores ranging from 20 to 80. Each exam lasts one hour. The Subject Tests are as follows:

English
Literature

History and Social Studies
U.S. History
World History

Mathematics
Mathematics Level 1
Mathematics Level 2

Science
Biology/EM
Chemistry
Physics

Languages
Chinese with Listening
French
French with Listening
German
German with Listening
Spanish
Spanish with Listening
Modern Hebrew
Italian
Latin
Japanese with Listening
Korean with Listening

The ACT

There is one way you can get out of taking the SAT. That is by taking another standardized test—the ACT. Most colleges accept either SAT or ACT scores.

The ACT lasts almost three hours and covers four subject areas: English, Math, Reading and Science. You will receive a score for each of the four subject areas and a composite (average) score for the entire test between 1 (the lowest possible score) and 36 (the highest possible score). The sub-scores range from 1 (lowest) to 18 (highest). Approximately half of students tend to earn composite scores of about 20 or higher.

There are four additional scores reported: English Language Arts (1-36), the average of the English, reading and writing scores; STEM (1-36), average of the math and science scores; Understanding Complex Texts (below proficient, proficient or above proficient), based on the reading test; and Progress Toward Career Readiness (1-36), an indicator for the ACT National Career Readiness Certificate, a career-focused credential.

The components of the ACT are the following:

The English Test (75 questions, 45 minutes). You'd better bone up on your parts of speech and comma placement because this part of the ACT has multiple-choice questions covering three areas: standard-written English (punctuation, grammar and sentence structure), production of writing (understanding the "purpose and focus of a piece of writing") and knowledge of language (word choice, style and tone). To test these skills, there are five reading passages, with questions about the passages and questions in which you select ways to improve the passage. You will receive four scores from the English Test: an overall score based on all 75 questions, a sub-score for Conventions of Standard English based on 40 questions, a sub-score for Production of Writing based on 23 questions and a sub-score for Knowledge of Language based on 12 questions.

The Optional Writing Test (1 prompt, 40 minutes). The writing test will allow you to demonstrate your skills through an essay. The prompt presents an issue and three perspectives. You will select a stand on the issue, either using one of the points of view given or your own point of view. This is an optional component of the ACT as colleges will decide whether or not to require this part of the exam. By taking the optional Writing Test, you will receive two additional scores, a Writing Test sub-score and an English Language Arts score (combines English, Reading and Writing scores). The overall Writing Test score is from 2 to 12, and there are four subscores for Ideas and Analysis, Development and Support, Organization and Language Use and Conventions. The score from this test does not change the subject area scores of the ACT or your composite score.

The Math Test (60 questions, 60 minutes). This test has multiple-choice questions covering mathematics courses taken up until the 12th grade: Number and Quantity (7 to 10 percent), Algebra (12 to 15 percent), Functions (12 to 15 percent), Geometry (12 to 15 percent) and Statistics and Probability (8 to 12 percent). Like the SAT, the ACT allows you to use a calculator. You will receive an overall score based on all 60 questions and sub-scores for each of the five subject areas.

The Reading Test (40 questions, 35 minutes). This test contains four college freshman-level reading passages on topics that range from the relationship between hunting and art in the Paleolithic era to the role of women in the development of Japanese literature. Following each passage are multiple-choice questions that test your understanding of the information presented and the inferences that you draw from the material. The passages cover a variety of areas including these: social studies, the natural sciences, prose fiction and the humanities. You will receive an overall Reading Test score based on all 40 questions and sub-scores for Key Ideas and Details, Craft and Structure and Integration of Knowledge and Ideas.

The Science Reasoning Test (40 questions, 35 minutes). You will read a series of seven reports on scientific experiments and mini-studies and then answer multiple-choice questions. There are three areas covered: data representation (graphs, tables and diagrams); research summaries (descriptions of related experiments) and conflicting viewpoints (descriptions of related and contrary perspectives). You will receive an overall score for the Science Reasoning Test and three category scores on Interpretation of Data, Scientific Investigation and Evaluation of Models, Inferences and Experimental Results.

For more information, refer to *Preparing for the ACT* available from your counselor or from the ACT at www.act.org.

Duel of the Three-Letter Acronyms: The SAT vs. ACT

Unfortunately, we have a lapse in our powers of divination and can not predict on which test you will score higher. However, you can make an educated guess by understanding what each test covers and how they are structured and scored. The main differences between the two exams are as follows:

Content

- The ACT contains the Science Reasoning Test which covers the use of data representation, research summaries and conflicting viewpoints in the natural sciences. The SAT does not.

- About 7 percent of the ACT math questions are based on trigonometry. The SAT does not test trigonometry.

Structure

- The test questions on the SAT get increasingly harder within each section. They do not on the ACT.

- The ACT is all multiple choice. The SAT has "Student-Produced Response" mathematics questions.

- Both tests are about three hours long. The ACT has 215 questions while the SAT has about 154, meaning that you will have less average time to spend on each question on the ACT.

Scoring

- There is no longer a penalty for wrong answers on the SAT. There is also no penalty on the ACT.

- For the ACT there are scores for the four components of the test, two insight scores and a composite score that is the average of the four scores. The SAT is broken into the Math, Reading and Writing scores as well as numerous sub-scores and insight scores.

Our advice: Check out the requirements for the schools to which you are interested in applying. Some accept both exams, but some prefer one. Then, take practice exams in books or online and opt for whichever you score higher on and the one that makes you feel most confident.

Advanced Placement Tests (APs)

Advanced Placement exams (APs) are the only exams that have the potential to make your parents love you more than they already do. If you take enough of these tests, which allow you to earn college credit, you can knock a year off your college career. This means, of course, that you also knock a year's worth of tuition off your parents' tab. However, be aware that each college has its own rules on converting AP scores to credit.

APs are different from the other exams: They can be taken any time during high school and they are not required by colleges. Many schools offer courses to prepare for the exams, although you don't have to take an AP course in order to take a test. The benefits of taking these exams are earning college credit without even stepping onto a college campus as well as impressing admissions officers with your academic abilities. If you have taken some honors or AP courses, take the AP exams in the areas in which you are strong even if you don't intend to graduate early. Again, they demonstrate to the colleges that you can handle college coursework.

The AP exams are scored on a scale of one to five, with five signifying that you are practically ready to *teach* your own course on the subject, and one basically signifying that you wrote your name on the exam. (Most colleges consider a score of three or higher "passing".) AP tests are given in the following areas:

AP Capstone
AP Research
AP Seminar

Arts
AP Art History
AP Music Theory
AP Studio Art: 2-D Design
AP Studio Art: 3-D Design
AP Studio Art: Drawing

English
AP English Language and
Composition
AP English Literature and Composition

History & Social Science
AP Comparative Government and
Politics
AP European History
AP Human Geography
AP Macroeconomics
AP Microeconomics
AP Psychology
AP United States Government and
Politics
AP United States History
AP World History: Modern

Math & Computer Science
AP Calculus AB
AP Calculus BC
AP Computer Science A
AP Computer Science Principles
AP Statistics

Sciences
AP Biology
AP Chemistry
AP Environmental Science
AP Physics C: Electricity and
Magnetism
AP Physics C: Mechanics
AP Physics 1: Algebra-Based
AP Physics 2: Algebra-Based

World Languages & Cultures
AP Chinese Language and Culture
AP French Language and Culture
AP German Language and Culture
AP Italian Language and Culture
AP Japanese Language and Culture
AP Latin
AP Spanish Language and Culture
AP Spanish Literature and Culture

An additional benefit of taking AP exams is that you may qualify for an AP Scholar Award. These are not monetary awards but are noted on score reports sent to colleges. They are based on the number of AP exams in which you score three or higher. For example, the distinction of AP Scholar is given to students who score three or higher on three or more full-year or equivalent AP exams.

International Baccalaureate Program
Headquartered in Switzerland, the International Baccalaureate (IB) organization offers an international educational program with over 1,000 participating schools in 100 countries. The Middle Years program is for students ages 11 to 16, and the Diploma Programme is for students ages 16 to 19. Similar

to AP exams, IB exams qualify students to enter college with sophomore standing.

There are three core areas and six academic areas:

CORE AREAS

Theory of Knowledge: Designed to enhance critical thinking experiences inside and outside of the classroom.

Creativity, activity, service: Encourages non-academic work in theater, sports, community service and other extracurricular activities.

Extended Essay: 4,000-word essay containing original research in one of 60 subjects.

ACADEMIC AREAS

Studies in Language and Literature

Language Acquisition

Individuals and Societies: Business and management, economics, geography, history, information technology in a global society, philosophy, psychology, social and cultural anthropology and world religions.

Sciences

Mathematics

Arts

Students take IB exams, which are graded from 1 (the lowest score) to 7 (the highest score possible). To receive a diploma, students must earn a minimum of 24 points and complete the three core areas. The highest score possible is 45, seven points each on six exams and one point for each of the three core areas. Even if you don't earn an IB diploma, the courses show that you challenge yourself academically.

TOEFL

The Test of English as a Foreign Language (TOEFL) measures English proficiency and is for international students whose native language is not English and some residents who are recent immigrants.

More than 2,400 colleges and universities in the U.S. require TOEFL scores for incoming international students. There are four sections to the Internet-based exam: Reading, Listening, Speaking and Writing Skills.

For more information, visit the TOEFL website at www.ets.org/toefl.

How to Increase Your Scores

If you are like a friend of ours from Harvard who was one question short of a perfect score on the SAT and knows precisely which question he missed, you have absolutely nothing to worry about when it comes to your scores. Maybe the next time around you'll achieve perfection.

But if you are like the rest of us and need to increase your score, there is plenty that you can do. In fact, the paragraphs that follow list and explain the strategies that we used to increase our own SAT scores. We chose to take the SAT, but these are general test-taking strategies that are applicable to all of the college entrance exams.

Before we get to the good stuff on how you can pump up your scores, know that preparation requires time: The earlier you begin preparing for the tests and becoming familiar with their formats, the higher your scores will be. If it's already too late to give yourself an early start (meaning that the time remaining before you must take the test can be measured in days or even hours), don't try to cram but just focus on staying calm. Become as familiar as possible with the structure and directions of the exams and do the best that you can. If you have several weeks or months before the tests, read the sections that follow to see what you should do.

Become familiar with the format, content and timing of the exams. Figure out how long it takes you to complete a section. Try to get a feel for when you have spent too long on one question and should move on. Don't forget to study the actual answer sheet so you know which bubbles to fill.

Know the directions by heart. By knowing the directions, you won't waste valuable time reading them during the exam.

Take practice exams. You can probably think of about a gazillion other things you'd rather do in your free time than take tests, but unfortunately, there is no better way to prepare for these tests than to take them for practice. And there are no better tests to take than those that have actually been given. There are previous exams and test questions on the websites of the College Board for the SAT and AP exams and ACT. It is best to take these real previous tests because they will be most similar to the actual exams that you will be facing.

For the other exams, scout out a bookstore for test preparation books or online. With the hundreds of titles available, you will have no problem finding one for your test.

Don't cheat! Take the practice tests under the same conditions as the actual test. Time each section and stop when you are supposed to. Don't use your phone, books or other aids to check your answers. Don't take a break in the middle of a section to watch a TV show and then come back to it later. Use a number two pencil and fill in the ovals on the answer sheet, and practice with the calculator that you will use on the real test.

Grade your tests. Look at the questions you missed and find out why you missed them. You may see a pattern develop after taking several practice tests and you will want to review the material you don't know well. If you ran out of time before you finished, figure out which areas took the most time. It may be better to save these parts until last and do the areas that you are confident you can answer more quickly first. Remember that the SAT questions are arranged in an ascending order of difficulty, yet they are all worth the same points. So do the easy ones first and when you have extra time tackle the harder ones. Remember that the questions on the ACT are *not* in order of increasing difficulty.

Review old notes and textbooks. It would be great if we could remember everything that we once read or learned, but unfortunately, as we all know from the experience of cramming the night before for exams, we can't. Thus it is necessary, especially for the Math, AP and SAT Subject Tests, to dig out your forgotten notes and dust-covered textbooks from years before to review.

Identify and work on foreign material. You may have taken a course that matches one of the AP or SAT Subject Tests, but you may not have covered all of the material that is included on the test (or you may not remember it even if you did). Commit to covering it now. Get more information on the areas that each test covers at www.collegeboard.org.

Think about coughing up a few hundred bucks for a review class. Want to raise your SAT score by 150 points? How much are you willing to pay? As you probably already know, there are countless businesses that are designed to prepare students for standardized tests. They often specialize in courses for the SAT or ACT, and some of them even promise that your scores, as determined by tests taken before and after their course, will increase by a specific number of points.

It would be really nice if the businesses could always deliver on their promises and if you had the several hundred dollars or so to pay for the course. Unfortunately, not every business delivers, and not everyone has this kind of spare change.

Still, don't rule out test preparation courses. If you have the money or you can convince your parents that this is a worthy investment, test preparation courses are good for students who find it difficult to motivate themselves to study on their own. Courses also offer helpful shortcuts, review of materials and practice.

We suggest that you take advantage of the free introductions that many of the test preparation businesses offer even if you don't plan to take the course. During these introductory meetings, they usually offer tips and hints. You'll also have the opportunity to take a practice exam under real test-taking conditions. By attending an introductory meeting, you'll get a better idea of whether a test preparation course is for you. Best of all, it's free!

Don't overlook test preparation courses offered by your school or local college. Many high schools offer some form of free after-school test prep. If your school does not, make such a suggestion to your teachers and administration.

If you are comfortable studying online, Khan Academy offers free SAT test preparation in partnership with the College Board, the makers of the SAT. If you have the self-discipline to study independently, this is an incredible free option.

Set up your own review schedule. Of course, you can always prep yourself. But you will need to be serious and disciplined to do so. Set up a study schedule with specific dates that you will give yourself real tests under actual conditions. And, needless to say, make sure you religiously stick to your plan.

How to Master English and Reading Tests

Read like crazy. The more you read, the faster you'll read, which is important for the SAT Reading and Writing questions and ACT Reading Test. Start reading everything you can, covering as many subject areas, writing styles and viewpoints as possible. Always read with a dictionary and look up unfamiliar words. Be sure to read works that are of literary merit and that cover a broad range of subjects such as *The New Yorker, New York Times, National Geographic, Newsweek* or *Harper's*.

Study vocabulary as often as you brush your teeth. (Which we hope is at least twice a day!) One of the secrets to success for verbal and reading tests is vocabulary, pure and simple. Even though an exam may not test vocabulary directly, it is essential to scoring well on the reading comprehension, sentence structure analysis and writing tests.

Use a vocabulary builder book or app. There are literally thousands of books offering different methods for remembering vocabulary words. Select the method that works best for you and use it. Set a goal—one chapter, 25 words a week or whatever is realistic for you—and, most important, stick to it.

Study etymology, the origins of words. By studying etymology, you can learn the historical roots of words. Often these roots can be used to figure out the meaning of the words that you don't know. In fact, by understanding how these root words combine, you can often figure out the meaning of hundreds of other words.

If all this root talk is confusing you, take a look at the following example. By studying etymology, you would learn that "bio" means life and "log" means the study of. Hence, "biology" is the study of life. Now you may have already known this, but with etymology you could also figure out (or at least take a good guess at) the meanings of such words as "biosphere," "biorhythm," "toxicology," "microbiology," "symbiosis," "sociology," "astrology" and "ethnology." By studying a few roots, you can decipher a tremendous number of other words. A great etymology-based book to try is *Word Power Made Easy*.

Carry flashcards wherever you go or download a flashcard app. Make vocabulary flashcards of unknown words, and carry them *everywhere*. That way you can make the most of your time studying while standing in line, waiting for the bus or even during a lull in a telephone conversation with your boyfriend or girlfriend (be discreet). You'd be surprised how many words you can learn in your spare time.

Get Mom and Dad involved. To help motivate you to follow through on your study plans, offer Mom and Dad the following proposition: Using one or more of the above methods, if you manage to meet your goal of learning X number of words per week, they reward you with $5 for that week. By the time your exam rolls around, you will not only be ready to ace the reading and writing sections but will have accumulated a sizable nest egg! If your parents won't go for this, consider paying yourself $5 a week to be used for anything you want after you take the test.

Remember that words can have multiple meanings. You may be thinking of one definition of a word while the test makers have another in mind. Study multiple definitions of a word since often, especially on the harder questions, the test makers will use the less-common meaning of a word.

Practice timed essay-writing. While writing practice essays in your spare time may not be your definition of fun, it will help boost your scores. Timed essays are not only a major part of the SAT Writing, ACT and AP tests but also of college mid-terms and finals. To prepare for the essays, gather the essay questions from previous tests, and practice writing essays within the given time limit. Here are some tips for timed essay-writing:

- **Have something to say.** You can be an incredibly talented writer, but without an idea to express, your essays will flop. You'd be surprised to learn just how many decent writers bomb the test because they simply don't have an idea to convey. Before you start writing, think about the question and plan out your answer. Make sure your essay has a clearly defined thesis statement.

- **Think of several canned introductions that can be applied to a variety of topics.** Find a few quotes (but ones that are not so well known that they have become clichés) that you could use to start your essay. Also think of a few good analogies.

- **I (Gen) liked the analogy of the "keystone," which if you know something about architecture, was the final stone placed in old stone bridges and archways to hold the whole structure together.** It was fairly easy to compare something to the "keystone," explaining how such-and-such a topic exemplified "keystone" qualities. Thinking of a few canned introductions will save you time and let you concentrate on the body of the essay, which is really where you should devote most of your writing time.

- **Keep your essays clear and organized.** Because the test graders are required to read a number of essays, they need to read quickly and efficiently. Help your ideas jump out at the readers by underlining your main points, especially if you have written a rather complex essay. If you run out of time, write a quick outline of your remaining points. This way the grader will know where you were headed and will most likely give you some points for it.

- **Find a kind soul to read your work.** It will be helpful to get feedback on your essay-writing style from someone else. Teachers make great editors. Share some of your samples, and ask for any suggestions for improvement.

- **Use examples.** To illustrate your points, use examples to show your mastery of the material and your writing skills.

- **Don't be a perfectionist.** The readers know you had a limited amount of time in which to write your essay. Get your thoughts out quickly, and don't get stuck trying to make a sentence perfect.

For reading comprehension questions, sneak a peek at the questions before reading the passage. If you scan the questions quickly before the passage, you will have a basic idea of what you are looking for when you read. Note: Some students find that reading the questions first does not help them since it takes too much time. Try practicing both ways before you actually take the test and do what works best for you.

Mark key parts when reading so you can find them easily when you are answering the questions. Certain words like "but," "however," and "except for" can completely change the meaning of a sentence. When you encounter these words, mark them in your test booklet. If an answer looks like it comes from one of these sentences, be extra sure that you know what the sentence actually means.

Note the style and attitude of the writer in the reading passages. Knowing this could help you select the correct answers by better understanding the author's point of view on a subject. Plus, there is almost always a question that asks you to guess the author's opinion or to select an appropriate title for the passage, both of which require that you have understood the author's position and attitude. This tip will help not only with Reading and English tests but also with the ACT Science Reasoning Test.

Read your answer (silently) to yourself. After you have selected your answer, double check that it is correct by reading it to yourself.

Do the quicker questions first on the SAT Reading and Writing sections. Since all questions are worth the same amount of points, do the ones that take you less time before the ones that take longer to decipher and complete.

Number Hunching and Crunching: How to Be a Math Whiz

You may be more creative than the test makers. When taking practice exams, you may discover that you found the answer in a different way than is presented in the answer key. That's okay. There are often several ways to arrive at most correct answers. What's important is not *how* you get it but *what* you get.

Memorize algebra and geometry formulas. Make a song of them, hypnotize yourself or chant them for 15 minutes a day. We don't care how you do it, just make sure you know the formulas cold. Although all the formulas you'll need will be given in the test booklet, don't rely on them since it will only waste your time flipping back and forth between pages. Plus, memorizing the formulas will help you to understand how to actually use them.

Experiment with different methods for solving problems. For some math problems that involve complicated formulas or a number of steps, it is easier to work backwards. To do this, plug the possible answers into the problem and then do the calculations, using that number. When you are taking practice tests, figure out if this method works for you, and if it does, decide on which kinds of problems it is most effective.

Plug in numbers for variables. On problems with complicated formulas and a number of variables, it can be faster to plug in actual numbers for each variable than to use formulas to figure out what the variables are.

Estimate if you can. If you see that the answers vary widely, use rounded off numbers in your calculations. For example, you can round off 4,867 X 6,732 to 5,000 X 7,000, which would give you 35,000,000. By estimating, you can easily eliminate choices that are not close to 35 million such as 35,000 or 35 billion.

Beware of the traps. When test writers design tests, they include a number of traps that catch most students. Don't be fooled. Typical tricks test makers try to get away with include these: 1) giving more information than you need to solve a problem which can waste a lot of time, 2) offering incorrect choices that you can arrive at by partially completing the problem or by using the correct information with wrong calculations and 3) giving numbers in the answer choices that remind you of numbers in the equation. Be cautious of answers that seem too easy to calculate, especially at the end of the SAT Math section when the problems are supposed to be the most difficult. On these difficult problems, the easy answers are probably wrong.

Know how to answer the SAT grid-in questions. There are no negative answers or answers greater than 9,999. Percentages must be filled in as .75 or 3/4, *not* 75.

Get friendly with your calculator. Use a reliable calculator with which you are familiar and take a backup just in case you need it.

The Day Before the Big Event

As the test day approaches, focus your energy on making sure that you are prepared. Review the directions and answer sheets. Being familiar with these is one of the most important things you can do.

Make sure the batteries are working in your calculator or any other devices you'll need (e.g., CD player for SAT Language Subject Tests with Listening).

Gather all of the materials you'll need such as these: admission ticket, identification, number two pencils, erasers, calculator (two if possible), non-beeping wristwatch, snack and CD player with earphones (if needed for SAT Language Subject Test with Listening).

Don't forget to get lots of zzz's. A rested mind is your best test taking resource.

Test Time Tips

Knowing that your performance on the standardized tests will be used by admissions officers in their evaluation, it's perfectly natural for you to feel nervous when the actual day arrives. Try to calm your nerves by keeping in mind that your scores are only one factor of many that the admissions committee will take into account. If you are a junior or are taking the test early in your senior year, you will also be able to take the test again, if need be. When taking the exams, it is most important that you try to stay calm so that you can think clearly. The following are strategies to use during the actual exams.

Pace yourself. It is natural for you to be nervous when the test first starts, but try to remain focused. Neither sprint through the test nor lag behind. Keeping with the race analogy, pace yourself. If you speed through the exam, you will make careless errors. But if you take too much time on each question, you won't be able to finish within the allotted time period. Since you will have taken a number of tests for practice already, you should know just how fast you need to go.

Tick tock. Watch the clock. Make a note of the finish time of each section so you can pace yourself and leave enough time to get to all the questions.

Read all questions carefully and completely. Don't start figuring out the answer until you have all the information.

Consider all of the choices. After you have found what you believe to be the correct answer, look at the other choices too. There may be a better answer. Realize that an answer by itself may be true, but it still may not be the answer to the question. You must select the BEST answer.

Cross out the choices you know are incorrect so that you don't waste time reading them again. So much hype has been given to not making "stray marks" on test answer sheets that some students forget they can mark on their test *booklets*. Use the spaces in the margin of your test booklet to make notes and certainly cross out wrong answers as you eliminate them. You will find more ideas on how to use your test booklet in another paragraph in this section. Your test booklet itself can be an important tool for acing these tests.

It's not your imagination; the questions do get increasingly harder on the SAT. Except for the SAT Reading Section, the questions are arranged in increasing order of difficulty in each section. (In the Reading Section, the passages increase in difficulty, but the questions following the passages are in no particular order of difficulty.)

Knowing this, it is best for you to start at the beginning and answer the easier questions first. Remember that question #10 will be much harder than question #3. As you progress toward the end of the section, be very wary of answers that seem too easy since these will most likely be tricks and will not be correct.

If you can't get the answer, move on. Don't spend too much time on any one question. Mark ones you can't figure out, and come back to them if you have time at the end.

Don't be afraid to guess. For the SAT and ACT, guess even if you don't know the answer. There's no penalty! The same goes for the grid-in questions.

Examine the answers. Knowing how they differ may help you pick the right answer or at least make an educated guess.

Mark up your test booklet. Remember that it's the answer key you must avoid "marking up." Extra lines or marks could confuse the grading machines and cost you points, so you don't want to risk making stray marks on the key that the computer might pick up as an answer. However, your test booklet is quite another matter. Underline key parts of reading passages. Circle important numbers in mathematical problems. Use the white space in your booklets to do calculations. The test graders are not judging you on how much you can do in your head, so mark up your test booklet as much as you want.

Bubble correctly. It's common sense but bubbling "off count" has been done incorrectly often enough to merit mention. Make sure that you fill the correct bubble, especially when you skip questions. Since the answer sheets are boxed by fives, you can check to see that you are on the correct question every five questions. It only takes a second and it can save you having to go back over ten or even twenty problems because you discover on question number 32 that you are bubbling in 31.

Bring a snack. There will be a short break when you will be able to use the bathroom, get a drink of water and commiserate with your fellow test-takers. At this time you may want to wolf down a satisfying *Snickers* to give you that burst of sugar-induced energy that can get you through the second half of the exam.

A Timeline for Testing

Here is a quick summary of when to take the tests:

PSAT: The exam is in October. Definitely take it in your junior year. We recommend taking the PSAT 10 in your sophomore year for even more practice.

SAT: The exam is given throughout the school year. Take it in the spring of your junior year at least once and if you are not happy with the scores, try it again in the fall of your senior year. For early admissions, you may need to take the exam in the fall and spring of your junior year.

SAT Subject Tests: The exams are given throughout the school year. Take them as soon as possible after you have completed the related courses, unless you are signed up for a more advanced related course. You should plan to take the subject tests in the spring of your junior year or fall of your senior year. The point is to take the tests as quickly as possible after completion of the related course. It is easy to forget how to conjugate "estar" in Spanish or the intimacies of the causes of the American Revolution.

ACT: The exam is given throughout the school year. Take it at least once in the spring of your junior year and, if necessary, the fall of your senior year. For early admissions, you must take the ACT in the fall or spring of your junior year.

APs: The exams are given in May. Take them as soon as possible after you have taken the related courses. Remember, if you take the AP exams as a senior, your scores will not help you with admission since you'll be all done by then. However, the scores can still help you earn college credit.

Remember that if you plan to apply for early admission, you will need to take your exams as early as possible. Check with each school for the deadline.

If you plan to take exams again in the fall of your senior year, spend the summer studying. Take the exams as early in the fall as you can because later in the fall, you will be busy completing applications and will not want to worry about taking more tests.

A Second Chance

If you feel like you didn't do as well as you could the first time you took the SAT or ACT, the good news is that studies show that students typically increase their scores the second time. We recommend that you take the SAT or ACT at least two or three times. Almost all colleges count your highest score for each individual section.

While colleges wouldn't hold it against you if you took the exam more than three times, be careful that you don't get *SAT Tunnel Vision*. This is where you become so obsessed with achieving a certain score that you devote all of your effort and time to preparing. This is a huge mistake. You do need to prepare for these exams. However, if you make them your only priority to the exclusion of other things like participation in activities, class work, sports and hobbies, you will set yourself up for failure. Plus, you'd probably much rather sleep in on a Saturday morning than take another test.

Score Choice and Superscore

With Score Choice you are able to select which SAT scores to send the colleges. You may choose the scores by date but not by section. With Superscore, you can send the highest possible composite score across multiple ACT tests and ACT Section Retests. Superscore calculates the average of the four best subject scores from each time you've taken the ACT. However, some colleges do not participate in these programs and still require that you send all of your test scores.

How to Deal With a Bombed Test

It's not the end of the world if you don't do as well on a test as you expected. If you have the time, you can take the test again. If not, then try not to worry (what's done is done) and instead spend the rest of your time writing a killer application. Concentrate on getting good grades and finding teachers who will write strong evaluations. You can prove to a college that you are academically capable in ways other than test scores. Remember that plenty of successful students have less-than-perfect test scores.

IN THIS CHAPTER

- How to get your share of the $241.3 billion in financial aid
- Financial aid mumbo jumbo explained
- Where to find the best scholarships
- Story from real life: How I paid for college $150 at a time
- Asking for more money from colleges

CHAPTER 11

HOW TO WIN FREE CASH FOR COLLEGE

Money Is Everything

One student we know was presented with a tempting proposal after he was accepted to Harvard. His parents told him that they would either:

A) Pay for him to go to Harvard or

B) Pay for him to go to a much cheaper state university AND buy him a brand new Mercedes.

This student chose to go to Harvard and by his senior year had finally saved up enough money to buy a very used Toyota Corolla. The point of this story is to emphasize (in terms we can all relate to) the truly incredible cost of college. This student's parents would have spent *much less* had he chosen Option B. In fact they would have had to purchase FOUR fully-loaded Mercedes before they would even come close to spending what it cost for his four-year education.

The stark reality is that the annual cost of college (and private schools are especially guilty) is *more than what some families earn in an entire year.* The price tag is staggering—an average of $21,370 per year for tuition and room and board at four-year public schools and $48,510 at private schools. These costs have grown approximately 30 percent over the past 10 years, and, as if that were not bad enough, the cost is continuing to rise.

So, of course, it makes sense that when speaking about a college education, money is a major concern. For some, money is the most important factor of all.

Fortunately, the government, colleges, businesses, foundations and civic organizations can help you foot the bill. Last year over $241.3 billion in financial aid and scholarships were awarded. However, despite this promising number, do not expect your college to simply hand over a stack of cash. It's going to take a little work to get a piece of this financial aid pie.

In this chapter, we will show you how to squeeze the most money out of the schools, government and scholarships. And who knows, if you are able to save your parents a ton of money on college tuition and prevent them from taking out a second mortgage, they just might buy you that new car for graduation!

Financial Aid Mumbo Jumbo Explained

Applying for financial aid is very much like filling out tax forms. While there is a lot of technical mumbo jumbo, there are a few essential concepts and terms that you need to know to understand the process. The first thing to understand is that financial aid comes in various forms from the government, colleges and private organizations. These include:

- **Grants or scholarships.** Money with virtually no strings attached— meaning you don't have to pay it back. This is really the equivalent of hitting the financial aid jackpot.

- **Federal Work-Study (FWS).** This is a program sponsored by the government in which you hold a part-time job, typically on campus or off campus at a nonprofit organization or public agency, while you are a student. The downside is, of course, that since you will have to work you will have less time to goof off! (Not that you would do that.)

- **Loans.** These are typically the easiest to qualify for but that's because they must be paid back with interest. However, you will find that the terms are often more generous than non-education loans.

- **State aid.** Individual states also award money, usually through their education agencies. Examples of state aid include the California's CalGrants and Georgia's Hope Scholarship. Each state administers its own aid programs for students so be sure to find out what type of money is available from your own state.

There are two general criteria for getting money for college. The first is called *need-based*. From the various financial aid forms that you submit, the colleges and government will determine how much you (that's right—you are expected to contribute to your own education) and your parents can afford to pay. The difference between this number and the annual cost of your college education will be your financial need, which will be met by a combination of grants, work-study and loans.

The second criterion is *merit-based*. Merit-based aid is awarded for skills or talents that are not related to students' financial need. For example, you can win scholarships based on your athletic, leadership or academic achievement.

Besides money from colleges and the government, another important source of financial aid is private *scholarships*. These can be need-based, merit-based or both, and are sponsored by groups including businesses, civic organizations, foundations, charities, churches and individuals. Scholarships often require the most work but can also be more lucrative, with the most generous covering full tuition and expenses.

Money From Uncle Sam: Federal Financial Aid

If you've ever wondered where your parents' hard-earned taxes go, here's part of the answer. A significant chunk goes toward funding student financial aid programs. This is your golden opportunity to get back some of your parents' tax dollars.

Almost all government aid is based on financial need, except for unsubsidized Stafford loans, PLUS loans and consolidation loans. Here are descriptions and details of the various types of federal aid for which you may qualify:

- **Federal Pell Grants.** For undergraduate students who have not earned a bachelor's or professional degree. The maximum award amount for each school year is $6,195 per student. They do not need to be repaid. It goes without saying that if you are offered a grant, take it!

- **Iraq and Afghanistan Service Grant.** These grants of up to $6,195 are for students whose parent or guardian died while serving in the U.S. Armed Forces. Students must meet all qualifications for Federal Pell Grants except for the financial need requirement.

- **Teacher Education Assistance for College and Higher Education Grants (TEACH Grants).** Providing up to $3,736 per year, these grants support students who agree to teach for at least four years in a public or private elementary or secondary school that serves students from low-income families.

- **Federal Direct Stafford Loans.** These loans are available from the government through the Direct Loan Program. They were previously also available from banks, credit unions and other lenders through the Federal Family Education Loan (FFEL) Program. These loans come in two forms: *subsidized*, awarded based on financial need in which

STORY FROM REAL LIFE
HOW I PAID FOR COLLEGE $150 AT A TIME

Are you feeling pessimistic about scholarships? Jenny was too until she won enough to be able to attend her first-choice college. The first step to winning is you gotta apply. —Gen and Kelly

I used to think that if I could be born again I'd want to be a Trump, Gates or Rockefeller. It's not that I have expensive tastes or that I need more money than I could possibly spend (although that would be nice), but when I realized how much it would cost to go to college it seemed like you practically had to be an heir or heiress to afford it.

I come from a middle class family. I have never had to seriously worry about money before. As a child I may not have gotten Barbie's Dream Mansion for Christmas, but I did always get a new Barbie doll. So when it came time to apply for college I was shocked when my parents had their first serious talk about money with me. They told me that after checking their finances, they couldn't afford to send me to an expensive private school unless I could find a way to raise about $8,000 a year on my own. A summer job and working part time during the school year would take care of about half that amount, but I was still short by $4,000.

Since I really wanted to go to a private college, I knew I had to find a way to get the money. I visited my counselor, who advised me to apply for some scholarships. I was surprised to find that there were quite a few scholarships available, ranging from the local Lions Club to Wendy's. I applied for every scholarship that I thought fit me. I had my doubts, however, and each time I mailed off a completed application I wondered if I was wasting my time.

Was I shocked when I actually won awards from nine groups for varying amounts between $150 and $2,000. In total I won over $5,000! What really made the difference were the little awards for $150 to $500 which added up quickly. With this money I was able to attend my dream (and very expensive) private school.

I've learned that if you make the effort, you can make almost any school affordable. The money is there—you just need to put in the work to get it.

—Jenny, who happily accepts any amount of free money

the government pays the interest for the loan until you begin to pay it off, and *unsubsidized*, in which you owe the interest as soon as you take out the loan. Typically, you begin to repay Direct Loans as soon as you graduate or leave school. The current maximum loan amounts are $5,500 for first-year students, $6,500 for second-year students, $7,500 for third-year and later students and $20,500 for graduate students. The interest rate is currently fixed at 4.53 percent. There is also a fee of up to 1.059 percent of the loan.

- **Federal PLUS Loans.** These are loans for your parents. The maximum amount that your parents can borrow is your Cost of Attendance minus other financial aid that you receive. For example, if your Cost of Attendance is $10,000 and you receive $6,000 in financial aid, the maximum amount your parents could borrow is $4,000. The interest rate is fixed at 7.08 percent for Direct PLUS Loans, and there is a fee for the loan of up to 4.236 percent. FFEL PLUS Loans from private lenders are no longer offered. Your parents will begin repaying the loan about two months after the final loan disbursement your senior year.

- **Consolidation Loans.** These combine the different federal student loans that you receive so that it is simpler—and less expensive—for you to repay them. The interest rate is fixed throughout the repayment period and is the weighted average of the loans being consolidated. To consolidate your loans, speak with your financial aid officer or visit https://studentaid.ed.gov/sa/repay-loans/consolidation.

The following types of aid are Campus-Based Programs, which means that they are administered by the college financial aid offices. The colleges are responsible for disbursing the funds they receive from the government for each program.

- **Federal Supplemental Educational Opportunity Grants (FSEOG).** Awarded to students with the greatest financial need. There is no guarantee that every eligible student will receive this type of grant because of their limited availability. The grants range from $100 to $4,000 per year.

- **Federal Work-Study (FWS).** This program will help provide you with a job so that you can work and study at the same time. Most jobs are on campus, although some, which usually involve work with non-profit or public agencies, are not.

For more information on federal aid programs, see the Appendix to contact the U.S. Department of Education.

All the Forms You Need to Fill Out

You will not appreciate the true monotony of filling out forms until you have finished applying for financial aid. You will calculate so many figures and fill in so many blanks that you will be begging for multiple-choice answers like those on the SAT.

Remember that while applying for financial aid from the colleges and the government can be a tedious process, it is well worth the effort.

You will need your parents' help in filling out the forms since they ask for tax return information and details of your family's income and assets. The following is a list of the major forms that you will need to complete:

- **Free Application For Federal Student Aid (FAFSA).** The government will use information from this form about you and your family to calculate your financial need and report the results to the colleges you have selected. After you are admitted, you will receive an aid package that may consist of grants, loans and work-study based on your need.

  This form is for U.S. citizens, permanent residents and eligible non-citizens. With questions about your family's income and assets, it can be completed on paper or via the Internet at www.fafsa.ed.gov. It is also available from your high school counseling office, the college financial aid offices and the Department of Education (see the Appendix). It should be completed as soon *after* October 1 as possible. The deadline for submitting the FAFSA for colleges to use it in their consideration is usually between mid-January and early February, but it can be earlier if you are applying for early admission or for state aid. Approximately one month after you submit the FAFSA, you will receive a Student Aid Report (SAR), which will indicate your Expected Family Contribution, the amount your family is expected to pay toward your education.

- **College Scholarship Service (CSS) Financial Aid PROFILE Service.** About 900 colleges, universities and scholarship programs accept or require this service for awarding aid. To register for the PROFILE, get a registration form from your high school counselor or college financial aid office, or go to the College Board website at www.collegeboard.org. In general, you should register as soon as possible. After you receive the PROFILE application, submit it as early as you can. Each college sets its own deadline, but the earliest deadline for registering is usually December 15, and the last deadline for submitting the application is usually between mid-January and early February. For early action, the deadlines are about two to three months earlier.

- **Business/Farm Supplement.** A part of the PROFILE application, this form is required of all students whose parents own a business or farm. Some colleges may require their own form instead of or in addition to the PROFILE form.

- **Non-custodial Parent's Statement.** Required from the non-custodial parent (whether divorced, separated or never married), this form is also a part of the PROFILE application. Note that some colleges may also require you to complete additional forms.

- **College's Financial Aid Form.** Some colleges have their own form with information about you and your family that you must complete. The colleges basically want to know your available assets—like that $20 million trust fund. However, this form also has a section where you can explain (often by attaching a separate letter) any special circumstances—such as an impending layoff of one of your parents or special medical expenses—that would affect your family's finances. Consult with your parents and don't be afraid to honestly describe your family's financial situation.

- **Federal Income Tax Returns.** The IRS isn't the only one who wants these. The colleges may need to see copies of your parents' and your federal tax forms and W-2 forms. Even if not required, you will need the information on these forms to complete your financial aid applications.

Tips for Filling Out the Forms

Here are some important guidelines to keep in mind while filling out the myriad forms.

- **Know which forms you need to complete.** Check with your school and scholarship programs and make a list of all the forms you are required to submit for each.

- **Dedicate the time needed.** A mistake that many students and parents make is not setting aside enough time to complete all the forms. Don't leave them until the last minute.

- **Follow directions.** Prevent delays in processing your paperwork by carefully reading and following directions.

- **Be thorough.** Complete every blank and include as much information as you have.

- **Be honest.** You don't want lies about your financial aid application coming to haunt you as a student. And you won't be a student for long if this happens.

- **Show that you need aid (if indeed you do).** If you are in need of support, which is the case for most students, demonstrate it. In the space provided on the application or in a separate letter, explain any factors that you think might affect your family's ability to pay you college expenses. Make sure to note any extenuating circumstances that the government or colleges may overlook. Such circumstances include unusual medical or dental expenses, costs for a sibling's education or a parent's recent unemployment.

- **Save copies as cheat sheets.** Make sure that you save a copy of all your forms. You will be using some of this information when applying to other scholarships and also when applying for aid for the following year. You've been through the grueling process once. Make it easier for yourself the next year by having a copy to use as a cheat sheet so that you don't have to look up all the information again.

- **Be on time.** Don't risk losing financial aid opportunities by turning in forms late.

- **Don't think you're on your own.** Take advantage of help from your high school, college financial aid office and the government's Federal Student Aid Information Center.

What Happens Next?

From the multitude of forms you need to complete and submit, colleges and the government want to determine your financial need. This figure is calculated by subtracting the Cost of Attendance (COA), the estimated annual cost of the college including tuition, room and board, books and supplies and travel expenses from your Expected Family Contribution (EFC), the amount you and your parents can reasonably contribute:

$$\frac{\text{Cost of Attendance (COA)}}{- \text{ Expected Family Contribution (EFC)}}$$
$$= \text{Financial Need}$$

Once the Financial Aid Administrator (FAA) at your college knows your financial need, he or she puts together a financial aid package.

Now that you know everything you need to fill out, sign and submit, you might not want to do it. Resist this temptation. Even if you do not think you qualify for financial aid, it doesn't hurt to apply. You may find that the work-study and low-interest loans are just what you need to round out your ability to pay your tuition. Also see the appendices for worksheets on calculating the colleges' cost of attendance and comparing financial aid offers from different colleges.

Scholarships: The Best Free Cash in the World

Money for future circus performers. Money for left-handed students. Money for children of Republicans. Scholarships award money for every kind of family background, interest and skill imaginable. Unlike college and government aid, many scholarships are based solely on students' academic and personal achievements rather than financial need. Plus, some are renewable for all four years of college.

However, don't count on a free ride just yet. Because they offer money with virtually no strings attached, scholarships are very competitive. But if you are willing to spend time locating scholarships that fit you and your background and dedicate effort to completing the applications, you will become a strong candidate to win some of this free cash for school.

Map to the Financial Aid Jackpots

Each year there are thousands of scholarships awarded by groups including colleges, businesses, unions, civic organizations, churches, clubs, foundations and individuals who wish to assist students and further the missions of their organizations. There are some groups that have marketing budgets to publicize their awards, but there are many that you will need to seek out and find. Some of the best places to find scholarships are right in front of you:

- **Scholarship directories.** Scholarship directories list the requirements and details for thousands of scholarships. Naturally, we recommend the directory and strategy guide that we wrote, *The Ultimate Scholarship Book* and *Get Free Cash for College*.

- **Counselor or financial aid office.** Meet with your high school counselor and someone from your college's financial aid office. Explain your background and achievements, and ask if there are scholarships for which you should apply or for which they can nominate you. Your guidance counselor will be particularly knowledgeable about local and regional scholarships. Keep in touch with him or her so that you will know what's available.

- **Internet.** Search free databases of scholarships on the Internet. Try www.moolahspot.com or our website www.supercollege.com to find awards that match your background and experience.

- **School activities.** Bands, newspapers, academic clubs, athletic organizations and service organizations often have scholarships for outstanding members. Inquire with the officers or advisors of the organization about scholarship funds.

- **Your parents' and your employers.** Many companies offer scholarships to their employees' children as a fringe benefit. Ask your parents to inquire with their employers' human resources department. They

STORY FROM REAL LIFE
HOW I GOT MY SCHOOL TO GIVE ME MORE MONEY

If you are dissatisfied with the financial aid package you are offered, do something about it. Speak with your financial aid officer and explain your circumstances, especially if something about your financial situation has changed. There may be nothing that your college can do, but it doesn't hurt to ask. —Gen and Kelly

I was ecstatic when I first opened the letter. I had been admitted to the private university of my dreams. However, my enthusiasm waned when my parents said that it was going to be difficult to pay for my education with only the small loan that the school offered. They wanted me to go to our state's public university instead, which had offered me a full scholarship. That was when I decided that I had to do everything I could to sweeten the deal from the private school.

I wrote them a letter explaining my situation. I said that I would love to attend the college but that the state university's offer of a full scholarship was difficult to refuse. Then, I asked if there was anything that they could do to make their offer more comparable. To my surprise the school responded by offering a $5,000 grant and a significantly larger loan. Of course I never told the financial aid officer that I would have attended the school even if they hadn't offered me anything else. But it sure would have been difficult on my family had I not asked for more aid.

—Christina, who is happy at her college and whose parents are even happier that their daughter made the bold move

should also check with any unions or professional organizations to which they belong.

- **Community organizations.** Groups such as Lions, Rotary, Kiwanis, American Legion and other civic groups often offer scholarships to local high school students. To find out where and when you need to apply, check with your guidance counselor or call or write the groups directly.

- **Local government.** Some cities and counties provide scholarships for local students. Call city hall to find out if such programs exist in your area.

- **Local businesses.** As a way to support their community, many local businesses provide awards to students.

- **Local newspaper.** Some local newspapers make announcements about students who win scholarships. Look at back issues to find out about awards and contact the sponsoring organizations to see if you can enter the next time the scholarship is offered.

Strategies for Winning Scholarships

Similar to applying for college, most scholarships require that you complete an application form, write an essay and submit reference letters. Some even require interviews with the judges. Because competition for scholarships can be high, you'll need to dedicate time to apply. Here are some strategies to maximize your chances:

Apply to those that fit you best. Don't let visions of dollar signs dancing in your head color your judgment. Groups that provide scholarships print guidelines and restrictions for a reason: They follow them. If you find a scholarship for students who plan to be future journalists, don't apply when all you've done is write a letter to the editor of the school newspaper. There are a lot of students who have written for their school newspapers since they were in kindergarten, and they will win the money. No matter how big the jackpot, don't apply for scholarships for which you do not meet the guidelines and restrictions.

Check out the competition. Before you decide to apply for any scholarship, know your competition. It may be better for you to concentrate your energy on applying to regional scholarships rather than national scholarships. In regional scholarships you will compete against the best students in your city or county, which is tough; but competing nationally is even tougher. Of course, don't *rule out* national scholarships. Many national scholarships offer significantly higher support than regional scholarships. After all, someone has to win these cash cows and it might as well be you.

Show why you should win. Throughout your application, focus on demonstrating why you fulfill the mission of the award. If the scholarship is meant to support students who contribute to their community, highlight public service in your application, recommendations, essays and interview. Try to prove that you are the most qualified applicant.

Write a powerful essay. Most scholarship competitions require an essay, which is important to show the committee who you are and what your goals are beyond what you write in applications. More on this in the next section.

Select the right recommenders. Ask teachers, advisors, coaches or others who can describe your qualities and accomplishments that match the goal of the awards.

Practice for interviews. Some competitions include interviews with the scholarship judges. Get a friend or family member to pretend to be a judge and do a mock interview.

Be realistic about your financial need. If you apply for a scholarship that is based on financial need, be truthful about how great your financial need really is. If it's clear on paper that you really don't need the funds, don't waste your time applying for a scholarship that will be awarded to someone who does.

Follow directions. Answer every question, supply all of the materials requested and submit your information on time. Because awarding organizations receive so many applications, one missing piece can instantly eliminate your application.

Refer to our books, *The Ultimate Scholarship Book* and *Get Free Cash For College*, for additional scholarship secrets and strategies. Plus, you'll find awards to match your background and needs in the directory of thousands of scholarships.

How to Write a Winning Scholarship Essay

If you think that writing essays for college applications was an exhausting experience, we're sorry to break the bad news to you—there are more to come. Many scholarship applications require at least one essay. Scholarship committees use essays to measure how you match up with the awards.

Before you wonder if it's worth the trouble to apply, the good news is that because you have already written quality essays for your college applications, you have some very good recycling possibilities. Plus, you have the motivation of writing to be *paid* money instead of writing to *spend* money as you did for the college application essays.

Similar to admissions officers, members of scholarship committees see the essay as a window into the hearts and minds of the applicants. Because of this, essays for scholarships should have many of the same qualities as college essays. They should be original, well written and honest and they should describe something meaningful about you. Scholarship essays should captivate the readers and make them care about the writer. All the strategies that you learned in the college essay writing chapters also apply to scholarship essays.

The biggest difference between the two essays is that for college essays you want to show why you are an overall good fit for an entering freshman class. For scholarship essays, you need to show why you are the best fit for the often very specific requirements of the award. In other words, for college essays you show why you are an overall good person. For scholarship essays, you show why you are the best English major, future physician or environmentalist, depending on the award for which you are applying.

While a scholarship application may give you the luxury of writing on any subject—in which case you can easily submit one of your college essays—most give you a much more focused topic. For example, if you are applying to an organization dedicated to promoting world peace, they may ask you to write about—what a coincidence—world peace. If you are applying to a civic group, they may ask you to write about your volunteer experience. In these cases, demonstrate in your essay that you are strong in that particular field or area or that you are the most suitable candidate because you fulfill the specific criteria of the award better than anyone else. This may mean that you will have to write a new essay.

The final thing to keep in mind when writing is to consider the kinds of people who will read your essay. An essay about how you wished you were born in a communist country because of your love for Marx may not go over well for an American Legion scholarship—many of whose members risked their lives fighting communism. An essay about the evils perpetrated by big business may not find much sympathy in a scholarship committee composed of Rotarians. At all times, keep your readers in mind and write an essay that will appeal to their interests.

Strategies to Get More Money

Colleges do their best to provide financial aid packages that make their schools affordable, but there are times when their offer is not enough for even the most resourceful families to pay the bills. This is especially true when unexpected changes occur such as a parent being laid off or a family member becoming ill. When this happens, be honest with the school and tell them that their offer is simply not enough, given your circumstances.

First, compose a letter in which you outline the reasons why you need more aid. When writing your reasons, be as specific as possible. For example, lay out your parents' annual income after taxes and how it is broken down to pay for your families' living expenses. Demonstrate how if your parents contribute as much as the college asks them to, they will be unable to meet the family's financial obligations. Also, explain any extenuating circumstances that might not be reflected in the information you submitted with the financial aid form.

Second, if you have received more aid from one school than another, you can try to use this difference as leverage. In other words, you can write a letter to College A asking them to match or at least increase your aid so that it is closer to the offer from College B. Explain that you would like to attend College A, but that because College B has offered more aid, you may be forced to attend it out of financial necessity. While colleges may not always be able to increase your award, it is certainly worth the time writing a letter to try.

How to Write a Letter to Ask for More

If you find it hard to believe that a single letter can result in a larger financial aid package, here is proof. The following is an actual letter one student wrote to the Harvard financial aid office. Before writing the letter, the student had received only a small loan from Harvard despite the fact that her father had been laid off for over a year. The student composed this letter to explain her family's extenuating circumstances, describing their actual income and expenses. Her letter paid off—she was awarded a $8,500 grant for the semester!

Letter to Harvard

Dear Sir or Madam:

I am writing to request that my financial aid package for the fall semester be reconsidered. My family and I were disappointed with the amount we were offered because in addition to my father having been unemployed for over a year, my sister will be a sophomore in college; and my mother, a part-time teacher, has received no income since June because of summer break.

We understand that nearly every family must undergo an amount of hardship to send its members to college. However, because my parents wish to continue financing my sister's and my education, they are worried about how they will pay for their own expenses. They have been using my mother's income to basically cover their mortgage payments and their savings to pay for everything else. In February, my parents had $33,000 in savings. In the last six months, their savings has decreased by about $15,000. They now have about $18,000 to contribute to my sister's and my college expenses as well as to spend on their and my younger brother's food and basic necessities. They don't know how long their savings will last without a change in the amount of aid I will receive.

At the end of this month, my sister will begin her sophomore year at USC. The cost will be $72,273, and she has received $48,901 in financial aid. This makes my parents' contribution amount to $23,372, of which they will borrow about half. One of the things you might be able to address is why my sister's financial aid package was dramatically higher than mine.

Since July of last year my father has been unemployed. His severance pay ended in October, and his unemployment benefits have been depleted since February. Although he has applied for over a dozen positions, his prospects for finding a job in his specialty are slim.

My parents and I have discussed the possibility of having me take a year off so that I may work to help pay for tuition, but we'd much rather that I finish school and work after I have received my degree.

Please contact my parents or me with any further questions you may have. Thank you very much for your time and consideration. I hope that this information is helpful in your review of my application.

Sincerely,
[Name withheld]

Get the Latest Scholarship Information

This chapter is meant to give you the *basics* of financial aid and scholarships. For more information, consider our other books:

- *Get Free Cash for College* is a scholarship strategy guide

- *The Ultimate Scholarship Book* is a scholarship directory

- *1001 Ways to Pay for College* discusses every conceivable way to fund your education and

- *How to Write a Winning Scholarship Essay* walks you through crafting a successful essay.

Be sure to also check our website at www.supercollege.com.

THE TRUE COST OF COLLEGE: PUBLIC VS. PRIVATE

A lot of families automatically rule out private colleges because the sticker price is higher than that of public colleges. It is critical to look at the net price of the college, which is how much your family will pay after taking into account financial aid. Perhaps even more importantly, you should research how many years it takes to graduate from the college. Many students find that it will take only four years to graduate from a private college but five, or even six, years to graduate from a public college (gasp!). At some public institutions, it can be challenging to enroll in the classes you need for your major or to graduate. You may find that it is more economical to attend a private college and graduate in a timely four years than to spend more time at a public college.

IN THIS CHAPTER YOU'LL LEARN SPECIFIC STRATEGIES FOR:

- Student athletes
- Transfer students
- International students
- Students with disabilities
- Home-schooled students

CHAPTER 12

ADMISSIONS FOR SPECIAL GROUPS

Special Considerations for Special Groups

Whether you are athletically gifted, desire to transfer from your current college or have a learning disability, there are special requirements and considerations when it comes to college admissions and financial aid. In this chapter, we will give some advice for students who belong to these special groups.

Student Athletes

You're the best dribbler, kicker, runner, pitcher or sprinter at your school. How do you use that talent to get into and pay for college? One answer is with an athletic scholarship.

Athletic scholarships are the Holy Grail of scholarships. At their best, they can cover tuition and fees, room and board and books. That's not bad for doing something that you enjoy.

College athletic scholarships are funded by membership revenue from the National Collegiate Athletic Association (NCAA), which encompasses over 950 colleges. The colleges are divided into three divisions, with athletic scholarships awarded for Division I and Division II schools, which are the most competitive. At Division III schools, student athletes receive scholarships based on financial need but not based on athletic talent.

However, don't think that every talented athlete is instantly showered with a full-ride scholarship. It takes more than talent to win and keep one of these awards. Here are some strategies for winning and managing an athletic scholarship:

Academics rule. You can be the number one player in the country, but if you don't have the grades or test scores, you won't play competitively in college. The minimum academic requirements for eligibility are the following:

- Graduate from high school.

- Complete a curriculum of at least 16 academic courses including: English: Four years; Mathematics: Three years of courses at the level of algebra I or above; Natural or physical science (including at least one laboratory course, if offered by the high school): Two years; Additional courses: English, mathematics or natural or physical science: One year; Social science: Two years; Additional academic courses: In any of the above subject areas or foreign language, philosophy or comparative religion courses: Four years.

- Before the seventh semester, you must complete 10 core courses, including at least seven in English, math or natural or physical science. After starting your seventh semester, you may not repeat any of the 10 courses to improve your GPA.

- Have a core-course grade-point average and a combined score on the SAT or a sum score on the ACT based on the NCAA Core GPA and Test Score Sliding Scale.

- Earn a minimum 2.3 GPA in core courses.

You don't have to be a football or basketball star to win athletic scholarships. In fact, you may have better opportunities to win scholarships for less-publicized sports like crew, rugby, volleyball or field hockey.

Find schools that match both your athletic and academic goals. Don't choose a college solely because of its athletic program. The great majority of student athletes don't go professional after graduating. They go to graduate school or find jobs. Select a college that fulfills your academic needs so that you will be prepared for the next step.

Coaches will not find you. You must find them. Unless you are a true super-star, the reality is that coaches don't have the resources to do national searches for student athletes. If you want to be noticed, you are going to need to take the initiative. Do this by writing an email to coaches at prospective colleges and sending them a portfolio of your athletic ability. However, be sure to follow the NCAA's rules for communicating with coaches. Your portfolio should include the following:

- Athletic statistics such as win-loss record, times, averages, etc.
- Records set
- Honors or awards won
- Titles won
- Newspaper or website clips
- Video links or videos on DVD or CD
- Letters of recommendation from coaches
- Playing schedule
- Contact information

Keep in touch with the coaches. Follow up to make sure they received your letter and portfolio. Ask if they need additional information. Get your high school coach to call on your behalf. Try to keep yourself at the top of the list of the players they want on next year's team.

If you are fortunate enough to receive an athletic scholarship, realize that you are not guaranteed a free ride for the rest of your academic career. Contrary to popular belief, there are no guaranteed four-year athletic scholarships. Athletic scholarships are awarded for a maximum of one academic year and may be renewed each year for a maximum of five years within a six-year period.

Don't count on that $7 million contract yet. For a very, very small minority, college segues into professional athletics. According to the NCAA, the odds of a high school football player making it to a professional team are about 6,000 to 1, and the odds for a high school basketball player are 10,000 to 1.

Get more information. The more information you have, the better equipped you'll be for facing the stiff competition for athletic scholarships. Speak with your coach and guidance counselors. Read *The Student Athlete's Guide to Getting Recruited* by Stewart Brown. Also, get more detailed information on eligibility and a directory of schools that have scholarships for each sport from the NCAA (www.ncaa.org/student-athletes). Contact information for the NCAA can be found in the Appendix.

Transfer Students

It's not uncommon for students to figure out after spending a year or two at a college that it is not the right match for them. Sometimes students will first enroll in a community college and then transfer to a university that offers a four-year degree. If you are considering transferring schools, there are things you should think about before making the switch and strategies to use if you decide to make the move. A little research will help to make sure you find the right match and make as smooth a transition as possible.

Before You Transfer

Understand that transferring schools can be a huge academic and personal change. Moving to a new school means re-adjusting to the new college's academic system, building relationships and getting involved in campus life.

You may have to take additional courses. Depending on how much credit you received for your courses, you may have to take summer school or extra courses to earn the credits that you need to graduate.

Think about your reasons for transferring. Are you certain that it is your college in particular with which you are dissatisfied? Would transferring improve your ability to learn? Can you change what you dislike about your current college to have a better experience? Are there other circumstances outside of college that are making you displeased?

Transferring is a difficult process. Some students opt not to transfer and adapt to their college while others have found transferring to be a difficult choice but the right decision. Don't make a hasty decision, and weigh all of your options.

Selecting a College for the Transfer

Among the most important factors in deciding where to transfer are your academic and personal goals. What do you hope to accomplish at the college? To help, here are some points to consider:

Selectivity. Colleges range in their rates of acceptance of transfer students. Last year Berkeley admitted approximately 4,800 of its 19,000 transfer applicants while Harvard admitted only 16 students from over 1,500 transfer applicants. When applying, look at the acceptance rates for transfer students. Apply to schools with high, medium and low selectivity to maximize the number of options you have.

Requirements and limits. The federal requirements for being a transfer student are that you must complete one year of post-secondary studies with a minimum 2.0 GPA at an accredited institution. Many schools have additional or higher requirements, such as an additional year of study or a higher GPA. Many also limit how much credit you can receive from your previous school, typically two years of academic work. Check both the requirements and credit transfer limits at the schools you are considering.

Course credits. Colleges have different policies for giving credit for courses you've taken elsewhere and for the number of courses required for a major. Check with both your current college and at those to which you want to transfer. You may have to take summer school courses to make up any difference in credits.

Timing. Know when you are eligible to transfer. Some colleges accept transfers only for the fall semester or only accept students in their junior or senior years.

Questions to ask yourself. In addition to the factors above, ponder the questions in Chapter 2 for selecting a college. Look for a school that is strong in your course of study, will prepare you for your post-college future and offers student life and activities that match your desires. It's important to spend the time to find the right match.

Transfer Student Admissions

Treat applying to college as a transfer student differently than applying as a freshman. Because you have already been a college student, admissions officers expect a higher level of maturity and more thorough definition of what your goals are. Here are some strategies for applying:

Highlight your academic goals. As someone already in college, you have a more realistic idea of what your post-graduation goals are. Demonstrate the clarity you've gained by focusing on your accomplishments in your area of study and commitment to your field in your application. Stress how well you've done in classes, academic issues you've tackled and contributions you've made to your academic department. Identify as specifically as possible what you want to do with your degree after graduating.

Highlight nonacademic strengths too. While your academic achievements are the most important, colleges also consider your nonacademic achievements. These include leadership, public service, honors and awards and other accomplishments that you've made at your current college.

Be aware of deadlines. Deadlines for applying as a transfer student may or may not be the same as those for freshman students.

Complete all the paperwork. The Common Application or Coalition Application can save time by allowing you to complete one application to submit to several schools, but make sure you provide any supplemental application materials as well.

Investigate financial aid opportunities. Review Chapter 11, and check in with the financial aid offices of the schools to which you may transfer. You will need to reapply for financial aid when you transfer.

After You're Accepted

First congratulate yourself on making this change and working to improve your educational experience. Then, consider a few more tips before making the actual move:

Do your research. Do the same investigating that you would as an entering freshman. Before deciding on a school, speak with faculty, students and members of the administration. Read the college's website and its materials. Visit the campus to get the best feel for what it's like to be a student at the institution.

Know what to expect. Expect differences. A large difference is student life, especially if you are moving from a mostly commuter school to a mostly residential one. You will find that much of student life revolves around what happens on campus. Another difference is in the academic curriculum. A new school may have different teaching methods, grading systems, exam schedules, class sizes and levels of interaction with professors.

Take advantage of orientation programs. Some schools offer special orientation programs for transfer students. Attend these to meet your future classmates and get familiarized with the campus and the way it works. Don't be lost on the first day of classes.

Get used to being on your own. Many students not only change schools but move from living at home to living on or near campus. This can mean learning to cook and clean for yourself, furnishing an apartment and not having parents or siblings nearby.

Give yourself time to get acquainted. Because the school is a new environment, don't take on too much right away. You'll need some time to get used to the different personal and academic lifestyle. Take it easy academically at least for the first semester.

Get involved. Meet people. Students may have already formed cliques during their first or second years of college, but most are always open to new friends. Get out there, and participate in activities. Don't be afraid to introduce yourself and get to know as many people as you can.

International Students: Coming to America

With over 3,500 colleges and universities and one of the most respected higher education systems in the world, the United States is a desirable place for international students to study. In fact, according to the Institute of International Education, there are more than one million international students attending U.S. colleges.

Studying in the U.S. has several advantages. There are thousands of schools from which to choose, some focusing on providing a broad education base (liberal arts education) and some providing pre-professional training. American schools are widely respected for their research and curriculums, and they offer a rich and varied student life.

However, there are important things to keep in mind when considering attending school in the U.S. First, it is competitive to be admitted to colleges, as schools typically accept between 9 and 33 percent of their applicants. Second, it is expensive. Financial aid for international students is difficult to find, especially for undergraduate students. The following are strategies to use as you are considering, applying for and figuring out how to pay for your education in the U.S.:

Considering Studying in the U.S.

While there are benefits of studying in the U.S., first take a look at how this education would fit with your goals. Here are some questions to ask yourself:

- What do you hope to accomplish by studying in the U.S.?

- Will your education be transferable so that it can be used in your home country?

- Will your career advancement justify the expense of attending college in the U.S.?

- Do you have the academic qualifications to study at an American college? Investigate a college directory to see grade and test score requirements.

- Are your English skills refined enough to do academic work?

- Can you live in the U.S. for a number of years and adapt to its culture?

- Do you have the funds to support your education? See below for more information on financial aid.

International Student Admissions

Your goals. Consider your goals for studying in the U.S. and your post-college career plans. This will help you select a program that fits your goals.

Do your research on the colleges. Consider the questions in Chapter 2 for selecting a college. Does the college have a strong program in the field you want to study? Does it have a strong support system for international students? How large is the international student population? Is it located in an environment in which you'd like to study? What kind of financial aid does the school offer for international students?

Get help. The U.S. Department of State operates over 350 Overseas Educational Advising Centers designed to assist students who wish to study in the U.S. Colleges also have international student offices to help students make the transition to attending school in the U.S.

Take the tests. In addition to the SAT or ACT, most colleges require you to take an English proficiency test if English is not your native language. The TOEFL is the most common test, but some colleges also accept the Advanced Placement English Language and Composition exam. See Chapter 10 for more details about the TOEFL.

The AP English exam tests skills from English teaching programs around the world and has a focus that is compatible with students who have completed several years of English language study. The exam tests your potential to participate in university-level coursework on the same level as native English speakers. For more information, see the Appendix to contact the College Board.

International Student Financial Aid

Finding financial aid for international students is difficult, particularly at the undergraduate level. According to NAFSA, 81 percent of international students pay for their education in the U.S. with personal funds. Still, international students with persistence and talent have been successful. Here are some tips:

Know what your expenses will be. Understand that even for state-sponsored institutions, students still bear a large cost in the form of tuition and fees. This is true for both U.S. and international students. Private universities are the most expensive, followed by public colleges and then by community colleges. Expenses include application and test fees, tuition and fees, rent or room and board, books and supplies, travel, personal expenses and health insurance.

Learn about living costs. The U.S. can have a substantially higher cost of living than other countries. Research the costs of housing, food and other expenses.

Investigate financial aid options. Unfortunately, international students are not eligible for funding from the U.S. government, but you should investigate other options, which may include aid from private organizations, colleges or universities, private loans or exchange programs. See Chapter 11 for more information on nonfederal financial aid.

Think about how you will finance your education on an on-going basis, not just the first year. Also, include expenses if you are planning to bring your family. Often you will need to provide evidence that you have the funds for your education.

Communicate with the colleges' financial aid officers. The personnel who work in the financial aid offices may have additional information on funding for international students.

Investigate funding sources in your home country. Some countries sponsor scholarships or loans for students who attend colleges abroad.

Typically when you are accepted, the college will provide an I-20 Form. You will apply for your student (F1) visa by providing your I-20 Form to the American Consulate in your home country.

For more information, see the Appendix to contact the College Board, United States Network for Education Information and NAFSA: Association of International Educators.

Students With Disabilities

If you have a physical or learning disability, many colleges will make a special effort to accommodate your needs. In addition, here are some tips for selecting colleges and finding out what they offer:

Get accommodations for standardized tests. Contact the Services for Students with Disabilities at the College Board if you are taking the SAT, SAT Subject Tests, AP or PSAT or at the ACT if you are taking the ACT. See the Appendix for their contact information. Students with professionally diagnosed and documented disabilities including blindness, deafness, ADHD, learning disabilities and physical handicaps may be eligible for special accommodations or extended time to complete the tests.

Explain your situation to the colleges. Make the college aware of your disability so that the admissions officers will have a framework for your performance and so you can get more information on how the school will support you. To get the most useful information, it is often best to meet with a representative or speak with one on the telephone rather than try to communicate in writing.

Factors for selecting a college. Consider these qualities in addition to the characteristics outlined in Chapter 2: level of support the college will offer, extent of support programs, success rate of other students with disabilities, availability of individualized tutoring and other special programs, availability of special accommodations for rooming, transportation and study, class size and the availability of professors.

Investigate what services the college will provide. Many have special offices that offer support programs such as tutoring, time with a disability specialist or note taking. You may also receive special accommodations including extended time on exams, a private room for taking exams, the ability to take exams at home or alternative exam formats. Meet with a member of the staff, visit the offices and sit in on a program. Ask about the experiences of other students with disabilities, how the office would serve you, what programs and advising services the office offers, special arrangements you might have for taking exams and special housing arrangements, if necessary.

Speak with current or former students with disabilities. More important than anything else, ask the college to put you in touch with current students who have a similar disability. Verify the support that they received and ask about their interaction with the special services office, professors and other students.

Home-Schooled Students

According to the National Home Education Research Institute, there are over two million students who are home-schooled, representing about two percent of those who are of school age. If you are one of the growing number of home-schooled students, consider these tips when applying to college:

Check home-school admittance policies with the colleges in which you are interested. Admission rates and procedures can vary by college. Understand the requirements that the colleges have and their acceptance rates.

Watch the deadlines. You probably don't have the advantage of a guidance counselor to remind you of deadlines, which means that you will need to keep track of them on your own or with your parents' help.

Academic record. If you don't have a transcript, be prepared to provide colleges with a detailed record of your academic coursework. This may include tests, research papers and a syllabus of courses and their descriptions. You may also want to include samples of some of your best work and a description of a day's work. Check with the admissions office to see if the extra documentation will help them in their decision regarding admittance.

Testing requirements. To verify your academic potential, you will be required to take the standardized tests including the SAT or ACT.

Show college credit, if you can. If you have the time, try to take some community college course so that you can show the admission officers that you are ready for college-level work. You can also take the AP exams or the College-Level Examination Program (CLEP) tests. Both of these tests demonstrate your knowledge of a specific subject and help the colleges quantify your academic ability.

Evaluations. Some colleges will not accept evaluations from a parent, even if your parent is your primary instructor. Think about other adults who have taught you in a formal setting at a community college or high school or with whom you've interacted in extracurricular activities. These make good evaluators and/or recommenders.

Get involved in your community. Even though you may not have access to activities at a high school, participate in activities in your community. While your academic promise is the most important factor in admissions, it is also important that you show other ways you will contribute to the college.

Embrace the fact that applying will be difficult. Even today colleges are slow to provide reasonable application alternatives for home-schooled students. Therefore, you need to accept that fact that it will be more difficult to apply than it would if you were a "traditional" student. But you should relish this opportunity to highlight what you have learned and accomplished. For example, since you have to create your own "transcript," use this opportunity to focus on your academic strengths and give examples of projects that you've done. This is something that students from traditional schools simply cannot do and yet can help you to stand out from other applicants. Be creative in how you adapt to the college's requirements. Always remember that the school doesn't really care about the forms and records as much as they do care about what your entire application says about you and why you would make a valuable addition to their student body.

CHAPTER 13

GET STARTED BEFORE YOUR SENIOR YEAR

WHAT FRESHMEN, SOPHOMORES AND JUNIORS NEED TO KNOW

Catch the Early Bird Worms

My (Kelly) mother used to say in her inspired attempts to wake me, "The early bird catches the worm." My reply would always be, "I don't want any worms," as I rolled over in my bed and burrowed deeper beneath the covers. In the case of college admissions, you definitely want the worm. In fact, you want a whole bucket of worms.

If you are a junior, sophomore or even freshman reading this, then kudos to you! You are giving yourself an advantage that most seniors only *wish* they had. There are so many ways you can prepare for college admission that the earlier you start, the more successful you will be. In this chapter we will look at specific strategies you can use now to raise your chances of getting in later.

Before we begin, however, we should warn you that your goal in getting an early start is to accomplish as much as possible, given your limited time.

Don't feel like you have to do everything that we suggest in this chapter—if you did, you would not have any time left to enjoy your pre-senior youth.

Everything an Underclassman Needs to Know About College Admissions (But Is Afraid to Ask)

You have a lot of important things on your mind right now—finding a prom date, passing your driving test, what's for dinner—but even with all these crucial life decisions to ponder, it is important to devote some time to thinking about where you want to apply to college. Many seniors have no idea where they want to go to school and often make uninformed decisions.

Start now by asking your parents, teachers, counselors, older siblings and friends about colleges. Talk to alumni from your high school about their experiences. Ask them about their courses, activities and social life. Get a college directory with detailed descriptions of colleges and universities. Or, search databases of colleges online. Our website SuperCollege.com offers a free database of thousands of colleges and descriptions of their academics, student bodies, admissions and financial aid. Visit the homepages of colleges. If your family is taking a summer trip, why not visit a few college campuses at the same time?

Having some idea of where you might want to apply will come in handy when it comes time to make the real decision. While you are considering various colleges, try to keep the following general questions in mind:

- What is the strength of the school's academic program, and does it offer courses in the fields in which you might be interested? A school that is strong in computer science may have a terrible comparative literature department. If you are unsure about what you might want to major in, think about which subjects in school you enjoy. See if your guidance office offers career assessment tests to give you some direction. Speak with people in fields in which you might be interested. Remember too that your interest may change. While science may be your favorite subject now, you might find that in college there are more fulfilling ways to spend your time than cooped up in a lab.

- How is the campus environment? Is there a large or small student body? Is the school in the middle of a city or out in the country? Do you like the climate? You can learn a lot just by visiting the schools and walking the campus. Also, information on class size and professor-to-student ratios can be found in most college guide books. Of course, to get the real story on what the school is like, try to talk to some current students.

- What kind of social environment, including kinds of activities, does the college offer? If hiking and fishing are hobbies you need to stay sane, don't go to a school in the middle of an urban wasteland. (Then again some people find wastelands charming.)

Visit College Campuses

If flipping through brochures and looking at websites does not give you a full enough picture of the colleges—which it shouldn't—another way to learn about them is to take a field trip. The next time your family goes on a vacation, see if you will be near any of the colleges you might want to attend. If you will, why not stop by for a short visit?

While you're there, take a campus tour, sit in on a class or just take a walk around the campus, absorbing its ambiance. Speak to students, peek inside the dorms and have a meal in the cafeteria. You can learn a lot from observing: the size and environment of the campus, what surrounds the campus and how happy the students appear. It's still early and right now you just want to get a feel for your options and have a sense of what's out there.

By getting an early start on thinking about where you want to apply, you will have a tremendous advantage when the time comes to actually begin the college selection and admission process.

The Application? What's That?

Once you have decided which schools you'd like to attend, you need to apply. During the summer before your senior year, you can start completing college applications. In general, these applications do not vary much from year to year. In fact, you can even look at this year's applications as a preview. College applications almost always include the following:

Application form. This is a collection of blanks, spaces and short questions about your education, test scores, family background, activities, awards and work experience.

Essays. Usually the colleges ask you to write your autobiography in the generous space of 650 words or less. Sometimes colleges give you a choice of topics to write on, such as a memorable experience, a personal hero or an issue that is important to you. Usually, there will also be one to four shorter questions that might quiz you about your favorite extracurricular activity, book or why you have chosen to apply to the college.

Evaluations. You'd better start getting on the good side of everyone you know. Colleges usually require three or more evaluations from your teachers, counselors and (maybe) even your boss. Your recommenders will comment on aspects of their relationship with you including your academic promise, maturity and integrity.

Interviews. These one-on-one discussions with an alumnus or admissions officer are the only times you will interact directly with a human being during the admissions process. Interviews are your opportunity to share information that is not easily conveyed through applications or essays and to ask questions about the college. Note: Not all schools require the interview.

Test scores and transcript. Most colleges require that you take the SAT or ACT, and many require two SAT Subject Tests. It is also highly recommended that you take some Advanced Placement (AP) or International Baccalaureate (IB) tests. In addition, you will send each college a transcript listing courses and grades and score reports from the tests you take.

For some of these parts of the admission procedure, let the procrastinator in you rejoice because you really can't do much until your senior year. However, for the worm-hungry part of you, there are several things you can do right now. Read on.

Challenge Your Brain

One of the most important factors in being admitted to college is, as your parents have probably lectured to you more times than you would like to remember, your grades. To get into college, you need to have a competitive grade point average.

However, understand that not all grades are considered equal. An "A" in an honors or Advanced Placement course is much better than an "A" in a non-honors course. After all, it's not fair to compare an "A" in regular physics to an "A" in AP physics, is it? In fact, colleges often recalculate your GPA based on how many courses are honors or Advanced Placement.

Some students make the mistake of trying to get a high GPA by taking the easiest classes offered like "Woodshop: How to Cut Wood." Colleges want to see that you are motivated and willing to challenge yourself academically. If you can handle the workload, sign up for honors, Advanced Placement or International Baccalaureate classes. Yes, this means that you will voluntarily ask for more homework, spend more time studying and take more difficult tests, but keep in mind that an acceptance letter will be your reward.

Meet with your guidance counselor to plan out courses for your remaining years in high school. Be realistic about what kind of course load will be challenging enough but manageable.

Practice for and Take the Alphabet Soup of Tests

There is no avoiding it. You will, before graduation, spend at least a dozen exciting hours filling in bubbles while taking a battery of standardized tests that have names that sound like they were created in a bowl of alphabet soup. These tests will include the PSAT, APs or IBs, SAT or ACT and SAT Subject Tests. Colleges use standardized tests as an additional measure of your academic promise and as a way to compare students from across the country whose high schools have different ways of testing and grading.

To learn what each of these mysterious combinations of letters stands for and for a cheat sheet on how to prepare for them, refer to Chapter 10. You will notice that the tests are concentrated in your junior and senior years. But some, like the PSAT, APs, IBs and SAT Subject Tests, may be taken earlier. For example, if you finish a world history class in your sophomore year, you'll want to take the subject exam in world history while the material is still fresh in your mind. Things like the terms of the Treaty of Versailles tend to slip the mind quickly.

Your most immediate concern is probably the PSAT, which you can take in your sophomore or junior year, the PSAT 10 in sophomore year or the PSAT 8/9 in eighth or ninth grade. These practice tests are designed to prepare you for the SAT, so in a sense, you don't have to stress too much. However, the score from your junior year PSAT will be used to determine if you qualify for scholarships and special programs including National Merit Scholarships, which aside from the honor, come with a cash prize to help defray college tuition. So, it is worth taking the PSAT seriously and putting in some study time as if it were the SAT.

While Chapter 10 contains a battery of strategies for preparing for these tests, the important thing to remember is to start early. Even if you don't consider reviewing your math book or drilling yourself with reading comprehension passages a blast, convince yourself that taking some practice exams is a hoot. The real secret of test preparation services is that they force students to get familiar with the test and become comfortable with the type of questions asked. This alone can boost your scores tremendously. Buy a book of past exams and review it regularly.

The Importance of Extracurricular Activities

Even though grades are the most important factor in admissions, colleges want to know that you do more than study. They seek students who will not only do well in classes but who will also contribute to the college community through activities. Show that you are this kind of student by getting involved in activities during high school. Activities include clubs and organizations, sports, student government and volunteer work.

When applying to college, much of your application is not only based on your classroom life but also on your out-of-classroom life. You will be able to brag about your extracurricular activities on the application form, and most students find that they use some experience connected with these activities in their college essays. To help you understand the importance of extracurricular activities, here are the most common questions that we get asked:

How important are extracurricular activities? Are grades or extracurricular activities more important?

The most important factor in admissions is grades. Admissions officers want students who have the academic ability to perform well in college-level courses. What you do outside of the classroom is also important, but it is secondary. Colleges want students who will contribute both inside and outside of the classroom. With few exceptions—such as finding the cure to a deadly disease, founding a multimillion-dollar business or being a nationally recognized athlete—you will not be admitted based on your extracurricular activities alone. Focus first on your grades, and then spend time on activities.

In which activities should you participate?

There is no magic combination of activities that will guarantee acceptance. Our advice may seem like common sense, but it is true: Get involved in activities that you enjoy. If you like writing, think about the newspaper or literary magazine. Don't think that there are certain activities that you must be involved in to gain admission. You will excel most in activities you enjoy.

What if there are no activities at school you'd like to join?

Your choices are these: a) start your own club or organization, or b) look outside of your school. Starting your own organization will take work finding an advisor, getting it officially recognized by your school and marketing it to potential members. However, it is very fulfilling to start an organization based on your interests and to leave a legacy at your high school. Admissions officers will also appreciate your initiative. If you can't find an activity within your school, don't hesitate to look in your community. There is a group dedicated to almost every interest imaginable.

In how many activities should you participate?

Again, there is no magic number of activities in which you need to participate. It will depend on how much free time you have outside of your schoolwork, how involved you are in each and what other commitments you have. There is no rule, but the students we've interviewed typically participate in between two and five activities at a time.

Will you be penalized for not participating in sports?

Colleges recognize that not every student is athletically oriented. Yes, athletes recognized on the state and national levels are heavily recruited by colleges, but you don't have to be an athletic superstar to be recruited by or gain admission to college. I (Kelly) was especially untalented at every ball-, net- or pool-related activity, but that didn't prevent me from getting accepted. Instead of worrying about not being athletically inclined, you can focus on other non-athletic activities. These are just as important to colleges (minus the opinion of the athletic department, of course.)

Do you have to be a leader in activities?

Being a leader in activities is not a requirement for getting admitted, but it helps. There is nothing more impressive to admissions officers than students

THE JUNIOR YEAR PROJECT

We always encourage students do so something significant during their junior year. Ideally, it is a project that you conceive that combines your unique passions and skills. There is no limit to what this project can be. The key is that it must have a tangible or quantifiable result. For example, working in a research lab during the summer is great. But it's not as impressive as if it resulted in the publication (even in your school newspaper) of some interesting findings.

So what kind of project can you do? Take a look at some of these examples, and brainstorm some way to merge your passions with a project that you can do before your senior year.

Sara loved martial arts (she was a brown belt) and writing. For her project she approached her community newspaper and pitched the idea of an article series on the history of the different martial arts schools in her community. The newspaper loved the idea. Sara spent the summer researching and writing, which resulted in a three-piece article series published during the fall of her senior year.

Jonathan loved computers and was an expert at all things technical. He was also active in his church. For his project Jonathan decided to set aside part of the summer to "wire" his church. He single-handedly installed thousands of feet of data cable, Internet routers and media servers to bring his church into the 21st century.

Lacy's passion was the environment, specifically ocean pollution. She had a friend who wanted to be a filmmaker and owned all of the latest digital video gear. Together the two decided to make a public service announcement (PSA) video about keeping the ocean clean. Lacy wrote the script while her friend shot and directed. They ended up with a slick 60-second video that they were able to run on their local cable access channel. They also entered it into several film contests.

As you can see, a junior year project is a great experience even if it doesn't have any impact on college admission. The fact that you can write about it in essays and list it on applications is only a bonus. Whatever your idea may be, just make sure that the project is realistic—especially given your time constraints—and has a tangible end result.

So what are you going to do this year?

who take initiative. This demonstrates that you are not just a member in name but that you make concrete contributions. In fact, more important than what particular activity you choose to participate in is the quality of your participation, meaning how much you contribute as a member and leader.

Run for office in clubs or school government. Try to be the captain of your sports team. Volunteer to head a project for your service organization. Start a group or club of your own. This will demonstrate your leadership skills as well as your ability to take initiative. Also, try to stick with the activities you enjoy for a number of years. It's important to show that you are grounded. Membership in the Yoga Club for four straight years, for example, is certainly a reflection of dedication. It is also the only way to become a leader.

Understand that to be a leader, you don't have to hold an official elected position. You can take charge of a special project or organize an event. It takes just as much leadership to put together a successful canned food drive as it does to run a student council meeting. This type of leadership is valued.

Compete to Stand Out

It should not be a surprise that colleges like winners. In fact, on the college application form, there is a section for listing all of your awards and honors. These include both academic awards like the county-wide spelling bee and non-academic honors like grand prize in a ukulele playoff. Thus, for competitions or contests you have a chance at winning, compete.

Luckily, there is an abundance of competitions out there for you to win. These include speech, writing, art, musical, scientific, debate, athletic events and more. Watch for the competitions that you think you have a chance of winning, and take the time to enter them. Keep in mind that winning does not necessarily mean taking first place. Being a runner-up in a state or national competition is just as impressive as winning a local award.

There are even many awards that you do not have to officially enter to win. For example, your teacher may award you a certificate for being Super Math Citizen of the Month or your school may vote you Outstanding Volunteer. The more awards and honors you can muster, the more the colleges will think you are a winner (which, of course, you are).

Keep a Record of All Your Accomplishments

You're too young for Alzheimer's disease, but you'd be surprised at how much you can forget in four years. In your senior year, you will need to recall exactly what you have done since the first day of your freshman year. It might be easy to remember now, but in a few years it won't be.

Keep a record of everything you do. Include brief descriptions of your activities, especially if you made a special contribution or were a leader of a special project, when you received a specific award or honor, what years you participated in activities and an estimate of how many hours you spent on each activity. This list will help you immensely when completing the applications and will ensure that you don't leave anything out. Don't forget to store this list in a safe place where you can find it easily.

Kiss Up To Teachers, Employers and Advisors

Now is the time to set your pride aside, dish out all the compliments you are capable of giving without gagging and hone your skills of flattery. Because you will need two or more evaluations from teachers, one from your counselor or principal and possibly one from an employer or advisor, now is a great time to foster your relationships with these key people in your life. By the time you are ready to apply, your goal is to have them adore you as if you were their own child.

Participate actively in class. Yes, this means raising your hand and answering questions, volunteering to erase the board and other such related sycophantic (sycophantic means obsequious and these words could both be on your ACT or SAT, so look them up!) activities. Put your best effort into all of your work. Stay after class or go early to ask questions. Volunteer to help your teachers with projects or try to give them extra help if they need it.

If it sounds like your goal is to become your teachers' pet, it is. Stand out from the other students in your class by developing a strong, personal relationship with your teachers. By doing this, your teachers will write the strongest evaluations possible. It will be evident that they feel you are not only a good student, but also an extraordinary person.

Also maintain your relationship with teachers after you have completed their courses. Drop by to chat when you have a free moment. Tell them what you enjoyed most about their class. Volunteer to help them in any way that you can. Since you have already taken the course, perhaps you could help plan an activity for this year's class or give suggestions for a new way of presenting the material. Your objective is to show your teachers that you are concerned and thoughtful enough to help even after you have nothing to gain from them (besides excellent evaluations).

To impress your employers, of course do your best at work. Be punctual, friendly and the fastest burger flipper this side of the Mississippi. But also volunteer for additional responsibilities or work overtime when your employer needs the help. Get to know your employer beyond the employer-employee relationship so that he or she will learn what kind of person you really are. Also, give feedback on your job and the company—what works, and if you feel comfortable enough, what doesn't. Even if you end up not asking your manager for an evaluation, your efforts may result in a promotion and maybe even a raise.

Many colleges also want a report from a school counselor or advisor. If you are thinking to yourself, "Who in the world is that?" you are probably not alone. Many students do not take the time to get to know their counselors until late in their high school careers. This can be a disadvantage when it comes time for counselors to complete the required school reports.

See your counselor or advisor as frequently as possible. Don't badger him or her, but drop by from time to time. Ask for advice on college planning. Consult with your counselor whenever you have academic or extracurricular questions. By seeking guidance, you will emphasize your desire to pursue a higher education as well as ensure that your counselor gets to know you well.

Avoid Appliphobia by Previewing Applications

Fear, anxiety and nausea are perhaps the most common symptoms. Unfortunately, we're not talking about the flu. Rather, we are describing an acute case of "Appliphobia," or students' initial reactions to seeing a college application. As you will soon discover, at first glance college applications are a maze of lists, questions and blanks. They can be quite intimidating because they are about five to eight pages of questions that you must not only answer but do so skillfully and thoughtfully.

That is why now is a perfect time for you to take a look at some applications so that you can overcome the ill effects of "Appliphobia" before you actually have to apply. Usually the earliest you can start applications is during the late summer between your junior and senior years. However, you can always look at last year's applications to get an exciting sneak preview.

Once you have an application or two, read through them. Not only will you find out more about the college application process, but you will also discover information about the colleges themselves. Take a look at the admissions section of the college's website. It will have photos of students so happy you wonder if they actually study, as well as information about the college ranging from its history to its academic focus to its extracurricular activities.

You will also find the basic components of the application: the application form, essay, interview (sometimes) and evaluations. You will see that, yes, there is a lot of work ahead of you, but it is manageable, and you will be able to do it. By taking a look at the applications now, you will eliminate surprises and be ready for the real thing. Who knows—you may even become so excited at the prospect of packaging yourself to the colleges that you start on them right away.

We hope this chapter has given you some ideas on how to prepare for your senior year. We recommend that you look over the other chapters of this book for more detailed information on the various areas of the application process.

Oh, and enjoy yourself before the stress of college admissions peaks!

CHAPTER 14

GET YOUR CHILD READY FOR COLLEGE

WHAT EVERY PARENT NEEDS TO KNOW

The Difficult Role of Being a Parent

As you probably have realized, things have changed since you were in school. And we're not just talking about hairstyles and fashion. In particular, competition has become astronomically fierce for entrance into college.

Nowadays students spend a lot of time and money just preparing for college admissions. Many of our friends at Harvard attended special test preparation schools during the summer—some had even begun in *elementary school!* A few hired "educational consultants," who charged as much as *$300 an hour* to advise them on where to apply to college. How much all of this helped we do not know, but one thing was certain: Their parents doled out hundreds, and in many cases, thousands of dollars.

It is safe to say that the competition your son or daughter will face will be extremely tough. Fortunately, you have two things working for you and your child: 1) Your child can use this book as a guide through every step of the admissions process (you knew we were going to say this, didn't you?); and 2)

As a concerned parent, there are things you can do to help. However, while your desire to help is sincere, we need to warn you up front that there will be times when you must combat your natural parental instinct to help your child because there are some things that your child needs to do solo. More on this later, but first let's look at two things that you can do.

First, learn as much as you can about college admissions. Since by virtue of being a parent we know you are busy, we have included a brief summary of this process in the next section. Remember that what was true when or if you ever applied to colleges may no longer be so.

Second, look into various sources of funding—hey, who do you think is going to end up paying for these four years of education? As you will see, there are many sources of funding you can take advantage of to help defray the costs of tuition. (We know this will make you smile.) But first let's take a look at the nuts and bolts of today's college admissions process.

A Galloping Overview of the Admissions Process and How You Can Help

Unless your hobby is reading the latest literature from the College Board, you could probably use a refresher course on today's college admissions process. Although each area is examined in more detail in the various chapters of the book, the following is a quick overview of what is expected of your son or daughter and a few suggestions on what you should and should not do to help.

The Application

This is the "stats" sheet for college admissions officers. It is a multi-page form for personal data such as test scores, academic honors, extracurricular activities and work experience. With this information, the admissions officers get a quick summary of your child's achievements and can easily compare him or her to other students.

How you can help: Begin by assisting your child in packing the most impressive information about him or her within the very limited space of the application form. To do this, your child should highlight academic achievements because this will indicate academic readiness for college. Your child should also emphasize the leadership roles that he or she has played in school and extracurricular activities. Admissions officers like to see that students are not just participating in activities but are also leading them. Leadership does not mean only elected positions. Any time your child took on responsibility could be an example of leadership. Your student should focus on any projects he or she has initiated and any special contributions he or she has made. Help your child recall all of the things that he or she did during the last four years. Parents frequently remember significant events that their children overlook.

Even if your child has trouble keeping his or her room clean, he or she needs to keep the application clean. Since not much creative writing is required, neatness counts. Because the application form is usually the last thing that gets done (often in the wee hours of the morning), it is also where most of the carelessness occurs. As the final proofreader of the application, ensure that every blank is filled and all appropriate boxes have been checked. Also make sure that there are no typos—misspelling the name of the school will certainly not improve your son or daughter's chances. Review the final version of the application form before it is submitted.

Essays

If you sometimes feel that you don't understand what goes on in the mind of your teenage son or daughter, here is an opportunity to find out how your child thinks. The essay, usually 650 words or less, is the admissions officers' window into the thoughts of your child. It allows them to form an image of the applicant beyond impersonal test scores and straightforward biographical information. Students often focus their essays on themselves, their experiences and their thoughts.

How you can help: Since this is one of the most important parts of the application, read Chapter 5 on writing the essay and even a few of the example essays in Chapter 7. As you will find, the college essay can be a very personal piece, and depending on how your child feels, he or she may not be comfortable sharing it with you. Respect his or her decision. It may sound strange that your son or daughter is willing to allow such a personal essay to be read by unknown college admissions officers and yet does not want Mom or Dad to see it, but it is certainly not uncommon. Don't take it personally.

If, however, your son or daughter does not mind, then make yourself available for editing and proofreading the essay. One word of caution: Some parents get so overzealous in their desire to help that they end up nearly writing the essay themselves. This must be avoided at all costs. College admissions officers read literally thousands of essays, and they are able to easily spot the "mommy-daddies." These are essays clearly written in a style, with language and on topics that betray the age and generation of the author. There is a rejection pile for these essays. So take care not to "edit" your child's essays to the point where your suggestions evolve into actually writing them.

That said, be as objective as you can, putting aside for a moment your pride in your child, and give constructive criticism on the following points:

- Is the essay creative and interesting?

- Does it draw you in and make you want to read more?

● Does the essay show a unique or outstanding attribute? This does not mean that the essay has to refer to the author overtly since the essay's style will also reflect on the character and sensibilities of the author.

● After finishing the essay, would you like to meet the writer? (Pretend that you haven't known your child for the past 18 years.) Make sure that the essay does not portray the writer as arrogant or meek.

● Does the essay make you think about the issues it raises? Are the issues raised applicable to your life?

● Are any parts of the essay unclear?

● Do the paragraphs flow in a smooth and logical way?

● Is the essay true? Does it sound sincere?

● Is the image you form of the writer a positive one? (It may be very hard to be objective on this one!)

When you are finished reading your son or daughter's essay, meet with your child to discuss your reactions. Try to make general comments or suggestions, and only use your red ink to make specific changes on technical errors such as grammar, punctuation and spelling. Be honest but not overly critical. Praise the essay's strong aspects and offer positive solutions for improving the weaknesses. No matter how busy you are, make yourself available to read your child's work as many times as necessary. Remember, each error you catch is one that the admissions officers won't.

Teacher and Others' Evaluations

Admissions officers already know that you think your child is the perfect candidate to attend their college. The evaluations provide the opportunity for teachers, employers, advisors and others to verify this. These forms cover areas like your child's leadership ability, motivation and ability to work with others.

How you can help: Without resorting to bribery (which we strongly disapprove of), there is not much you can do about evaluations. Fight your parental urge to intervene since it certainly won't help to badger your child's potential recommenders. They are the last people you want to annoy. Trust that your son or daughter has a pretty good idea of which teachers will write favorable evaluations. Make sure these evaluations are handed out to the evaluators early (two to three months before the application deadline) since it takes time to compose a solid evaluation.

Interviews

Interviews, required by many schools, can be downright frightening. Unlike the other components of the admissions process, interviews require interaction with real life admissions officers or alumni. Topics up for discussion may include everything from academic interests to hobbies to current events. Interviews are also the time for students to ask questions of the colleges' representatives.

How you can help: Fortunately, we walk your child through the interview process in Chapter 8 to ease his or her nerves. One of the best ways you can help prepare your child is to do a mock interview. At first, your son or daughter may be hesitant or embarrassed to do a mock interview with you as the interviewer, but encourage him or her to try it. In Chapter 8 you will find a list of commonly asked questions to which you can add a few of your own. The most important thing to remember is to give your child constructive feedback on his or her performance. Do not concentrate on weaknesses as much as strengths. Tell your student which questions he or she answered particularly well so that he or she will be confident during the real interview.

Also, never under any circumstances, go into the interview with your child. Some parents have the mistaken idea that it will help their child if they go in and explain what a good son or daughter they have and why he or she deserves to attend X university. Such attempts have a 100 percent chance of failing. Realize that the college interviewer wants to interview your child, not you. If you intervene, the interviewer will think your child is too reliant on you and not ready for the independence of college. Thus, unless you are planning to attend college together, restrict yourself to helping your son or daughter prepare for—not conduct—the interview.

Grades and Coursework

This is not a radical idea, but naturally the harder the courses and the higher your child's grades, the better.

How you can help: If you're like most parents, you've been badgering—ah, we mean encouraging—your child to get good grades. Keep that up! But what you also need to do is make sure that he or she is also taking challenging courses. Avoid demanding that your child take the hardest courses offered all of the time, especially if they really are too difficult for him or her. (Most students take between one and four honors courses a year depending on what is offered and what they can handle.) Also avoid making your son or daughter do nothing else besides study. From others' experiences, this usually results in triple bypass level arguments at best and total rebellion at worst. What seems to work best in instilling good study behavior is positive reinforcement through praise.

Test Scores

Your child will take what we call an alphabet soup of standardized tests. These are tests with enough acronyms to be the ingredients of alphabet soup including the following:

- *SAT.* Contains Math, Reading and Writing sections.

- *ACT.* Test with English, Math, Reading and Science sections. Usually students take either the SAT or the ACT.

- *SAT Subject Tests.* Specific subject tests including English, math, foreign languages, social sciences and sciences.

- *APs.* Advanced Placement tests for attaining college credit during high school. Students should take these tests after completing an Advanced Placement or honors course in the test subject.

- *IBs.* International Baccalaureate tests for earning college credit during high school. Individual colleges have their own rules for whether or not these scores can translate into credit.

- *PSAT.* Given to juniors and some sophomores to prepare for the SAT and used as a basis for awards and special programs including National Merit Scholarships. Your child should take this test in the junior year and, if possible, earlier for practice. The PSAT 10 is given to sophomores, and the PSAT 8/9 is given to eighth and ninth grade students.

How you can help: The SAT and ACT websites offer free practice exams and test preparation tips. There are also many books available that you can use to assist your child in preparing for the ACT and SAT tests as well as numerous test preparation courses. In general, if you can afford it and your child wants to go, allow him or her to take a test preparation class. The best time for students to take these courses is a couple of months before they plan to take the actual test. This is usually during the winter or spring of the junior year or the summer between junior and senior year.

Don't expect miracles from any test preparation course, although they have been known to happen occasionally. But do expect that by virtue of systematically studying for the exams and becoming familiar with their structure, your child will perform better on the actual test.

We have also included more details about the tests and strategies for self-study in Chapter 10.

That's it for the tests. Again, when you have some free time ("What's that?" you ask), refer to the specific chapters in this book for more details about what colleges expect. But, your main goal is to give your child positive encouragement and maybe to cut him or her a little slack when it comes to doing chores between September and January of the senior year.

How to Pay for College Without Filing for Chapter 11

After stressing you out with all that your child must do to be admitted to college, we are now going to help you relax a little by discussing how you can save some money. Each year the government and colleges award over $241.3 billion in financial aid. Even at schools like Harvard, about two-thirds of the students receive some form of financial assistance. (Are you smiling yet?)

There are several forms of aid and some are definitely more desirable than others. At the top of the financial aid food chain are grants and scholarships. This money has no strings attached, except that it must be used for tuition. Scholarships and grants do not need to be repaid. Next comes Federal Work-Study, in which the government helps subsidize your child's wages for term-time work. Finally, various low-interest and deferred-interest loans are often offered as well.

To tap into these funds, you and your child will need to fill out—you guessed it!—more forms. These include the Free Application for Federal Student Aid (FAFSA), the College Scholarship Service (CSS) Financial Aid PROFILE form, federal income tax returns and, if necessary, colleges' financial aid forms which come with the applications, the CSS' Business/Farm Supplement and CSS' Non-custodial Parent's Statement. For details on each of these forms and to determine which are relevant to you, see Chapter 11 (no pun intended) and the instructions on the specific college application form. Colleges vary as to which forms they require, and many will also have their own supplemental forms.

Regardless of who completes the pile of paperwork, you will need to provide information about your annual income, savings, mortgages, loans, stock portfolios, etc. All of this information is kept confidential and is used to determine if you meet the requirements for various federal, state and college-sponsored grants and loans. Also, make sure that your child is aware of any special circumstances that your family has as a result of unemployment, job instability, a sick family member, other family members' educational costs or a recent addition to the family. Colleges take these factors into account, and they can have a huge impact on aid packages. Your child will receive a letter after being accepted outlining the specific aid package offered.

For more information on how your child can win scholarships, review Chapter 11, where we have compiled strategies for finding and applying for scholarships. Also consider our scholarship guidebook, *Get Free Cash For College*, which contains a strategy guide and scholarship directory of thousands of awards. Ordering information is at the end of this book.

Don't forget that the most lucrative forms of scholarships are often the closest to you. For example, start with your employer. One student we know won a $20,000 scholarship from her father's company and $10,000 from her mother's union. Consider this one of the unwritten perks of your job. Inquire with your human resources department about the availability of scholarships for children of employees. (If your company does not offer such scholarships, suggest that they do.) Aside from your company, check with professional and community organizations that you belong to such as your church, PTA, Lions Club and Rotary Club.

100 Percent Freedom for Your Child

Okay, maybe you shouldn't give your child 100 percent freedom (possibly a frightening thought), but once your child is accepted, give him or her as much freedom as your checkbook can handle in choosing where to attend. After all, it is your child—not you—who is going to be at the school for the next four years.

Obviously since you are probably the one who will foot the bill, you can express your preferences to your child; but for the most part, let him or her choose among the schools you can afford.

Both of my (Kelly) parents are University of Southern California alumni, and if you are familiar with USC, you know that there is something so powerfully inherent in being a USC alumnus that it convinces you that your offspring, your offspring's offspring and the next 17 generations of offspring must attend that college. Thus, when I earned a full-tuition scholarship to USC, it was a very difficult offer to turn down.

Somehow, however, my mother and father combated their natural USC alumni instinct and allowed me to make my own decision about where to go. I think my parents agree with me that it was worth it for me to have no regrets about my decision to go to Harvard.

Be as supportive as possible about which school your child wants to attend, and emphasize that you are proud whatever his or her decision may be. After all, it matters less which college your child goes to than what he or she makes of the experience.

Get an Early Start With Freshmen, Sophomores and Juniors

As you may have guessed, college students are not created overnight. Being the modest Harvard graduates that we are, we like to think that it takes a lifetime of training and self-discipline to reach the pinnacle of perfection. Truthfully, however, there is no regimen that you should have been prescribing for your child since birth. But there are a few things you *can* help your child do before his or her senior year in high school.

The earlier you and your child start thinking about the admissions process, the better. Below we have summarized a few points that apply specifically to parents, but we recommend that both you and your child read Chapter 13, which is devoted to juniors, sophomores and freshmen.

Preparing for college admittance in advance allows your child to select courses, get involved in activities and cultivate relationships with teachers that will help him or her tremendously when it comes time to apply to college. Being knowledgeable about the admissions process yourself, you can encourage your child to make decisions that will help make him or her a stronger candidate.

The following are some guidelines for advising your child. Please do not force any of these suggestions on your child, especially if he or she is the kind of person who resists recommendations from mom or dad. But if possible, advise your child with these principles in mind.

Aim for a high GPA. Admissions officers see all of your child's academic records from the time he or she hits the ninth grade. Advise him or her that grades count. Of course, it is not necessary that your child have a 4.0 grade point average, but the closer he or she can get to that, the better. The exception is when it comes to honors versus non-honors courses as explained below.

Don't punish your child for bad grades or bribe your child for good grades, but do encourage him or her to focus on studying. We know of some parents of our high school classmates who did not heed this advice and the results were disastrous. There was one student whose parents offered him a new car if he received straight "A's." The bribe worked for that semester and his parents were very happy. Unfortunately, it did not work when it came time for college admissions. The many rejections that he received from colleges were due in no small part to the fact that he had started taking such classes as auto shop, wood shop and speech to earn his high grades while his classmates were taking Advanced Placement English, math and science. This example leads directly into our next point.

Don't go for the easy "A." Encourage your child to take rigorous honors and Advanced Placement courses. It doesn't matter that he or she might be able to get a higher grade in an easier course. Almost all colleges recalculate grade point averages taking into account the difficulty of the courses. It is much better for your child to get an "A" in an Advanced Placement or honors course than to get an "A" in a non-honors course.

Concentrate on value rather than volume. Encourage your child to lead, not follow. When it comes to extracurricular activities such as clubs, sports and volunteer work, encourage him or her to make valuable contributions to the organizations. Admissions officers are more impressed by the quality of a student's participation in extracurricular activities—leadership positions held, honors won, programs started—than by the quantity of activities. Your child should work to attain as many leadership positions as possible and excel in whatever activities he or she chooses to join. Entering contests, publishing essays or poems and starting organizations or clubs are also great ways for students to distinguish themselves from the thousands of other applicants to college.

Don't groom a bookworm. In addition to promoting strong study skills, allow your child to relax, have fun and be a kid. Don't require that he or she study incessantly or take courses that are obviously over his or her head. After all, what good is it for your child to be accepted by his or her dream college if he or she is already burned out? Also, consider that academic achievement is not the sole basis for admission. Colleges are looking for bright, but also well-rounded and interesting individuals.

Be positive. Even the best students are not accepted by every school. Depending on each college's individual pool of applicants and needs, admission officers may accept your child or they may be looking for a student with slightly different, not necessarily better, skills. Do not push your child to attend one of the elite schools, and do not equate being denied with failure. Remember that even if your child does everything right, he or she may, for reasons totally beyond his or her control, not get accepted.

A tragic but true story is of a family with two daughters who were accepted by Stanford. When the youngest child, a son, did not get in and had to "settle" for a state school, his parents did not hide their disappointment and frequently berated him as a failure. This boy eventually took his own life and from the note he left behind made it very clear that he could not live with the guilt of having let down his parents.

While this is an extreme example, be aware of how much emphasis you are placing, whether consciously or not, on your son or daughter getting accepted into a certain school. The truth of the matter is that college admissions is always a gamble to some degree. Even the most qualified and deserving students are sometimes denied, simply because the college does not have enough space in the freshman class.

Plus, as you already know, success in life is not dependent on where you go to school but on what you do there. All colleges produce their share of losers. In the end the best rule is to support your child in his or her decision and to be proud of whatever the result.

CHAPTER 15

DECIDE WHICH COLLEGE TO ENTER

The Waiting Game

Submitting your applications is a big relief. However, once it sinks in that the decision is now in *their* hands, the wait can cause more than a little apprehension. Unfortunately, there is not much you can do but wait it out. Each year admissions offices receive thousands and even tens of thousands of applications. As each is evaluated individually, the whole process takes some time.

Most decisions arrive by mid-December for early admissions and at the beginning of April for regular admissions. Let us congratulate you in advance for the acceptances that you will receive.

If you want a hint, good news usually comes in thick envelopes, although this is not always the case since some schools send acceptances by email or in business-sized envelopes—which some students don't even open since they are sure they are denial letters. Inside, however, is a simple letter that reads something like this: "Congratulations! You have been accepted. More information to follow."

The Quality of Parties and Other Important Criteria for Making Your Final Decision

If the quality of parties is your highest priority in selecting a college, then you will have no problem deciding which school to attend. One student contacted the local beer suppliers surrounding the various colleges to which he was accepted. The college that purchased the most kegs of beer won his favor.

However, if you have more mundane criteria such as financial feasibility, academics, campus environment, class sizes, location, weather and extracurricular activities, then your decision becomes a bit more difficult—and practical.

Once you have a stack of acceptance letters, you have the enviable task of choosing which school to attend. If you've been accepted at your first-choice school, congratulations on your accomplishment! Still, before you send in that acceptance card, consider all of your options and never make a decision until you have your financial aid award letters.

Look back at the questions in Chapter 2 that you used to select where to apply. The same questions are still valid in deciding where to attend. In addition, now that money is a consideration, ask yourself the following questions to evaluate the economics of going to a certain college:

- Will you be able to afford to attend school *and* eat? Before answering this, make sure you have read Chapter 11: *How to Win Free Cash for College.*

- What kind of financial aid package has the college offered? Financial aid letters usually arrive after acceptance letters. Be patient to see what kind of offers you get.

- Is asking for more aid an option? Do you have an aid offer from another college that you can share with the college to request more?

- Putting aside the complex formulas that the colleges use, how much can your parents realistically contribute?

- How many years will you need to repay student loans? How much do you think you can pay after you graduate? Don't be afraid to take out loans, however, since your education is certainly a good investment.

Besides thinking about these questions, re-read the colleges' websites. Go to the library and look up your schools again in the college guidebooks. Also, speak with graduates from your high school who are currently attending the colleges, as well as alumni, teachers, counselors, family and friends who can provide some insight.

Some colleges will give you a contact number of a current student you can call to ask any burning questions. If not, call the admissions office and ask to be referred to someone who can answer your specific questions about the school. Don't be afraid to ask a question, no matter how trivial you think it may be.

It may sound nerdy, but make a list of the pros and cons of each school. Don't let the excitement of receiving the acceptance letter cause you to act too quickly. And never make a decision until you have heard from all of the schools, with the exception of Early Decision because you've already made your choice.

Keep in mind that while choosing a college is one of the biggest decisions you'll have to make, there is still no absolutely right or absolutely wrong decision. All of the schools have their own strengths and weaknesses. Plus, no matter where you choose to attend college, you will grow to love it.

The Campus Visit: A Crash Course on College Life

The best way to get the fullest picture of life at the colleges ranging from the quality (or lack of quality) of their cuisine to what it's really like to live in a 10 foot by 10 foot cage (i.e., the dorm) is to participate in the colleges' pre-frosh or visitation events. These are usually overnight stays offered by the colleges to accepted students. Often these include a stay in the dorm, meals at the cafeteria and the opportunity to attend as many lectures as you can stay awake through. If you are lucky, you may even find a party.

During these pre-frosh events, you will usually also have the opportunity to meet your potential classmates; speak with advisors, professors and administrators and hear speeches about all of the wonderful reasons why you should attend the college. Most useful, however, is that you will stay with a current student in his or her dorm and you'll be able to sample college life for a few days.

If you cannot attend one of the college-sponsored pre-frosh events, visit the college on your own. Walk around the campus, eat the food, sit in on a lecture and visit the dorms. Don't be afraid to ask the students you encounter a few questions; they are usually helpful and will provide you with candid (sometimes too candid) answers.

Although you do not have to actually visit any schools to make a choice, we highly recommend that you do. Too many students have found out too late that the schools they selected only faintly resemble the pictures on the colleges' websites, which quite understandably portray only the good sides.

Don't Wait for the Wait List

If you get wait-listed instead of accepted, you may feel like you are living in a state of purgatory. It leaves your admissions status in limbo, suspended in between acceptance and denial. If not enough students who are accepted choose to attend the college, then students on the wait list may be admitted. It is a way for colleges to ensure they have the right number of students enrolled in the fall. Unfortunately, it means your life will be in flux by not knowing whether you will be admitted later.

If you are accepted at another school and know that you do not want to attend the school that has wait-listed you, remove yourself from the limbo state. Let them know that you don't want to still be considered. However,

STORY FROM REAL LIFE
HOW AWFUL SOUP MADE ME CHOOSE HARVARD

Consider all of your options before deciding where to go to college. You may be surprised to find that your first-choice school changes after some re-consideration. —Gen and Kelly

Okay, I didn't really base my entire decision on oxtail soup, but it certainly played a role. Before I even applied to schools, I had already decided which college I wanted to attend. I am a native Californian and never fathomed living farther than an hour from the Pacific Ocean. I only applied to Harvard on a whim, just to see if I could get accepted. I had no intention of living on the East Coast.

When I received my accepted letters I was surprised that not only did I get into my dream college in California but I also got into Harvard. I still had no intention of going to school in the east but to be fair I decided to visit both my dream college as well as Harvard.

During pre-frosh weekend I discovered that my dream school had a few flaws. I was at a dinner for prospective students when they served incredibly awful oxtail soup. The fact that the oxtail soup (a personal favorite of mine) was so unsavory made me look at this school with a more critical eye. I soon discovered other things I didn't like: like the fact that it was way out in the suburbs and I would need a car in order to go anywhere exciting. I also realized that this college felt a lot like my high school—same weather, scenery and types of students. Maybe, I began to thing, a change might not be such a bad idea.

When I visited Harvard I was impressed with the well laid out campus and beautiful brick buildings. I found the East Coast refreshing and exciting. The other students who I met were hardly the stuffy heirs and heiresses that I had imagined. But they were different from my high school friends in California.

I came to realize that the dream college that I thought I would attend from the time I was an infant was not the place I wanted to spend the next four years. I ended up selecting Harvard and have never regretted the decision. And, by the way, Harvard's oxtail soup is quite delectable.

—Gloria, who loves more than the cuisine at Harvard

if you would like to attend the school where you are wait-listed, get used to limbo.

The good news is that you aren't completely powerless. There are a couple of ways you can demonstrate to the admissions officers that you would love to make the jump from the wait list to the accept list. The basic idea is to keep reminding them that they should admit you. Here's what you should do:

Write an email. Write to the admissions officers to let them know that you are still interested in attending the school. Stress why you believe you should be accepted. Let them know about any great things you have done since you submitted your application, e.g. good grades earned or additional honors and awards won.

Escalate to calling. Verbalize your letter: Speak to an admissions officer about why you should be dewait-listed and what incredible feats you have accomplished.

Bring your teacher or advisor in on the act. Ask one or more of your teachers and/or advisors to write or call the college on your behalf and present your case.

We hope that this helps toward dewait-listing you. Keep in mind that colleges accept few students from their wait lists, but showing your continued interest can only help.

Your Last Letter to the Admissions Office

Once you've finished weighing all the factors, completing your research and working out how to pay for your education, notify all the schools of your final decision. Make sure to do it before your college's deadline—this is one deadline you can't miss!

Now, all you have to do is wait to receive a collection of brochures, welcome letters and, of course, bills from your new college. As for college admissions, you are finished! You've made it through one of the toughest, most stressful times in your life. Be proud of your accomplishment, enjoy the rest of your senior year and get ready for the four best years to come! Congratulations!

SuperCollege.com
2713 Newlands Avenue
Belmont, CA 94002
Phone: 650-618-2221
Website: www.supercollege.com

ACT Test
Phone: 319-337-1270
Website: www.act.org

College Board
250 Vesey Street, New York, NY
10281
Phone: 866-630-9305
Website: www.collegeboard.org

College Fairs
National Association for College
Admission Counseling, College Fair
Desk, 1050 N. Highland Street, Suite
400, Arlington, VA 22201
Website: www.nacacnet.org

Common Application
Website: www.commonapp.org

**International Baccalaureate
Organization (IB)**
Phone: 301-202-3000
Website: www.ibo.org

IRS
Phone: 800-829-1040
Website: www.irs.gov

**NAFSA: Association of International
Educators**
1307 New York Avenue, NW, Eighth
Floor, Washington, DC 20005
Phone: 202-737-3699
Website: www.nafsa.org

**National Association of
Intercollegiate Athletics**
1200 Grand Boulevard, Kansas City,
MO 64106
Phone: 816-595-8000
Website: www.naia.org

**National Collegiate Athletic
Association (NCAA)**
700 West Washington Street, P.O. Box
6222, Indianapolis, IN 46206
Phone: 317-917-6222
Website: www.ncaa.org

**National Junior College Athletic
Association**
Phone: 719-590-9788
Website: www.njcaa.org

**National Merit Scholarship
Corporation (NMSC)**
1560 Sherman Avenue, Suite 200,
Evanston, IL 60201-4897
Phone: 847-866-5100
Website: www.nationalmerit.org

**PROFILE from the College
Scholarship Service (CSS)**
Phone: 844-202-0524
Website: css.collegeboard.org

Sallie Mae
Phone: 800-472-5543
Website: www.salliemae.com

STATE FINANCIAL AID

Alabama	800-960-7773
Alaska	800-441-2962
Arizona	602-542-7230
Arkansas	501-371-2000
California	888-224-7268
Colorado	303-862-3001
Connecticut	860-947-1800
Delaware	800-292-7935
D.C.	202-727-6436
Florida	888-827-2004
Georgia	800-505-4732
Hawaii	808-956-8213
Idaho	208-334-2270
Illinois	800-899-4722
Indiana	888-528-4719
Iowa	877-272-4456
Kansas	785-430-4240
Kentucky	800-928-8926
Louisiana	800-259-5626 x1012
Maine	800-228-3734
Maryland	800-974-0203
Massachusetts	617-994-6950
Michigan	800-642-5626 x37054
Minnesota	800-657-3866
Mississippi	800-327-2980
Missouri	800-473-6757
Montana	406-444-6570
Nebraska	402-471-2847
Nevada	702-889-8426
New Hampshire	603-271-3494
New Jersey	800-792-8670
New Mexico	505-476-8400
New York	888-697-4372
North Carolina	866-866-2362
North Dakota	701-328-2960
Ohio	614-466-6000
Oklahoma	800-858-1840
Oregon	800-452-8807
Pennsylvania	800-692-7392
Rhode Island	401-736-1100
South Carolina	803-737-2260
South Dakota	605-773-3455
Tennessee	615-741-3605
Texas	800-242-3062
Utah	800-418-8757
Vermont	800-642-3177
Virginia	804-225-2600
Washington	360-753-7800
West Virginia	304-558-2101
Wisconsin	608-267-2206
Wyoming	307-777-7763
Puerto Rico	787-641-7100

U.S. Department of Education and Federal Student Aid Information Center

Phone: 800-4-FED-AID toll-free

Website:

https://studentaid.ed.gov or www. ed.gov for general information

www.fafsa.ed.gov to download the FAFSA application

https://studentaid.ed.gov/sa/repay-loans/consolidation for Direct Consolidation Loans

Make a copy of this worksheet for each of the colleges that you are considering.

Name of college: _____

Location: _____

Number of undergraduates: _____

Email: _____

Phone: _____

Academics

Faculty/student ratio: _____

Department(s) that I'm most interested in: _____

Requirements (senior project/thesis, required courses, etc.): _____

Classes that I'd like to take: _____

_____

_____

Research or other special academic program opportunities: _____

_____

_____

Study abroad opportunities: _____

_____

_____

Student Life

Clubs or organizations I'd like to join: _____

_____

_____

Role of Greek organizations on campus: _____

Role of athletics on campus: _____

Intercollegiate or intramural athletic prospects: _____

Prevalence of drinking/parties: _____

Fun things to do off campus: _____

_____

_____

Notable things about the dorms, whether students usually live on or off campus, availability and cost of off-campus housing: _____

_____

Notable things about the quality of the food and meal plans offered: _____

_____

Notable things about campus such as the student center or on-campus pub:

_____

Admissions

For accepted freshmen:_____

SAT Reading range: _____ ❏ Required ❏ Recommended

SAT Math range: _____ ❏ Required ❏ Recommended

SAT Writing range: _____ ❏ Required ❏ Recommended

ACT composite range: _____ ❏ Required ❏ Recommended

ACT Writing test: _____ ❏ Required ❏ Recommended

SAT Subject tests: _____ ❏ Required ❏ Recommended

Average GPA: _____

Percentage accepted early: _____
Percentage accepted regular decision: _____

❏ Reach college ❏ Good chance of being admitted to
❏ Very likely to be admitted

If early admission is offered, description of: _____

Early admission deadline: _____
Regular admission deadline: _____

Requirements:
❏ Common Application accepted
❏ Supplementary forms required
❏ Online application form accepted
❏ Number of long essays: _____
❏ Number of short essays: _____
❏ Counselor evaluation
❏ Number of teacher evaluations: _____
❏ Interview recommended
❏ Interview required

Financial Aid

Email: _____

Phone: _____

Annual tuition: _____

Room and board: _____

Fees: _____

Average financial aid package: _____
❏ Need-blind admission
❏ Meets all demonstrated financial need
❏ Merit-based aid

Priority financial aid deadline: _____
Regular financial aid deadline: _____

Forms required:
❏ FAFSA
❏ CSS/PROFILE
❏ College's own form

Average student loan debt for graduates: _____

Summary

Notes from campus visits/talking with people from the college: _____
_____
_____

What I like the most about the college: _____
_____
_____

What I like the least about the college: _____
_____
_____

APPENDIX C: EVALUATION/ RECOMMENDATION WORKSHEET

This is helpful information to give your counselors and teachers who are writing evaluations for you.

Name: _____

Email: _____

Phone: _____

Colleges That I'm Applying To

Name of college: _____

Deadline: _____

Address/website to submit evaluation: _____

Reasons I'd like to attend this college: _____
_____
_____

Name of college: _____

Deadline: _____

Address/website to submit evaluation: _____

Reasons I'd like to attend this college: _____
_____
_____

Name of college: _____

Deadline: _____

Address/website to submit evaluation: _____

Reasons I'd like to attend this college: _____
_____
_____

Name of college: _____

Deadline: _____

Address/website to submit evaluation: _____

Reasons I'd like to attend this college: _____
_____
_____

Name of college: _____

Deadline: _____

Address/website to submit evaluation: _____

Reasons I'd like to attend this college: _____
_____
_____

Here is an example of an academic experience that I've had in which I've excelled or learned significantly from: _____
_____
_____
_____

Here is an experience that I've had outside of the classroom and how it's
changed me as a person: (This may be from an extracurricular activity, sport, job,
church, your family, etc.) _____
_____
_____
_____

Here is an example of a time that I've demonstrated initiative or leadership:
_____
_____
_____

Here is information about my academic and career goals: _____
_____
_____
_____

Here is an example written by _____ (friend/parent/other)
that describes my character: _____
_____
_____
_____

Here is information about special circumstances that I'd appreciate being included in my evaluation: (This can be extenuating family or other circumstances,
special talents or something that your teacher or counselor may not know about
you that would be helpful to have in the evaluation.) _____
_____
_____
_____

My greatest strengths are: _____
_____
_____
_____

I've also attached these materials to help you:

❑   Copy of my essay

❑   Resume

❑   Transcript

College					
Tuition and fees					
Room and board/rent and food					
Books and other supplies					
Personal items					
Medical insurance					
Travel					
Total cost of attendance					

College					
Financial aid phone number					
Financial aid email					
Total Cost of Attendance (from Appendix D)					
Financial Aid Offered					
Scholarships/ grants					
Loans					
Work-study					
Total					
Expected Family Contribution (EFC)					
Student contribution					
Parent contribution					
Total					
Unmet Need					

Cost of Attendance – Financial Aid Offered – Expected Family Contribution = Unmet Need

ABOUT THE AUTHORS

HARVARD GRADUATES GEN AND KELLY TANABE are the founders of SuperCollege and the award-winning authors of 14 books including: *50 Successful Ivy League Application Essays, Accepted! 50 Successful College Admission Essays, The Ultimate Guide to America's Best Colleges, The Ultimate Scholarship Book, Get Free Cash for College, 1001 Ways to Pay for College, How to Write a Winning Scholarship Essay, 501 Ways for Adult Students to Pay for College* and *Accepted! 50 Successful Business School Admission Essays.*

Together, Gen and Kelly were accepted to every school to which they applied: all of the Ivy League colleges plus other prestigious universities including Stanford, Berkeley, Duke and Rice. They earned over $100,000 in merit-based scholarships and left Harvard debt free.

Gen and Kelly lecture at high schools across the country and write the "Ask The SuperCollege.com Experts" column syndicated in local and school newspapers nationwide. They have made dozens of appearances on television and radio programs and have served as expert sources for respected publications including *USA Today*, the *New York Times, U.S. News & World Report* and the *Chronicle of Higher Education*.

Gen grew up in Waialua, Hawaii. Between eating banana-flavored shave ice, he was president of the Student Council, captain of the speech team and a member of the tennis team. A graduate of Waialua High School, he was the first student from his school to be accepted at Harvard. In college, Gen was chair of the Eliot House committee and graduated *magna cum laude* in History and East Asian Studies.

Kelly attended Whitney High School, a nationally ranked public school in Cerritos, California. She was editor of the newspaper, assistant editor of the yearbook and founder of a service club for literacy. In college, she was co-director of the HAND public service program and co-leader of a Brownie Troop. She graduated *magna cum laude* in Sociology.

The Tanabes approach college admissions from a practical, hands-on point of view. Drawing on the experiences of real students, they provide strategies students can use to increase their chances of getting into their dream school and paying for their education.

Gen, Kelly and their sons Zane and Kane live in Belmont, California. Contact the Tanabes at gen_kelly@supercollege.com.